Advance Praise

"Turning It Around . . . *will help a lot of people all over the world.*"
— Dr. Alice Oliveira – Pediatrician, Brazil

"*Bill Allin's . . . revolutionary approach will be (required) reading for professionals and laymen, politicians and educators.*"
— Marveen Craig, AA, RDMS, FSDMS

"*Accurate with a lot of facts and evidence, thoughtful, objective, universal, and very well written.*"
— Vihar Andonov – Bulgaria

"*Very informative, helpful, easy to read and understand. Every educator, parent and grandparent should read this book.*"
— Yvonne Belchoubek, C.C.C. – Canada

"*You have done a great job for the next generation, helping the world solve its social problems . . . all of the world needs* Turning It Around.*"
— Qin Yi, Professional Engineer – China

"*Turning It Around . . . addresses issues with government, parenthood, education and society with fervor. Reading this gave me hope that we can make a difference if we just look at our common goals and not at our differences. Every world citizen should read* Turning It Around.*"
— Bonnie Hobson, PhD – USA

Turning It Around

Turning It Around

Causes and Cures for Today's Epidemic Social Problems

Bill Allin

The Writers' Collective
Independent Books for Independent Readers

Turning It Around © 2005 Bill Allin

Cover Designer: Barbara Hodge
Interior Design: Mary Jo Zazueta

ISBN-13: 978-1-59411-015-3
ISBN-10: 1-59411-015-8

All rights reserved. No part of this book may be reproduced, stored in a retrieval system, or transmitted in any form by any means electronic, mechanical, photocopying, recording, or otherwise except in brief extracts for the purpose of review, without the permission of the publisher and copyright owner.

Library of Congress Cataloging-in-Publication Data

Allin, Bill, 1942-
  Turning it around / by Bill Allin
    p. cm.
Includes index.
  ISBN 1-59411-015-8 (Trade Paper : alk. paper)
  1. Social problems. 2. Social history--1945- I. Title
HN17.5A465 2005
361.1--dc21   2003012584

Printed in the United States of America
10 9 8 7 6 5 4 3 2 1

Published by The Writers' Collective ▲ Cranston, Rhode Island

For Trish, who understood that TIA is not a dream but a plan to fill a great worldwide need, for the benefit of all people;

For each person who believes that one voice, one will, can inspire others to make the world a better, safer, saner place for everyone.

Contents

Preface	xi
Acknowledgments	xv
Social Problems in Your Life	1
Looking Around Us Today	5
Social Problems Affect Everyone	11
Plans for the Future	17
Extremes of Behavior	23
Rage	33
Humanity Versus Nature	39
Ignorance	47
Violence	53
Fear	65
The Fight (or Flight) of Our Lives	77
Staring Into the Future	83
Governments	91
The Rudderless Ship of State	101
Loss of Innocence, Embrace of Guilt	109
Education	119
Education 2100	129
The Pyramid of Living System	159

Building the Pyramid	167
How to Begin	181
Toward a Meaningful and Lasting Future	185
They-Sayers	195
Strategies for the Long Term	205
Preparing the Guardians of Humanity	219
Preparing Citizens for the Twenty-First Century	231
Moving to Action	245
Appendix A: Course Material for New Parents	253
Appendix B: Program Topics for the Primary Grades	263
Resources	275
Bibliography	277
About the Author	279
Index	281

Preface

Any one of us or someone we love could be the next victim of road rage, home invasion or an accidental killing in a drug war. Social problems like these and others we read about on the front pages of newspapers affect everyone. They affect our families, our homes, our relationships, even our personal well-being. Until this book, solutions to these problems seemed impossible. Most people have given up hope that they can ever be free of these threats.

Let's consider how this came about.

Survival and teaching of the young are the most important responsibilities of adults in any civilization, in any age. Primitive bands, tribes and clans in the prehistorical years of modern humans had thousands of years to develop their skills of survival and their methods of teaching their young so that their way of life could be maintained, could thrive and flourish. In those days, everyone knew their social responsibilities. They were taught to every child. Social problems were minimized because everyone knew their role in guarding the welfare of the group.

Parents and other adults in modern megasocieties have the same responsibilities. Teaching our young is no less important today because there are more of us around. It's as critical to our survival today as it was to our ancient ancestors who lived in caves. When educating the young is not done properly and thoroughly, social problems will result. It's simple. When people don't know what to do, they're apt to make the wrong choices.

Since the beginning of the Industrial Revolution, the human population has grown so rapidly and lifestyles have changed so quickly that survival has become the dominant need. New ways of teaching our young were needed so that our values, our beliefs, our family institutions, the traditions of our way of life could be passed to the next generation. For many of us today, the need for teaching our young beyond knowledge and skills related to future job skills is fuzzy. There are no standards, no norms that we teach for all families.

We believe that we fulfill our primary responsibilities as parents and teachers when we teach our children a core set of information and skills, plus what they will require to earn a living. To us, to earn a living is to survive. To a lesser extent, we teach them values and social skills, but most of this is not direct teaching. Children tend to acquire these incidentally, such as from television, friends and events they experience.

Children inherently know, though they are unable to express, the fact that they need more from adults than they receive. Whether they are consciously aware of this unknown, missing "other" or not, they experience stress and even anxiety knowing that they need something they don't know how to get. Children with needs they can't satisfy act out and misbehave.

A large majority of children accommodate themselves, over time, to become properly functioning adults in our communities. A small minority, unable to cope with an adult-dominated world they can't understand and that can't teach them what they need to feel significant and worthy, strikes back.

This latter group forms the core of our future social problems. Their behavior, often anti-social and intentionally so, affects the rest of us. We read about them in newspapers, watch stories about them on television, hear about them from neighbors, friends and work associates, and sometimes suffer direct attacks on our privacy by them. Most are in their teens, twenties or thirties.

By not fulfilling our roles of teaching our young children the knowledge and skills they require to live comfortably and securely as adults, we create the conditions for potential social problems.

Teaching of essential life skills has been a basic role of adults both through human history and in the larger world of animals. When it does not happen properly, problems result. Not surprisingly, those who are most unable to cope with their lives fill that vacuum with values, beliefs, skills and information that may not be in line with the norms of their communities.

Parents are not guilty because their children break laws. That denies a basic tenet of humanity, which is freedom of choice, even for children. Children make their own decisions. But they make decisions based on what they know and believe, which might not be what are socially acceptable norms. That is, what kids believe and what we would like them to believe often are not the same.

Parents have always tried their best to raise their children properly. But, through generations of repeated change in the basics of family life over the past few hundreds of years, children are no longer taught those skills of parenting and of coping with life's thrills and terrors, its happiness and traumas by their parents. Today's parents, themselves unable to cope with the downturns of life in modern times, have no resources or knowledge base from which to teach their children. They were not taught these by their own parents.

While debate rages on between parents and school systems about who should teach what to children, both have lost track of what kids need to know to be good and productive adult citizens of their community. We want to teach them facts and skills. Kids need concepts to understand the world they are growing into. Computerized machines function on facts. People have a need to understand their world, to make sense of what is happening around them. If their world doesn't make sense to them, then some of them will make dreadful mistakes.

When people don't understand the world around them, they may develop psychological problems. When young people feel lost in their world, they have a greater potential for problems because they do not have other life structures such as jobs, positions in social clubs and family leadership roles to hold onto. Young people are in a constant learning mode every day. They have bosses wherever they go, except within their peer groups. Even then they choose leaders. When they don't feel secure in their world, they tend to band together with others in similar circumstances. The door to trouble is wide open. Most adults can't recognize this and wouldn't know what to do about it if they did.

Kids need to know how to cope with situations that happen in the lives of most adults, at one time or another. Examples are job loss, death of a loved one and a friend or loved one contracting a serious disease. When they see their own parents unable to cope in crisis situations, such as divorce, they become confused, stressed, anxious.

For most of them, their parents' marriage is how they came into existence. When that crashes around them, it affects their concept and value of their own being. It could be months or years later before that hidden anxiety plays itself out in their lives. By that time, they could become social problems along with others like them in their communities.

As parents, we teach children what we believe they need to know. The truth is that most of us don't know what they really need. We tend to teach our kids what our parents taught us. If our parents didn't teach us enough, we don't know enough to teach our own kids.

Most children manage to pick up the basics of what they need for their lives, from various sources, as they grow. Their parents consider themselves successful. Some children do not. The rest of us consider the parents of these kids to be failures. The difference may not be the parents themselves, but the coincidence of what the kids managed to learn along the way.

If we, as a society, knew what children really need and had programs for parents and children to provide for these needs, there would be no reason for failures. No need for anti-social behavior on a massive scale. No need for social problems we believe are beyond our ability to solve.

The purpose of this book is to help us learn what we need to know, to close the knowledge gap. Only when we understand the social problems around us will we be able to begin the process of correcting them.

Only then can we make a difference.

Acknowledgments

BONNIE Hobson inspired this book and urged me through the critical first draft. Donna Mosher kept me at it. Patti Farmer gave reactions from the heart, letting me know that I was writing for real people with genuine concerns. Nan Ross gave the project a magnificent overview. Peter Adams, MP, helped me to understand that politicians will listen when approached properly. Bob Richards, staunch ally and friend, lent support when the project seemed overwhelming. Marveen Craig provided encouragement and confidence that U.S. citizens would and could embrace new solutions for social problems. Qin Yi helped me to understand that Canada's social problems were the world's social problems, that people everywhere are looking for solutions to the same troubles. Ingrid Hedler provided flashes of brilliance with graphics when needed. Jeroo Vandrevala made me rewrite until it all made sense. These people are part of what TIA is.

Thanks to manuscript readers around the world for inspiring me to believe that Earth in this new century is truly a huge village where all citizens can work together to advance civilization and make each life better for the future.

While the concepts and manuscript for *Turning It Around: Causes and Cures for Today's Epidemic Social Problems* could not have come about without the critical input of each of these friends and colleagues, its implementation will only take effect if you join us to make it all work together. We are each responsible for making our communities, our world, a better place to live. This will be the best and most lasting legacy we can leave to our children.

When enough of us care, we will make it happen.

Social Problems in Your Life

VIOLENCE. Drugs. Suicide. Gangs. Teen subcultures. Home invasions. Dishonesty. Lawlessness. Fear. These and other characteristics of our communities that make us uncomfortable can be changed.

Most of us lock our doors at night. We never walk alone and always avoid some parts of town. Turn off the television news because it reports too much tragedy. Worry that our kids or grandchildren may get into trouble.

Such problems worry almost every one of us, but until now, no one knew what to do about them.

Social problems affect each of us, even if they don't take control of our whole lives or our community. Only a minority of the population participates in such things. Yet that small minority upsets almost everyone to some degree.

Social problems can only change depending on factors that influence them. They will not decrease on their own. Witness how they have increased over the past few decades. Think about how much simpler and safer life seemed to be twenty years ago.

If no one does anything about what causes them, nothing will improve. It will only get worse. This book will turn around the belief that the situation is hopeless and provide a process to improve the quality of everyone's life.

Until now we have depended on the police, courts, politicians and disciplinarians in the education system to act against anti-social behavior. The problems got worse. In parts of some cities in North America, the police are like night watchmen, observers in a territory governed by anarchy. Armed security people patrol the halls of some schools like prison guards.

We used to trust people in our communities. Now we don't know if we can trust our neighbors.

If we agree that something has to change or life in our cities will get worse, then read on. People's ways of thinking, their habits and attitudes can be changed. That means that we will have to make some changes too.

Two generations ago, television commercials advertised that cigarette smoking was good for us, that it made us sophisticated, successful, popular. The belief was widely held. No one in North America believes that any more. A majority of people in North America changed their attitude toward a once popular and loved habit.

At that same time, consuming alcohol in large quantities was considered a challenge of the brave, a way of life for the winners, the upwardly mobile, the successful. Of course they drove home when the bottles were empty. It was what people did. Not any more. At least not with the blessing of anyone else.

Driving while intoxicated and smoking are anti-social behaviors now in most communities. What a large majority of our society believed was good two generations ago is now believed to be wrong, bad, destructive.

If personal habits as dear to us as smoking and drinking can be curbed significantly, those other things that disturb us so much can be changed too. This book will propose a process for taking these huge burdens off each of us by making our communities safer and better places. In the process it will relieve us of great costs and make a better society for our children.

In a sense, this book is about ages: young, middle and wised-up by experience. For older people, it is about a civilization, a way of life, that we will pass on to younger generations. For children, it is about what they will learn about their world and how they can be taught to cope with its ups and downs. For parents, it is about how to guide their children through those wonderful and terrifying periods of childhood and adolescence.

To some extent, the book follows the political thinking of Canada's first female Prime Minister, and one of that position's shortest titleholders, the Right Honourable Kim Campbell. Her campaign referred to the "politics of inclusion". Ms. Campbell had the then-heretical plan of encouraging all citizens of Canada to participate in their own government. Her ideas were ahead of her time.

It also borrows from the thinking of another Canadian Prime Minister, the late Pierre Elliott Trudeau. Mr. Trudeau believed, at least in the early years of his sixteen-year period as his country's government leader, that Canadians deserved to know what their government was doing. This was a radical idea in the late 1960s, one that had not been tried before. Nor has it been attempted since in a meaningful way, as the media consider it their exclusive function to dole out the news in the form they want their readers and listeners to understand it. Because of the constant scrutiny of the media, politicians feel they have all they can manage without having to pay attention to the people that elect them.

The proposals in this book do not have a political or religious agenda. One reason is that the people who will support it will not be the major beneficiaries of it. The people who will benefit most from this plan are not even born yet or at best are still of school age. Another is that the plan is based on the common beliefs and values of most of the citizens of the country, not on the biased beliefs of any political party. The fortunes of a political party will wax and wane, but common beliefs and values remain in place among a majority of citizens over time.

We want to have a thriving civilization to pass along to future generations. We all want it to be a healthy one. This can happen, no matter where we live.

Meanwhile, we also want to make improvements that will begin to take effect within our lifetimes. Previous generations brought our country to where it is now. It's up to us to start to improve it.

We have a role to play in the evolution of the government of our country and the education of our fellow citizens. Except in time of civil war or insurrection, conditions we hope are long past, our participation and support is never more needed. The technology of the twenty-first century will make this possible. Never before in history has it been as easy for citizens to voice their opinions to their elected officials.

We have good reason to stand up and say to our governments, "We are good people. This is what we believe. This is who we are. We stand now together to ask our government to listen and to act. We ask you to do what is right. Make your decisions as legislators based on the beliefs and values we hold dear."

We don't have to be politicians to tell our government what we want of it. We don't have to be university scholars or lawyers to say what we mean, what we stand for, what we believe is good and right.

We just have to be citizens. Responsible human beings. Those are our only qualifications.

Citizens of thriving countries will have a different role to play than ever before in history. We have left the running of governments solely to egocentric, self-interested politicians long enough. If we want things to change, then we must do something about it.

If we believe that the condition of our country is not what it should be, then we should say so. We should say what we believe and believe that what we say is right. We have the right to complain if we don't like something, but we can't expect change if we refuse to speak up at the right time and place.

Politicians need to hear what we want, what we believe is good and right. They won't listen to complaints. They are unimpressed by shows of violence and confrontation. The approaches must be positive and constructive.

They also need a plan of action, which is what this book is about.

Bringing together good people with good intentions and values they hold in common is the primary objective of this book.

Read on. Let's see how much we all have in common.

Looking Around Us Today

Most of us have serious concerns about the world we live in. In some cases fear and worry play a significant role in our lives. Conditions in our communities seem so much beyond our understanding that they appear to be out of control.

It's not that we live in constant fear. The problems are relatively minor to our lives, but nagging and incessant. Changes could make the quality of our lives better. We want change, but feel helpless to control it. Helplessness is a perception, a widespread belief. But it is not reality. We look for short term solutions rather than long term cures.

Something can be done. One of our objectives will be to learn how to not be helpless. Another will be to learn what can be done to make our lives and those of our fellow citizens better. No bitter pills or great sacrifices to make here. Just some straight thinking.

The following may be familiar statements.

"We live in a sick world."

"I can't watch the news any more. It's all terror and drugs."

"Kids today don't have any respect for anyone or anything."

"People don't care about laws any more."

"The education system's at fault. Schools don't teach what kids need."

"Parents today don't take any responsibility for their kids. Things would be different if parents were put in jail for crimes their kids commit."

These words reflect the concerns and fears of people all over our country. Every country. They result from our anxiety at being unable to control many factors in our lives. We can't see anyone who is able to turn the situation around. No help means no hope.

Our society can be reshaped into communities that better reflect the wishes and values of the people who live in them. This book will illuminate the path that can be followed. We will consider what can be done, the objectives, goals and steps in the process toward improvement. First we will look at the realities that upset most of us and establish the extent of the damage that has been done. Once we understand the problem facing us as a nation and as individuals, we will consider solutions and options.

Consider these facts. They each relate to the problems. The examples are from Canada only because it is my home country and it is often looked to as a role model or example.

Eighty percent of Canadians over age sixty-five have low literacy skills, meaning that they have trouble with understanding and dealing effectively with printed materials that confront them frequently. Forty-five percent of all Canadians have low literacy skills. Twenty percent of recent high school graduates have literacy skills too low for entry-level jobs. Canada compares favorably with the U.S.*

A study done in 2002 found that twenty-two percent of adult Canadians have serious reading problems, according to ABC Canada, a literacy awareness group, quoting the International Adult Literacy Survey. Another twenty-six percent would have trouble reading such important written materials as a doctor's prescription information sheet or a road map, completing a job application or filling in a deposit slip at a bank. That's nearly half of all adult Canadians.†

Estimates by medical experts suggest as high as thirty percent of teens have some hearing loss due to ear damage resulting from listening to loud music. Most teens in North America are exposed to drug use and availability in school. For many teens, high school means living through four years of fear.

Alcohol is present in the blood of at least one driver in over half the cases of death in motor vehicle accidents in North America. That despite aggressive campaigns against drinking and driving, strict laws and stiff sentences including loss of driver's license.

A majority of people fear walking alone at night in most North American cities. In many cases people can't afford to move from a neighborhood where they are afraid twenty-four hours a day. Murders resulting from arguments between spouses, drugs, organized crime and untreated psychoses occur daily in many North American cities. Home invasions prove that even the inside of our own residence might not be safe.

Some problems with our communities are so powerful and pervasive that we avoid thinking about them. We turn our attention away and try to carry on with our lives despite the tragedies and travesties going on around us. But the anxiety lingers inside.

We live in the Information Age, a time when messages that used to require hours, days or weeks of research can be accessed in seconds. Yet literacy problems abound. It used to be that an illiterate person was one who could not read. Now there are many people who can read but do not understand some or all of what they read. These people consider themselves literate, although they may not be able to understand instructions for taking medicine, paying a bill or completing a tax form, for example. They can't understand why life is so hard for them.

Most of us know at least one person whose life has been profoundly affected by something violent, something invasive, something that changed that person's life forever. Personal violence is a problem that upsets many of us deeply. Lately even invasion of privacy by computer hackers has risen as a form of personal psychological violence.

The idea for this book grew out of a desperate need, expressed by many people around the world who communicate with each other regularly on the Internet. Many would be happy if only someone would put everything together as a package that could be presented to government leaders on all continents about undeniable, unignorable social illnesses and grievances that must be addressed. Otherwise, they don't know what to do.

Politicians avoid discussing causes of such problems as they don't have any idea what to do about them. They assume that these illnesses come with the pace and demands of life in our time. If they do anything, they spend tax money to make temporary patches to problems whose causes they don't understand. If anything, they pass stiffer laws, build more prisons and hire more police. The problems just get worse.

We will consider the path that may be followed to overcome these problems and set us on a smoother course. The program we propose will work toward a long term solution, one that will be effective for generations into the future. No one person will be required to make a lifelong commitment or costly investment to make it happen, but a minimum commitment by lots of people will be needed once in a while. How far along the path toward turning our communities around will depend on the will and determination of those who want change.

This is a book of big thoughts, big ideas, big plans. They will be presented in a form that will be easy for everyone to understand. Hope for our country, no matter in which country we live, rests with those who ask how it can be done, not with those who blindly claim that it can't be done. It's an impossible task only if there are enough people who believe it is. If we understand the causes of the problems and commit to the path toward solutions, there is every reason to be positive about the future and about our ability to improve the lives of everyone in our respective countries.

Our media pundits have become cynical. With rapier fashion they disembowel the ideas of anyone with the temerity to step forward with new ideas. They don't want to report on good intentions. They want to report trouble, violence, hurt and damage. It's what fills their news pages and sells their daily papers. Yet the media have much to gain from a transformation of the thinking of their audience. The media could be the force for good that will make the plan succeed. This book will give them lots of positive news to report to their audiences. The media will be allies when they realize how much they have to gain.

For a long time in the nineteenth and early twentieth centuries, newspapers in North America upheld causes, worked ceaselessly for change, held high standards of excellence and insisted that everyone, especially our leaders, should strive for these standards. Publishers today recognize that leaders are not perfect. Rather than relishing in their weaknesses, we should aim to get the best people we can in leadership roles.

Today's media search tirelessly for what is wrong, damaged, evil. It's often difficult to distinguish between the content of supermarket tabloids, some of which report fictitious material as facts, and the front pages of mainline newspapers, tabloid television programs and even magazine style television programs and news reports. What is fiction? What is fact? The lines blur. There is confusion, indecision, moral compasses spin, chaos and anarchy seem at hand. It makes us all dizzy and sick.

What is good and right? It's time to identify these. What do we believe? It's time we shared this among ourselves. What legacy do we want to pass on to future generations? It's time we plan to make it happen. Today's media look for villains if they can't find heroes. We will provide them with a heroic cause.

How can we effect changes to make our world better? Dare we even hope? Yes, it is possible and there is good reason to hope. We can each help. First, read this book to learn how.

Later in the book we will learn about some manageable changes for both our education systems and the long-term planning of our national and regional governments. We will suggest a role that all citizens need to play in bringing the necessary changes about. A role that we can each play, no matter what our feelings about politics and education. And a path for all of us to follow for decades into the future of our countries. This book is not about politics. It's about people. People like us and millions of others like us.

Before that, we will examine some of the problems we all agree about in our society. We will understand the solutions and recommendations for change easier if we first understand the problems themselves, their causes and the extent they affect us. These are root causes, not the actions of law breakers of today, but what brought the perpetrators of our problems, as children, to become who they are now. Just as we can't cure cancer with a bandage, providing more police today will not cure the causes of violence. It's difficult enough to cure a disease when it's caught early. Our plan will be to catch threats to the body of our country while there is still time, before it suffers too badly from the disease. Then we will have a chance to bring it back to health.

It will require a new form of national health and wellbeing, more befitting world conditions that exist today than the old ways. Nothing to be frightened of. We will find that the objectives of the plan closely match the kind of community we would like to live in. Remember, the problems are rooted in our people. It only makes sense that the solutions will be too.

Together we will explore the problems and the paths to follow to make improvements. Together we will work through the process and the goals. Our society, our collective determination, will provide the means to reach the destination we desire. The plan will need some help from us, a small contribution of our moral support.

We will learn, to the amazement of many of us, how much we have in common in our beliefs, our values and our morals. We will learn what we can build together based on our common beliefs, with each person making a small effort to bring about changes that we all believe are needed. Then we can share it with others who have yet to learn. Our respective countries will act as role models to other countries who desperately seek some guidance that will help them to gain cohesiveness, a national will that can make them more peaceful, secure and prosperous nations.

We will finally be able to build a road to peace, respect and mutual tolerance in our world.

First let's set the stage by examining some of the problems.

---

* "A Nation In Denial," Saturday Night, September, 1999, 2-7
† "The Quest for Literacy", MACLEANSBEHINDTHE SCENES, Macleans, October, 2002

Social Problems 3 Affect Everyone

Our primary focus through the book will be problems over which we believe we have no control. We all suffer from them without knowing what to do about them. We talk about them in lunchrooms, after church, on the Internet and at social gatherings. Television news programs, magazines and newspapers are full of them. We shake our heads, sympathize with each other, feel a little more uncomfortable with each exposure.

Problems are a way of life with us. We know the effects and costs of personal problems. They have a way of resolving themselves over time. Our personal problems mostly affect us and maybe a few others close to us. Social problems ring in at a different level. They rage through our communities, out of control because we believe their causes can't be addressed or even touched by us. They seem to be a necessary evil of modern life in cities.

How can we recognize a social problem? After all, we endure all problems personally. Social problems are shared among many people, not just a few. They usually involve anti-social behavior. But not always, since the perpetrators do not necessarily think they are doing anything wrong. They affect strangers as well as friends and family.

Our society pays to have social workers, police and other government employees deal with those involved with social problems. Yet the problems persist. Either these people are incompetent in every city of the world or we are approaching the problems in the wrong way. So we pay to take ourselves down the same dead end roads year after year.

When we find ourselves on a dead end road that will not take us where we want to go, we change course and find a different route. Finding that different route is the second step for this book. The first is to show that a new course is needed.

A social problem affects people directly and indirectly. An indirect effect would be fear or concern that is generated among members of a community over a particular problem they have in common. In a sense, we could say that "a personal problem is what I have" and "a social problem is what others have that affects me, even if I don't know the individuals involved."

For example, a divorce touches the lives of several people, most of whom know each other. A divorce rate around fifty percent is a social problem because it not only affects the individuals involved, but it has an impact on others. For example, school classes have trouble celebrating Mother's Day or Father's Day because some children lack a parent in their lives. Children may also lack the influence of one parent or gender role model in his or her life. This can affect their behavior in class, which in turn impacts on the rest of the class.

One of the ways in which we teach children respect and admiration for their parents is through activities relating to Mother's Day and Father's Day. When the celebrations in classrooms stop for reasons of political correctness, the occasions for teaching of respect and admiration for parents stop too. The ideal teaching moments vanish. School curricula provide little room for these losses of teaching opportunities to be replaced.

Some formerly common celebrations within schools, including Christmas, must be omitted entirely because we fear that some kids will find them unhappy occasions or be unable to participate. Although we eliminate Christmas trees and carols, the lessons of goodwill, of caring for others, of helping and sharing, of giving, disappear as well. Alternative teaching opportunities simply do not happen, at least not ones with the same impact on kids.

A high divorce rate affects the topics of television programs and stage plays, fiction and nonfiction books and even creates the need for support groups and sometimes intervention by civil authorities who should otherwise not be involved in family affairs. Divorce, as a social factor, affects our lives whether or not we are directly involved.

Those who are homeless have a personal problem. But homeless people collectively form a social problem. We believe that all people should have food to eat, shelter from the weather and clothing to wear. They need support from strangers because they cannot manage these on their own. Homeless people, for the most part, are unable to provide for themselves the basic necessities of life, at least not in a socially acceptable manner.

Illiteracy, even functional illiteracy where people can read but have trouble understanding and acting on the written documents that affect their lives, is a social problem, because our businesses slow down to accommodate employees who cannot keep up with the pace. Our health care system is plugged with people who suffer from stress they are unable to knowingly attribute to their own inability to cope with what they have read, either in their jobs or at home.

Speeding on residential roads and highways has become a social problem because people die or are injured in accidents. No one has a good explanation of why drivers greatly exceed the speed limit. Some of it involves thrill-seeking and risk-taking. A high-speed, high-stress lifestyle explains other examples. Some believe that speeding has become a social norm, acceptable to most drivers but frowned upon by police who need to fill the public coffers with fines.

Street gangs don't directly affect the lives of most of us. But they become social problems when their activities become violent or they sell illegal materials, behaviors that create fear of strangers because people worry that they might become the next victims. Repeated emphasis of these activities by the media causes fear, apprehension, even neuroses among citizens not otherwise involved.

Organized crime exists as a social problem mostly because participation in their activities is a moral issue. Even having to deal with such people in an official capacity is considered socially unpleasant.

Criminal organizations address the high demand for certain services and products for which there is a small or no legal supply. Honest citizens pay highly from their pockets for organized crime because they insist that their governments do not become involved directly in activities associated with organized crime. We pay much higher taxes because those who use the services of organized crime pay no tax and we must pay for police, court, legal and prison services so that our governments can remain at arm's length from these highly profitable business activities.

If the moral component associated with organized crime activities were removed, governments could provide clean, safe products and services, in controlled conditions. If, for example, governments licensed prostitutes and verified their state of health and controlled the distribution of street drugs, our streets, our social services and our health care system could be relieved of great burdens.

With the money saved by freeing up police and judicial services and the taxes earned from these activities, governments could easily conduct education campaigns that would lower participation in these now illegal activities. This is a short term solution that might not be acceptable to the majority of citizens. The purpose of this book is to provide long term solutions that are agreeable to a large majority of people.

Governments have no trouble collecting money from people for products and services which they fundamentally condemn. Cigarette smoking has become socially unacceptable in most parts of North America. Governments collect taxes from the legal sale of cigarettes, then use the money to campaign against smoking by educating citizens of its hazards. Yet there are less socially acceptable practices that governments do not tax.

Governments have begun to turn the corner on some social problems in our communities. They have not yet done so with others because they are not supported by their electorate and in some cases they don't know what to do.

Only when citizens authorize and encourage their governments to directly address social problems, without allowing ancient moralities and fears to interfere, can progress be made to eliminate them or at least lessen their impact over a short term. Those ancient moralities developed when civilization was in its tribal stage and religions needed to create rules to control the behavior of a few people. Now we have police and laws to serve the same function. Modern social agencies work within ancient moralities.

For our purposes, a social problem will be any behavior by groups of strangers that creates fear, worry or concern for us and others in our communities.

While many people participate in them, many more are affected, either as victims or by association (such as by watching television news reports). Social problems involve almost everyone in some way, even strangers. For the same reason, social problems require solutions where people who don't know each other act together to protect their personal and collective interests. They must act together to remedy situations that have gone beyond their control and the control of their governments, their churches and other agencies that directly influenced citizens and controlled behavior in the past.

If a particular problem worries us or concerns us in some way, then we must be a party to its solution. Social problems do not go away by themselves, as personal problems sometimes do. When people ignore them or urge their governments to provide quick solutions by using the police, courts and hospitals, the problems get worse. Only when the people affected by a problem acknowledge that it is a problem and work together on a collective solution can there be any possibility of resolving it.

There is no custom or tradition in large societies to create collective solutions to social problems. Large societies are a relatively new form of civilization, considering the history of humankind. In tribal societies, collective solutions to problems were as common as solutions devised by tribal leaders. Theft, for example, might be handled by social ostracism for a period of time, such that members of the tribe would not speak to the offender or help him. For the most part, our world has evolved past tribal societies into much larger forms of civilization. In the process of creating our modern world, we have not developed ways to address and resolve social problems created by our larger societies.

Our governments tend to involve us less and less in the daily operation of our countries as they grow, whether they be democracies, monarchies or other forms of administration. We don't have time to learn what our governments are doing. Or we have been led to believe that we don't have time. Our governments, in turn, believe that they don't have time to inform us. An uninformed public is the breeding ground for social problems when people do not act together to address them.

Some people don't vote because they don't know who is running in an election or anything about the issues of the day. These people unknowingly create another social problem called apathy.

Governments can run amok, following whatever policies and paths their leaders want. They know that most people don't know enough about what is going on to care.

People who don't care and don't vote affect us because politicians can rouse apathetic, uncaring people enough, when needed, to support what those politicians want. Unaware and uncaring citizens unknowingly become a non-participating, controlling interest in social policy. Apathetic citizens affect public policy.

Social problems can only be addressed and solutions formed when a majority of people agree that they should. The silence of the silent majority of people is a social problem in itself. It's up to those who care and who are interested to rouse the interest of those who don't. That means that they must read this book and come to realize that they can help to solve social problems, that they are needed, that they can make a difference. In fact, social problems cannot be solved without them. Our encouragement is needed.

Our modern cities have not created a lot of bad people. They have created a majority of people who are not conscious of the need for them to participate in solutions our own problems.

Those who care about finding solutions to social problems must become the ones who awaken others and keep up their spirits until we can form an active majority.

Apathetic people have become that way because they have given up hope that anything can be changed. They don't know the very important information that we will learn in this book. They don't know that solutions are within us. It's up to us to make them aware that there is reason for hope, that solutions are possible, that their participation is needed and valuable and that the solutions are based on what we all believe now.

We don't need to change our beliefs and values. On the contrary, it's critical that we keep them. We need to change what we do with them.

Plans for the Future

EVERYONE has pet peeves. Complaints, grouses and grumps, things we don't like about other people. Sometimes these are relatively minor things like someone picking his nose. Sometimes they are more serious, like lying or stealing. We may voice these differences between ourselves and others, or we may not. Either way, we feel them. They have an ugly way of embedding themselves inside of us.

Behavior, actions more than thoughts, tend to be what we disapprove of most. We don't want to be *seen* to influence the behavior of others. We just want them to change those habits that bother us. We don't want to manipulate the behavior of others, as that's interfering in someone else's life. Most often we talk behind their backs, which ensures that they never learn about how annoying their actions are. Interestingly, should we have those same behaviors ourselves, we don't think to change them. We don't find ourselves annoying.

An example of a common peeve might be people spitting on a sidewalk. Almost everyone disapproves of it, in others, not in ourselves, especially if we feel we have good cause to do it. Imagine driving through a city and pulling up to a stop. On the sidewalk is a shabbily dressed person who horks a gob that would make a baseball pitcher proud and spits it onto the public pathway. Many would find this disgusting. Later we might drive past a dead skunk, with our window down, and inhale the acrid smell. We could actually taste skunk stink. We might want to spit out the window ourselves then.

We don't want to step in to personally take action to prevent people from spitting. For one thing, we don't know what to do. (Where is a cop when we need one?) We would prefer to think of spitters as perpetrators rather than sufferers. This excuses us from taking any responsibility. Governments look after perpetrators; that's why we have police and courts, isn't it? And health institutions look after sufferers, so that lets us off the hook.

Spitting on sidewalks is an example of negative (socially unacceptable) behavior in many places. If we want to change behavior, it would require a long time to accomplish. It's an ingrained habit. If spitting could be changed easily or quickly, it would have happened in cities all over the world by now. Either no one knows how to change it or there is not the will necessary among people to make change happen. We don't know what to do. We don't want to do anything that would cause ourselves grief later. So we do nothing.

Changing behavior requires a long-term commitment. It would require a sea change of policy and practice in any country to change behaviors that a majority of people consider bad. In general, our societies have very little long-term commitment to anything, let alone behavior change. For example, are we committed to peace? There are around thirty wars going on in the world in any given year, including this year. We read about single incidents, but may not think of them as wars. Leading industrialized countries do very little to influence the peace process in these countries. We are more apt to sell weapons to both sides in a conflict.

When we examine the commitment of our governments to long-term plans for peace, we find little more than rhetoric. Mostly we try to keep the combatants away from each other by what we call peacekeeping efforts. These are inevitably short term projects and rarely have much effect other than to delay conflict.

Are we, as a society, committed to end genocide and large-scale atrocities? In principle, yes. But, in fact, what we are committed to is punishing those who commit such inhuman acts, such as in the new International Criminal Court, in The Hague, Netherlands. The only deterrent that we have put in place to prevent genocide and massive atrocities is the threat of punishment. That is the same deterrent that is in place to prevent violent crime, and we all know how effective that has been to decrease the number of people in our jails and prisons. The United States has the highest per capita prison population in the world. Canada's prisons are overflowing. Crime is increasing; the only thing we have to throw at it is punishment. It's not working.

We are committed in principle, but not in practice. Long-term plans do not exist on a world order, such as at the United Nations, to bring peace to any part of the world.

Some of us have personal long term commitments toward abstinence, such as from smoking, drinking alcohol, gambling or drugs. But these are individual commitments. As hard as such individual commitments are to fulfill sometimes, they are within our control.

If we consider individual commitments, especially our own, we can see how difficult it is to maintain them. Some people even have difficulty committing to personal hygiene or good health habits such as not smoking. How much more difficult must it be, then, to have a whole community, state or nation commit itself to a major behavioral change of its member constituents?

The solution is that the commitment must be made decades in advance of when it will have full effect and there must be positive incentives for change along the way. There must be a guiding policy to follow so that the short-term actions of special interest groups, governments and education systems will not subvert the plan. That sounds pretty heavy, but we will find solutions as we go along that will make it seem lighter and more manageable.

For now, let's leave it that if we want to change some behavior like spitting on sidewalks or even road rage, it will require a long-term commitment. Simply passing a law or changing a regulation will not work. The same will apply to other changes of behavior, especially the changes in society that we all really want. The hardest part is making the decision to begin the process.

There will have to be choices made, priorities established as to what will be important in, say, thirty years time. Someone will have to consider the possibilities. We will address how to form priorities later. Standards of behavior will have to be established.

Those who are old enough to remember the language used by newspapers, television broadcasters and book writers thirty years ago can fix that in our minds. Compare that with how language is used in these media now. What's more, compare it with language used on the Internet. If language can change that quickly, so can other forms of behavior. Language is one of the essential components of our lives.

The Internet, the Information Highway, is proposed to be the primary learning medium of the future. Yet much of the language used in emails and chat messages on the Internet makes the messages confusing, ambiguous, even unintelligible.

We can argue that as long as two people understand each other, the use of language patterns does not matter. More and more small interest groups are establishing their own language usage patterns for use on the Internet. Indeed, many are creating their own vocabulary as a form of coded communication. In time, these interest groups will have developed their own languages, thereby excluding others from the group, which will be done by conscious intent. New world languages are developing, although few of us realize it.

The Internet, then, could signal the creation of a modern day Tower of Babel. While ancient languages are becoming extinct at an alarming rate of about one hundred and fifty per year, new languages and dialects are forming on the Internet. This turnover of languages is developing so quickly that most people are unaware that it's happening. We have no way of knowing how many new languages could develop from Internet groups. They could be based on business, special interests of their speakers, clubs or crafts, rather than on social and food interests as in the past.

How does this affect the price of cantaloupes in Amsterdam? Not much today. But it will make the world a different place in thirty years time. Do we want things to change that way? Is such a change positive for the world? Will it create more problems or could it help to solve problems that exist now? Should we care?

The answers to these questions will not put food on our table or keep a roof over our head. But they might affect the way we live our lives in a profound way in the next thirty years. We must plan now or accept the consequences later.

Should we do anything about this now? Small things can make a difference. We just have to know what to look for to know what to do. That is why we must do this together.

What life will be like in thirty years time is affected by what we do today. Someone needs to look ahead thirty or fifty years, imagine how lifestyles will evolve, then tell us how we would have to change now if we want to avoid bad developments in our future.

That will take a bit of explaining. We'll work our way up to it as we move through the book. Our objective is change, positive and widely acceptable. First we'll discuss why change is needed. Then we'll get into how to go about it.

Extremes of Behavior

EVERYONE dislikes extreme behavior, especially in others. What qualifies as extreme varies from one person to another, but there are many kinds of behavior that a large majority of us disapprove of. Some make us feel uncomfortable.

The most obvious form of socially unacceptable extreme behavior is hate. Hate expresses itself as vandalism, terrorism, prejudice, murder, dominance, slavery, torture and even such slights as ostracism and avoidance.

Extreme or socially unacceptable behavior has always been with us. Not the ends of the normal range of accepted human behavior, but things beyond that, acts that most people strongly dislike. These extremes would be the kind of behavior that most of us would rather not see, hear or think about. We don't even want to know that other people do that stuff.

Why don't we want to know about it? It's not part of our belief set of acceptable behavior. They violate our norms, our bounds of acceptable behavior. Where did we get that belief set, those norms? We learned them as children and developed them through our own life experiences. The operative word here is "learned".

Most of the behavior that we don't like in others has to do with personal confrontation (arguments), excesses of sex in the media, violence, addictions having to do with drugs, alcohol, gambling, corruption of politicians, use of obscene language and expressions of hate as noted above. If offenses related to these behaviors could be eliminated from the world, most people could live more contented lives.

It isn't likely to happen soon. We could take steps in that direction. That's why we have this book.

Unacceptable extremes of sexual behavior might be date rape, sexual assault or even the creating, selling or watching of pornography, in addition to the excess of gratuitous sex found on television and in movies. The Internet is ablaze with pornographic sites, most with aggressive marketing programs to promote themselves.

Violence could be in groups, such as gangs; individual, such as muggings or beatings; familial, such as wife-beating; or even watching it in movies. Obscene language could be on the street, in a shopping mall, on television, at home, virtually anywhere now and mostly would include words relating to sex and violence. Addicts could be anywhere, even attacking us in our homes. Hate is shown on every mass medium.

Let's look at offenses of sex and violence. Perhaps a list of names will suffice to remind us of some of the famous stories of the past. Joseph Stalin. Adolf Hitler. Pol Pot. Al Capone. Jack The Ripper. The Marquis de Sade. Henry VIII (if his wife did not bear a son, he had her beheaded). Ghengis Khan. These at least are names that most people recognize.

How far back could we go until offenses of this nature did not exist? As far back as we have folk stories and history. There seems little doubt that offences of sex and violence preceded recorded history. In fact, they likely formed as part of our nature as a species. They arose as a consequence of competition surrounding reproduction among early humans.

Have humans always had extreme behaviors regarding sex and violence, right from our beginnings? Yes, without doubt. That does not mean that we can't rid our species of these uncivilized drives. If we want to change this pattern, we will have to take measures that are different from anything that has been tried before. Nothing has worked to date.

As recently as two generations ago children in some elementary schools learned things about the "civilized world". They had maps that listed large areas in Africa as "Dark" or "Unknown" or with no definition at all, just a large white patch in the middle. This was fairly recent, although such areas were explored and well defined half a century and more earlier. Children were told that we didn't know anything about the people who lived in those places, that they were likely very primitive, and warlike. In those years children learned through movies about the "uncivilized natives" of North America and other continents, also often referred to then as "savages".

(NOTE: It was not taught, as such, in school that certain people were "savage" or that people from certain places were "uncivilized". It was left for some children to conclude this. It is important to understand this distinction. Movies were more specific than classroom teaching about this subject. Good guys were always white and spoke better English, and wore white hats, safari garb, army uniforms or carried police badges.)

Did presented material in some school classes lead to this conclusion about the meaning of civilization without it being formally taught? Or were some children at fault for misinterpreting the lessons? We can only say that these are the conclusions some children reached. Saturday movies reinforced their conclusions and even took them further to an extreme dichotomy of understanding of the terms "civilized" and "uncivilized".

What was there about us that made us "civilized" and others not? The conclusion some reached was that we had given up physical violence among ourselves in favor of dialogue to resolve differences. We talked out our problems rather than fight to see who could defeat the other side. This might have been the case more in Canada, where independence from the colonial motherland was gained through non-violent means.

World War II, where millions of people died while trying to murder each other or avoid being killed, was explained as a temporary aberration. Not a normal way of life for a Canadian.

There were wars going on constantly in other lands, but not in my own, so that may have had an influence. Oddly, there was little discussion in my classrooms about the relationship between wars (and war movies) and the degree of "civilization" of the nations that fought them. We were to infer that our country was more civilized than the bad people in the countries we heard about.

Were we actually more civilized or was that a false understanding? The degree of civilization of a nation is more one of perception than of reality.

Opinions about how civilized a nation is differ among individual citizens and from one country to another.

Are we more civilized now as individuals than we were a century ago? A hundred years ago, more people settled their differences with their fists than by going to court, as people do now. The War To End All Wars, World War I, did not do the job completely, so the combatants went back at it two decades later. There has not been anything like it in scale since 1945, though tens of thousands of people have been slaughtered in many countries most of us did not recognize as being at war since that time.

Before the world wars, large armies stood lined up opposed to each other and fired weapons until no one was left standing on one side. Prior to that, soldiers used sharpened steel to pierce the bodies of their enemies or amputate their limbs.

Yes, there are wars and military ventures now. The biggest of them are shorter than ever in the past, at least among industrialized countries, as many countries band together now to act against one country that may be committing violent acts against people within its own or a neighboring country. The strategic effort of these allied countries is to damage military installations and equipment rather than people, as much as possible. The plan is to damage property, not kill people.

If there is a war-like situation in effect now where NATO troops are involved, killing other people is frowned upon. Stuff is destroyed, but as few innocent people as possible are killed with guided missile bombs. Where there are few major military installations with materiel available to be targeted by bombs, there is still much slaughter of unarmed innocents by armed, hateful ("uncivilized"?) military personnel.

Judging by the scale of wars in recent decades, North American countries are becoming less violent as peoples, as civilizations. Whether we are less violent in special interest groups or as individuals is another matter. Statistics suggest that violent crimes in North America are fewer now than in the past, at least in some cities.

Are we less violent as a species? That is, are we evolving (socially) away from violent ways as we have less need to kill our food? This is open to interpretation, especially when our news presents us daily with reports of acts of terror. We may assume that there is more violence around the world because we hear about it more now than in the past. Yet this has more to do with advancements in technology that can bring us breaking news instantly than an actual increase in violence. Also, with many more people in the world today, it only makes sense that there would be some increase in violence.

All over the world people want to avoid war, even countries with the military might to easily win a war against their neighbors. In the past, the only incentive needed for one country to attack another was the likelihood that it could defeat that neighbor. Conquest meant power. Power meant riches and not having to account for our actions.

The power that is respected most now is economic might, not military strength. The richest countries can afford the mightiest armed forces and the most powerful weapons because they have a wealthy tax base on which to draw. We spend more of our peacetime efforts accumulating wealth through trade than by military conquest.

In the last century, winning a war often meant more hardship for the winners than for the losers. Compare Germany and Japan with Britain and France after World War II. The power of economic might, rather than military strength, could be seen by the huge investments made by companies in the Allied nations into the homelands of the defeated Axis countries. Germany and Japan, the losers of the war, became economic powerhouses while Britain and France struggled to recover from the damage caused by two world wars into which they had so heavily invested.

Even countries that have had border conflicts, disagreements and wars within the past fifty years are trying to settle their differences peacefully. At least peacefully compared with the way it was done in the past. An example would be differences that India and Pakistan have over control of Kashmir, the disputed land between these two heavily populated countries. These two nuclear powers have the fire power to kill each other, but they did not do so in 1999 when they had a relatively minor battle around the Line of Control separating their area of mutual interest. Border skirmishes since have been relatively minor compared with the possible results of exploding nuclear weapons.

Did each refrain from annihilating the other because of the fear of reprisal in kind by the other? Of course. But the skirmish ended with the Line of Control being where it began. It ended, in effect, when the NATO powers told Pakistan to get out of Indian territory or face severe economic reprisals after the battle. Economic power overwhelmed political ambitions. The military junta ruling Pakistan backed off because of the threat of severe economic sanctions to their already ailing economy. The politicians of each side claimed at least a moral victory.

Why are these countries not fighting again now? Simply, it is because the rest of the world powers have told them not to fight and have threatened further economic sanctions if fighting continues. In fact, minor conflicts exist despite lessened international sanctions, but they are of a sufficiently low level to remain below the radar of NATO concerns. Terrorism fills their agendas now.

Enough countries got together to advance the belief that wars are not the way to settle border differences. Historically, wars create losers along with winners. Losers wait until they can build sufficient strength to regain what they lost. When nuclear weapons could be involved, everyone pays attention. The weight of sheer numbers of countries, be they military or economic, forced India and Pakistan to stop fighting. Economic arm twisting by the International Monetary Fund and the World Bank and major sanctions by the United States helped.

Fighting did not solve the political differences between northern and southern Korea in the early 1950s. Half a century later these two countries are making overtures toward eventual reunification. Their differences are primarily economic and political. Progress is slow because the leaders do not want to give up their power, no matter how bad the effect has been on their people. North Korea, unable to afford to feed its people, let alone fight a war, is sharing diplomatic initiatives with its ethnically similar southern neighbor. If they believe they can build a strong economy together, they will move to unify.

Fighting did not resolve the political differences between North and South Vietnam in the 1960s. Once the foreign troops pulled out, the north almost immediately defeated the south. Now the combined Vietnam is moving to become an economic powerhouse in southeast Asia. The days of fighting are over. The days of building a strong nation are upon them. Vietnamese people are more interested in prosperity than in political idealism. Vietnam relishes its economic possibilities as one of the Asian Tigers.

Fighting a war, considered extreme behavior for a member of the international community of nations, is now socially unacceptable. The world's most powerful nations, both economically and militarily, are moving to prevent wars as much as possible.

It is worth noting that the most powerful nations also have the highest proportions of educated citizens. Higher levels of education in a country correspond directly with greater aversion to military conflict of any kind, especially where lives are lost. If they must enter a battle, organizations such as NATO drop bombs on inanimate military targets as much as possible, avoiding the loss of human life. Bombing to kill people, such as the two atomic bombs dropped on Japan that killed nearly a quarter of a million people and ended World War II, is considered extreme behavior that is no longer acceptable in the international community, especially in countries with higher levels of education.

What will happen in the former Yugoslavia now that the fighting has stopped in Kosovo and Bosnia? That will depend entirely upon whether the religious differences are settled peacefully or with violence, whether economic benefit will take precedence over religious hatred. A Serbia in civil strife will not become strong again. Good living conditions do not result from violence. Nothing of permanent good comes from violence in modern times.

Even the traditional combatants in the United Kingdom, the Protestants and Roman Catholics of Northern Ireland, have agreed to stop fighting each other with weapons and use words in their own legislative assembly. Will they succeed after so many decades of killing? That will depend upon whether they are more interested in the welfare of Northern Ireland than of their religious differences and hatred. It will depend upon whether they want to talk about their mutual benefits or fight again for their mutual destruction.

Economic factors did not play a major role in the conflict in Northern Ireland. If they had, the issues would have been settled years ago. The people of Northern Ireland finally came to realize that they were suffering from death and deprivation while others elsewhere were not. There had been too much death and too much fear for too long. The thinking of the rest of the world had changed and the Irish changed theirs to keep pace.

Are these lands more civilized places to live now? Are the people more civilized? It doesn't really matter how we define that word. There is more talk and less violence.

The fact is that there is a predominant world opinion now that the age of wars is past, that the age for dialogue and negotiation has arrived. That is a message that has been repeated over and over, around the world, for decades.

The League of Nations that formed and failed between the two world wars was to have been a forum for dialogue. It was doomed from the beginning because the long-term plan did not include the means to implement plans it formed. Its successor, the United Nations, was weak for many years, but is much stronger now that enough world opinion stresses that peace is better than violence. There is a forum for nations to talk among themselves now.

When the majority speaks, others must listen.

Embattled areas now look to the large land masses in Europe and North America where there is peace and see that peace is bringing prosperity. There is peace in all of the most prosperous nations of the world. Even in Russia, which was devastated economically with the fall of the Soviet Union, people are working sometimes without pay to pull together to make their country successful again. They believe in themselves and they will make it happen.

If violence can be defeated at an international level, then it can happen at all levels, even personal ones. At an international level, the incentive is not just peace but prosperity. At a personal level, the incentive can be freedom from fear.

In the mid-1800s there was disagreement between the north and south of the United States. Dialogue did not work. Conflict was the order of the day. So the southern states separated and the American Civil War (War Between the States) began. The northern states forced the southern states to abide by the will of the majority and return to the union. The side that caused the most damage to the other won. The southern states suffered financially and in other ways until they accepted that they should be part of the nation and should work together with their fellow Americans of the north. As the Civil War slowly fades from memory in the south, prosperity is gaining hold.

In Canada, the province of Quebec has been holding referendums every few years about separation from the rest of Canada. Each referendum has been preceded by a claim that Quebec is being dominated by the rest of the country, which is predominantly English speaking. Quebeckers do not want to lose their language and their culture.

However, the loss or saving of language and culture will have little to do with whether or not Quebec remains with Canada or becomes an independent country. It will have to do with how Quebec participates in the English-language-dominated economy of today's world, and how much Quebeckers want to retain their language and culture, not laws or international boundaries. Yet everyone on both sides agrees that violent confrontation is out of the question.

When the rest of the world that is flourishing economically combines forces, usually through associations or alliances such as the European Union or the North American Free Trade Agreement, isolating our own country for any reason is akin to choosing poverty. Most people in a free vote would not choose independence to become an economic backwater.

Talking and being prepared to learn new ways is the key for all parties with disputes.

Talking and learning new ways will be benchmarks of progress for the future. In the past, forming military alliances was the key to success or at least survival. These successes were related to conditions of the times. The world is changing so rapidly that military alliances are not as valuable as they once were. Military alliances serve to secure the economic ties that have been arranged through negotiations among trading partners.

Does this mean that we are more civilized now than in the past? This could be so. As long as we can afford to worry less about whether or not we will be at war with some other nation or part of our own country, we can spend more time devoting ourselves to the real challenges of our own country and our own lives.

This would be real progress for the human species. It happened because we agreed it should happen.

The real troubles of our country are severe enough to warrant our attention. The biggest problem each country faces (no matter what country) is its people. The things we don't like about our own people, including extreme behaviors, can be solved through talking and learning new ways.

Of course this involves education, which is covered in other chapters of this book. Learning and education are equivalents, so long as we understand that education goes beyond what we learn in school.

If a world affliction such as war can be overcome by talking and learning new ways, solving problems such as excessive sex, violence, addictions and abusive language are smaller goals by comparison. A majority of countries of the world now believe that peaceful means must be found to settle political differences.

This is a shocking difference from all previous human history. Whatever name we give it, this happened because of education, albeit often of necessity, and acceptance of new ways.

A worldwide cultural belief set against war was likely accomplished without our even knowing it. The wars that are going on now are relatively small compared to those of the past. They are taking place in relatively poor countries. Whether we have the collective worldwide will to improve the situation in these strife-torn countries remains to be seen.

We can, however, move to solve our own problems at home. This movement will involve, indeed require, participation on the part of everyone who does not like the way things are in their country now. The means for change will be a new form of democracy, one in which everyone with an interest can and must participate to some extent.

As a new form of democracy becomes reality, we should be participants, not spectators. Participating in the process will mean that we will have to learn enough to vote knowledgeably. We must be prepared to accept new ways of involving ourselves as citizens of our country. If we don't, we will be effectively left to history, in an emotional/social sense. Our choice will be to keep up or be alienated.

A new form of democratic government will require a new form of politician to operate it. We can see the conflicts now among the old-style politicians and the new ones. The old style politicians still rule the roost, but their support is eroding. Real change will happen when the old patriarchs retire over the next decade. People want to be informed about what their government is doing.

Changes are happening around us now. It's our choice. Participate in the ways of the new century, observe what is changing around us and adapt to it, or run the risk of being ignored or bypassed by those who will.

Rage

ANGER. Rage. Bullying. Pretty bad stuff. They scare the life out of some of us. Even shouting. Vigorous arm actions, thrusting fingers and fists. Wide-eyed stares, frowning, grimacing and other terrifying facial expressions. A level of energy and activity we seldom see in anyone otherwise.

It does as much harm to those who project the rage as to those who receive it. That fact doesn't comfort anyone. Someone is out of control. At least two people are suffering, the victim and the perpetrator.

What do those who experience the rage of someone else, the victims, feel? Fear, in most cases. Fear of violence, of possibly being attacked, a feeling of being violated. Fear of seeing a fellow human out of control and not knowing what to do about it. Fear of physical violence to themselves and others. We may not think of it as fear. We may consider it extreme discomfort, as no one likes to admit fear, even to himself.

We've heard about drive-by shootings. We've read about people being beaten to death from uncontrolled impulses. We know how a car can be used as a weapon to attack a person in another car. We know what guns are used for. We've watched those homicide shows on television and in films. We have seen hatred expressed in news film.

Road rage is a well-known phenomenon that causes concern in more than just people who drive. Anger and bullying have become a surprisingly common occurrence in the workplace. While victims of road rage suffer a single incident that seldom goes on longer than a few minutes, workplace bullying and anger adds a level of stress to any job that most people find difficult to cope with, even to the point of causing an emotional breakdown. These experiences are intimidating because there is the fear that these might turn into physical violence at any time.

Fear of physical violence depresses our immune systems, affects our health.

We are uncomfortable with any emotion expressed strongly by another person in public, especially if that emotion is not expressed directly to us. Think about it. Someone who is deliriously happy. Someone who is laughing uproariously but not with us. Someone who is so deeply in love that he or she seems to be drugged. Someone who is extremely sad because of the recent breakup of a marriage. Unless the person is a close friend or we are an integral part of a social event with the person, we are wary about being near him. Many of us would go out of our way on a sidewalk to avoid a person who clearly is experiencing one of these strong emotions. A person experiencing a belly laugh on the street is exhibiting unconventional, unexpected and unacceptable behavior.

We live in a society that consciously inhibits emotions and punishes those who exhibit them. Think of a party. Someone who is experiencing great sadness is seldom the focal point of attention of most people in attendance. Yet sadness is part of each of our lives. A sad person may need attention more than anyone else there, but we tend to avoid that person. A belly laugh is said to be one of the healthiest things we can do for ourselves, but it is considered crude behavior at a party. We assume a person who would laugh like that at a party must be drunk. Anyone else who is experiencing a strong emotion of any sort is similarly avoided by the majority.

When it comes to behavior and emotions, we tend to take strong opinions and sometimes strong actions in the form of social pressure against those who exhibit the extremes.

Demonstration of strong emotion is socially unacceptable in our society. We tend to alienate people who show them. We could accept a drug addict, an alcoholic, a gambler, an extortionist as part of a social group for conversation, so long as he or she fits in with the accepted group behavior. Accepting an emotional person into a social setting is considered a risk.

Emotions are part of our basic makeup as people. Ironically, we fault anyone who expresses any emotion strongly. We urge people to suppress their emotions. We teach this to our children before they reach school age. We teach adults by socially ostracizing them. Yet strong emotions expressed by others are finding their way into our lives, often in an unacceptable manner. It's upsetting to most of us.

Road rage is viewed as unacceptable behavior by a majority of people, even though almost every one of us experiences the feelings to some extent in ourselves. Others show their bad manners and their anger behind the wheels of their vehicles. Not us. We don't admit it anyway.

What can be done about road rage? Or any kind of demonstration of emotions? Should anything be done about expressions of emotion? Most of us agree that emotions that threaten the safety or comfort of others should not be shown to others. People need to be trained how to behave in a way that is socially acceptable to the majority of people in the community.

Something can be done about rage and other problems involving strong emotions that make us uncomfortable. People can be taught not to victimize themselves when others are expressing positive emotions. And the perpetrators of fear-causing negative emotions such as rage can be taught how to control them. Indeed, we can avoid these entirely if we know what to do and take action collectively.

This book responds to needs expressed by people in many parts of the world to find a way to make their country a better place to live. The desperate cry for a way to make their cities safer and their lives more emotionally and psychologically comfortable has been echoing around North America for decades. People want a means of turning around a civilization that has lost its way and seems to be headed for disaster.

The course we have been following is self-destructive. We have become so used to a troubled world around us that we sometimes take it for granted. Most of the time we just pass off what we don't like, hoping that we can just forget it. It does not need to be that way.

The purpose of the book is to provide a means by which the collective consciousness of the people of any given country or region can achieve its own goals of improving the lives of its citizens. Each country can go in the direction the majority of its people want to go, instead of the way it is being dragged now by the personal interests of those with influence.

We will be offered a path to follow and the reasons for taking that path. We'll go through it together. Us and a few million other good people like us. Perfect people? No, just average folks who feel that it's time to change things if we possibly can. We will do it because we can and because it's the right thing to do.

One person can change the direction that is being taken by a whole country. Especially when that one voice joins with millions of others that want the same things. Needless to say, we could find dozens of reasons why this cannot be done. Everything from "it can't be done because the Bible (or Nostradamus) predicts the destruction of the world and that destruction is obviously near", to "it can't be done because I can't even fight City Hall let alone save a whole country."

It can be done. Our lives and those of our fellow citizens can be improved. The problem is that most of us don't know how. We could be a part of saving our own country from the mess that it's in. What is at stake is the country that our children and grandchildren will inherit, and our enjoyment of the rest of our lives.

First let's begin with the premise that our own country is made up of good people. This is important for us to believe. If we are expecting a forecast of a repeat of Sodom and Gomorrah, then there are plenty of books with sinister motives and predicted destruction to entertain that kind of gloom. If we believe that there can be hope, that one small voice can make a difference, this book has a major role to play.

If we have a country made up of good people, why is everything so wrong? Almost everyone wants their society to improve. Don't we elect governments to do that? Shouldn't the schools be filling some role in this? Shouldn't someone other than us be doing something to improve life in our country?

Let's focus on that last question, especially the "other than us" part. Logically, if everyone other than us did his part to make our nation better, then there would be no need for us to get involved. But, if not us, then who? If everyone who reads this book believes that someone else should act to make changes, then there would be no one left to make the changes. That is the situation we are in now, the situation that brought our countries to their present state.

This book is not about apathy or noisy demonstrations. It will not ask us to take up placards and march on our legislative buildings, scream at our elected officials, riot in the streets. That way has been tried and has failed many times. There are peaceful, practical ways to make our thoughts and beliefs known to the right people.

It's our inalienable right to do nothing and to complain how no one does anything to help the situation. That is what most of us have been doing. Let's think about it.

If everyone takes the attitude that he or she doesn't have to do anything, then nothing will get done. Others who feel strongly enough that they will work for their personal agendas to be put into effect will hold the most influence. Those agendas may not be to our liking. That leaves us where we are right now.

Let's get back on track. We have our own country mostly made up of good people. Let's go a step further and say that everyone who reads this book is a good person. If good people do not act to save their country, their society, their world, then who should do this? The bad ones?

What should we each do? First get comfortable for a good read and some serious thinking.

Before the end of this book, we will know what needs to be done to create the needed fixing and how we can each contribute to it. What's more, with a small effort, we will be a part of the saving of humanity, at least the part of it we belong to. That's important. How much more important could anything get?

However we came to where we are now, we must continue to exist as a civilized species by saving ourselves. Blaming others for the state of our world just has not worked. We can't climb to higher ground by digging a hole. Continually being negative won't work. We need solid ground to build on and we need to think positively in order to create a better world on it.

Good people need to have children and train them to be good people, too. Too old to have kids? No problem. We can do our part with someone else's kids or grandchildren. We're not talking tax deductions and retirement funds here. We are talking about a return on investment in the future of humanity. We can't put a price on that.

We have to begin with young people. The younger the better. Newborns? Good starting place.

We are each part of the human species. We should prepare ourselves to prolong the existence of our species. We have a duty to see that our species survives, that it does not destroy itself and that it does not destroy the rest of the world in the process. It's our responsibility. We'll work through this together.

There are many good people who don't have any idea of what to do to help themselves, let alone their country or their species. That's all right. Good people just need some guidance, a route to follow. That route has not been evident until now. We are good people. Good people must do the saving, to prevent the few bad people from taking over.

Get ready, we have important ground to cover.

7
Humanity Versus Nature

Humans and human nature. What complex subjects! The largest and most industrialized civilizations of modern Earth have lost their connection to nature. We no longer see ourselves as being an integral part of nature, especially as part of the food chain. Rather, we see ourselves as being harvesters of renewable and non-renewable resources, owners and managers of vast resources and industrial complexes. Earth, we believe, is provided for our exclusive benefit. We enjoy a privileged position in the universe. So we think that we are an exclusive, privileged and unassailable species.

Much of what we do happens because there is some recognizable benefit for us. We concern ourselves with air pollution because air contains oxygen that keeps us alive, not because it also keeps almost every other plant and animal species that lives on the planet alive, too. We concern ourselves with water pollution because we understand that water is a primary component of our bodies and we must consume it to live, not because almost every other species requires it as well. Our personal needs are always placed in higher priority than those of other species and even, in some cases, than those of humans in other countries.

We have separated ourselves, by our own choice, from nature. Rather than working with nature and within its confines and laws, we use what we want of it as if it were our birthright.

We are in conflict with nature. We are in conflict with our fellow humans. We are even in conflict with ourselves, what we call human nature.

The nature to be considered in this chapter is twofold. One is the nature of the human species, the nature of humankind. The other is nature as it refers to the natural world in which we live. The latter meaning requires little explanation, as we are confronted with messages about our assault on nature in the media every day. The nature of humans, however, is more of a mystery, both biologically and psychologically.

What is our nature as a species? In describing ourselves, the way we are, the kind of persons we are, our emotions (control of them and loss of them), our characteristics, our virtues and our vices, we are describing our individual natures. In turn, we would get a different explanation of our individual natures if we were to ask our friends, neighbors, work and social associates, as they perceive us differently from the way we perceive ourselves. We might get something still different if we were to ask a clergyman or psychologist who knows us well.

Do any of these descriptions describe the nature of us when we are part of a group, or the nature of people in general when they are in groups? Clearly, the answer is no, at least not necessarily. The nature of groups, social behavior, is different from that of the individuals who make up the group, in many cases. Members of clubs, gangs or social groups behave differently when they are together than they do when they are alone.

A person who is known to have a peaceful nature, habitually in control of his or her emotions and pleasant with everyone, can have a violent outburst in which either physical or verbal (emotional) violence is inflicted upon others. When might this outburst take place? At times of extreme anxiety or great fatigue, when under the influence of alcohol or drugs, or when he is in a group where such behavior is seen as normal or at least acceptable.

Consider the current presidents, business and religious leaders and elite of society who were rebels and demonstrators in the 1960s. Some were even arrested by the police for their behavior that was at that time socially unacceptable. What was acceptable to them in their idealistic, emotion-charged youth is not acceptable to them today.

When young people of today demonstrate similar behavior to the way our leaders acted in their own youth, they get confused and look for differences between what they did and what the young people of today are doing. They try to justify what they did and condemn what today's youth are doing. Did the nature of these people change over time? No, just the fact that the behavior of their youth was demonstrated in groups, while their behavior now is more confined and defined as that of the individual person. People behave differently in groups than they do when they are alone.

These same leaders behave differently at home among their families from the way they do when they are among their club or fraternity group, especially when it comes to ritualistic behavior. Fraternities and service clubs, for example, have some rituals that would be considered strange or weird to outsiders, so are kept secret within the group.

What is the nature of a person, especially as it applies to this book? Is it his nature as an individual or his nature when he is in groups? Or is it his function as part of the natural world? These are just different rooms of the same house.

Consider this question: are the quests of people to dominate and defeat the natural world and to dominate and defeat their fellow humans part of our nature as individuals or as groups?

Humans are in conflict with their own nature, as a result of learning (called *socialization* by social scientists) in the early years of life, since we are seldom taught as children to dominate or defeat other kids. Was this childhood learning supportive of what was already their basic nature as humans or was it contrary to it? This problem is too complex for a simple silver-bullet answer. We must consider the possibilities and potential answers as we move through the book. Consider us as examples.

What we have done is to dominate nature, not to supervise and care for its welfare. In doing so, we have taught ourselves to believe that this is our human nature, that it is a right given to us by God. It is, in fact, contrary to our nature as a species. It is also contrary to our best interests as a species and as members of the natural world. Such has been the effectiveness of our teachings.

At the present time, Canada is known to other members of the United Nations as peacekeepers to the world. The United States of America is known as police officers to the world. Little has changed in terms of the attitudes of the two neighbors towards each other over the past two centuries.

There is a role on the world stage for each. There are also lessons that may be learned from these differences. One might say the natures of the people of the two countries are different, although, generally speaking, their value systems are almost indistinguishable.

Canadians saw the connection that Britain had with its dominion in North America as a benign and helpful one, if somewhat greedy. Canadian schools taught British history and fought alongside British soldiers in several wars. Canadian children grew up learning much more British history than they did Canadian or American history. Americans saw the British as oppressors, enslavers, two hundred years ago, yet the militaries of these countries fought side by side several times during the twentieth century.

Why the differences in perceptions of the mother country? The answer is simply that each group had been trained to believe in its point of view. Each group had been taught that its beliefs were right, that its cause was a just one. It's the same reason why ordinary people who have little interest in politics and would never consider hurting anyone risk their lives in battle for their country in wartime.

They believed because they were taught to believe that way. Remember that, as it will become important later.

Teaching is part of nature. Every species that does not have a complete set of instinctual behaviors at birth teaches its young. The young follow the teaching of the adults because it is the only way they know. Teaching is a natural function of the human species, just as it is with other animals. We learn from our elders, good, bad or indifferent.

If we want people to believe something, we must teach them that way. Best of all, teach them while they are young and growing. It's the natural way of doing things. That way they will have at the core of their learning what we want them to know and believe.

Just how far away from nature have we gone? The reasons for separation will help us to understand.

The split seems to have been created when an agriculture-based society evolved into an industry-based society with the inventions of the steam and internal combustion engines. An agricultural society depended very much on both animals and plants. Their welfare and continuity were very important to the continuity of the people. There was a symbiosis between farmers and their animals that did the heavy work and between farmers and their plant crops. Each benefited from the other and each helped the other.

When people left farms and gathered more into cities and those cities depended more on industry than agriculture, the interest of people was in minerals more than in animals and plants. Industry produced greater wealth than agriculture and produced it faster and more dependably. It created more jobs than agriculture. There was an apparently inexhaustible supply of mineral wealth in the earth. As minerals have no apparent life in a sensate way, the tradition developed of taking what was on or under real property, without putting something back.

Great industrialists, the wealthy people who set behavioral standards the rest of us followed, taught us that ownership meant being able to take without having to account for the taking in any other way than legal ownership. This attitude even extended toward other people, as the slave trade in the Americas shifted into high gear during these years, although not in industrialized areas.

We now use phrases such as raping the land, desecrating our heritage, as we realize that our natural resources have been severely depleted. Our attitude toward human use of nature changed as the natural resources became more evidently finite. In other words, if there is going to be an end to them, we had better preserve them. We are learning that change of attitude as we have been taught that over the past few decades in North America.

Where are we now in terms of our recognition of nature and our part of it? Many school systems do not teach young people that humans are part of nature, that we humans will either function in a symbiotic relationship with nature or we will destroy it. Many teach that we have a responsibility to look after nature. But this teaching is not supported fully in the community, in business and industry, even in our homes. Thus the lessons do not fully set in our young people, as the messages are mixed.

We have people who refuse to eat meat because they disapprove of killing animals. And, ahem, do they wear leather on their feet, carry wallets or purses, use footballs and a variety of other products that could not be made without animal parts? These same people do not hesitate to kill and eat plants, which have been proven to be sensitive, if not sensate in our normal understanding of the term. Plants respond to their environment just as animals do. But they do it slower than we do and in a different manner.

Plants have lasted on this planet much longer than animals, despite enduring many experiences equivalent to plant holocausts. In terms of life achievements, plants have been more successful than most animal species. Like us, plants share a drive to survive and to reproduce.

Plants are life forms. Perhaps plants function in a different time dimension than we do, a much slower one. So slow we don't perceive it in the same way we understand our own time.

Watch a hummingbird swoop, turn, hover and dart around at a speed that is difficult for us to see. Our brains don't function that quickly. Think how slow we must seem to them. Maybe trees look at us and wonder why we rush around so much. Maybe they think of us the way we think of ants. Oh, right, we highly developed humans with superior intelligence can't communicate well with any other living species on Earth. Yet we search for extra terrestrials.

Our schools teach about animals from books and the Internet. They teach relatively little about plant life and the inanimate part of our planet until at least the senior grades of high school, if at all. As our main understanding of life is founded when we are small children, this learning separation between when we need to know and when we are taught creates a lack of understanding when we are adults. It's these same adults who can't understand the connection between humans and nature that control the education systems that are training young children.

Recently, computers are being placed into our schools. Computers have the potential to be the next level of abstraction between humans and their natural environment. It doesn't have to be so. In fact, computers could facilitate learning about nature and our part in it. Or they could have the same net effect as video games on our young people.

What do we suppose that young people learn from video games? Do we really believe that they are time-wasters or tools to keep young minds occupied instead of their getting into trouble? What are they learning from music, television and movies that are filled with drugs, gratuitous sex and violence? Remember the music and the movies we watched when we were in high school. Chances are our beliefs and values now reflect those in the forms of entertainment you loved then.

It is in our nature to believe what we have been taught. What we learn can be from informal sources such as entertainment media as well as from formal sources such as parents and schools.

We wouldn't invite a murderer, a sex offender or another criminal to spend the evening with us and our family in our living room. Most people would be uncomfortable with this situation, knowing that somehow this person might influence their children. Even with adults there, it would not be considered safe. Yet millions of parents leave their kids alone with such people every day. True, they can't do physical harm to the children via the television or video game. Too few parents give a thought to the psychological impressions that these people are placing into the minds of children whose brains are still in the formative stages.

Recent research suggests that the frontal lobes of teens are changing rapidly during these years. The frontal lobes of the brain are the parts where concepts of right and wrong are formed and consciousness of the moment is considered. Television appeals directly to this part of their consciousness. In other words, teens sometimes have trouble distinguishing between right and wrong at the best of times while this brain growth is taking place. Into that situation, millions of parents are inserting television programs, movies and video games with enough bad guys that a small minority of kids could be permanently affected.

We should ask ourselves, as adults with considerable responsibility for and interest in the future of our respective countries and societies, if our feelings about what young people are learning from television, movies and video games make us comfortable, given the way the world around us is evolving.

The guys in the white hats don't necessarily win any more, as in cowboy movies of old. The heroes of many of our young people are the bad guys they see in these media.

That is not the way of nature. It is the effect of how we have allowed things to become. We don't need to abolish television. It is an excellent learning medium. We need to teach all parents their responsibilities about how their kids use the family television or ones they may have in their bedrooms.

The content of this chapter may be a bit confusing. Its purpose was to help us to understand how much confusion and contradiction we live in. We are a confused species. We don't know ourselves and we don't know how we fit in with the rest of nature, with the rest of our planet. We are trying to understand ourselves and understand everything around us. It's happening at an unprecedented rate, by historical standards.

We are so confused that we have come to accept our own confusion as a part of life. If anything, we think that our confusion results from our own lack of understanding of what others comprehend. Most of us are not aware that we are so confused. It's no wonder we make mistakes and are not certain we have made mistakes until it is proven that harm has been done. We shut the door after the horse has left the barn. We took action against smoking, for example, only after immense health damage had been done and untold thousands of people suffered and died from diseases caused by cigarette smoke.

We must decide where we want to be as a human species in the future, how we want to relate to the rest of our environment. That's a big job. If we don't, our civilization will get worse until we make it change. More confusion, more alienation, more suppression of our fear. The more confusion we feel, the more inclined we are to leave the teaching of our children up to others.

Until we decide what we want to be and how we want ourselves to be, we will not have objectives to aim for. Until we decide what our place is in relation to the natural world, we will continue to abuse it until, eventually, it may fail us and cause the collapse that will end human life as we know it.

Once we decide how we want our society to be, we can take positive steps to make it happen. We can set goals. That decision must result from a majority of people in our country speaking up, together, expressing their feelings and beliefs in such a way that decisions can be made and programs put into effect.

What we would like a country where we live to be will not come about until we and a majority of our fellow citizens say what we want. No politician will listen until he knows we have something to say. Complaints alone don't make the grade with them.

A majority can only be formed when many individuals speak up together, in unison when necessary and each in their turn at other times. A small effort by each individual can make a big difference this way.

One candle can light the way for one person or it can light many candles so that multitudes will be able to see.

Ignorance

WE live in an age of ignorance. At a time when history is being made at an unprecedented rate and more information is at our disposal than ever before, many of us don't know what we need to know. The problem is not just what we don't know, it's also that most of us are not aware of how little we know. In many cases, we don't even know where to go to learn what we need to learn.

Worse still, most of us deny it, a form of self deception. We claim that life is too fast, too complicated, anything to avoid admitting we don't know enough to function properly. We blame others for our difficulties. We long for a simpler life that not only doesn't exist, but never did in history.

Who cares about ignorance! Ignorance is what other people have, right? Not so. Everyone in today's world is ignorant to a greater degree than most of us could imagine. Several times each month we may be victims of our own ignorance. This inadequate knowledge can affect our lives in many ways.

Each time we take our car to a new shop for repair, we may become victims of our own ignorance. Of course it is wise if we take our car to be repaired by someone who has the skills and knowledge to do the repairs efficiently and accurately. But when we pay the bill, do we know for certain that we needed all of the parts that were installed, that the repairs corresponded with the symptoms of trouble, that it really took as long as the shop said it did, that the parts were installed properly, that the installer did the other prescribed checks that go with the repair that was done? Not likely. Most of us trust, pay and hope for the best.

Sometimes we will ask a friend for a recommendation about where to get our car repaired, often not. Between car repairs, we can survey people we know about their experiences with car repairs, looking always for the best deals. It could be that our ignorance about car repairs and limited opportunities for learning from both good and bad experiences will take too long for us to gain real expertise. We need input from other people in order to help us decide where to spend our money.

By acknowledging my ignorance about car repairs and seeking advice from other people, we can cope with our ignorance in a way that gives us an advantage over someone else who just takes his car to the nearest repair shop, trusts and hopes for the best. It gives us a slight advantage in distinguishing an unscrupulous repair shop from a good one, by combining our personal experience and knowledge with those of others.

Any time we spend money we are leaving ourselves open to becoming victims of our own ignorance, whether we know it or not. If we are unable to understand our electric bill, we may be charged incorrectly and not know. If we need to repair our kitchen sink, bedside lamp or barbecue and don't know how to find someone who can help us learn how, we may end up buying new or paying a high price for a professional who will do what we might have done competently ourselves.

At election time, those who don't know the issues and the positions of the candidates will be shooting in the dark. Our elected representatives may be the results of lots of guessing by ignorant voters, not necessarily of the wisest choices by an informed electorate.

Should we have an opinion as to whether our country supports a peacekeeping effort in a warring nation in Africa or the inclusion of India as a senior member of the United Nations Security Council? These decisions could affect us or our families in years to come, in ways we could not imagine now. Our children or grandchild might be called to defend our country or might be victims of violence by militants unhappy with our country's participation in peacekeeping in their country.

We should only have a right to express our opinion if we have sufficient background knowledge on which to base our beliefs. Ignorance on these subjects should bar us from having the power to make a contribution to such decision making. Participation by uninformed voters in decisions about important matters could be worse than leaving the decisions to crooked politicians.

The more we fail to recognize our ignorance on so many subjects, the smaller our personal world becomes. We humans tend to avoid any subject about which we don't know much. Those who know very little have a very small personal world. Ignorance also is the breeding ground for prejudice and oppression. We fear what we don't understand and resent or hate those who do. People with very small personal worlds tend to be the most intolerant.

The more we recognize and accept our own ignorance, learn to cope with it and overcome it when necessary, the smaller the physical world seems and the better we can manage our lives as part of it, and the more people of different races, colors, religions and homelands seem like our brothers and sisters.

In the past, it could have been said by an arrogant expert in a particular subject to another who was not, "What you don't know would fill a book (or an encyclopedia)." At the time, what any one person, even the most well-read person, did not know about all subjects combined would fill an entire library. Those were the good old days when we didn't know much about any given subject. Now all the information available to us can't be contained in ten giant libraries.

With the arrival of the Information Superhighway, the Internet is the reservoir that comes closest to holding the sum of human knowledge. It is nearly impossible for any one person to become extremely knowledgeable about more than one subject, let alone many subjects, as was possible in the past.

Now people with access to the Internet can learn what they need to know. Yet we are limited in many ways, time being the greatest, from becoming well-read on many subjects. Sometimes a little information is enough to cause us to make incorrect conclusions and dangerous decisions. Even those who know how to cope with their own ignorance will be challenged.

Through most of the second millennium CE, humanity's knowledge base grew slowly, requiring several hundred years to double in size. It required only the first half of the twentieth century to double again. By the end of the century, with all of the research going on in the world, the total of human knowledge was doubling every few years.

How much can one person absorb?

How much knowledge does one person need to know to function reasonably well in our society? What knowledge would that be, if we intended to make it compulsory in our schools? Who would select this material and what criteria would be used? This is important. The people who are making those decisions on our behalf now might not be qualified.

In the future, if all human knowledge could be dealt out carefully and selectively, should we all have a base set of the same knowledge and each have public access to expert sources? Should each of us hold a portion of human knowledge as preservers of what our species has learned? That is, it might be possible for a few select individuals to each have expert knowledge in one subject area, each being the bearer of one section of the total puzzle. That, in theory but not in practice, is the system we have now.

In a sense, this was tried unsuccessfully in the last century, through professions such as medicine and social sciences, each with their various specialties. The trouble arose because many problems required input from several specialties and the professionals consulted each had a vested interest (pride) in providing the most significant contribution to the solution of a problem.

Experts in different disciplines and areas of expertise sometimes would not work well together. Dominance in the area of recognition (the leader/boss) became more important than getting the most effective solution for the problem.

Each of us has a need, maybe even a right, to understand who knows what in our society and where to find these people. If we don't, we will live surrounded by ignorance. Real social problems grow in an atmosphere where ignorant people are not aware of their own ignorance, in other words, where we aren't certain of what we don't know. In a world of ignorance, everyone is a potential enemy. Everyone could be a threat. Paranoia and hatred are real possibilities.

During the early part of the last millennium, political leaders and feudal lords believed that knowledge beyond what one absolutely needed was not only unnecessary, but dangerous. The theory, which proved to be remarkably effective, was to keep the masses ignorant so they would not know what they were missing. There was actually a net loss of stored human knowledge for several hundreds of years. Libraries were destroyed. No one knows now how much we lost during that period. If it had not been for monasteries in Ireland and a few other select places, the entire base of Western thought would have been lost forever.

Through the Middle Ages, there were only a few repositories in the world where human knowledge was stored. In what we now call the Western World, the best were the monasteries of Ireland. The monks painstakingly copied and preserved all important written works that exist now from earlier days.

That changed with the Renaissance, which brought about a new era of thought and creativity. Now we are on the brink of a new Renaissance.

The alarming rate at which we repeat the disastrous lessons of history suggests that we have put more emphasis on the history of products than we have on the history of people.

With teachers being forced more and more into accountability regimes where their effectiveness (and sometimes even their pay rate) is judged on the ability of their students to memorize facts to be spewed back on standardized tests at this turn of the century, teachers are being forced into rote learning situations not significantly different from the way kids were taught a century ago, and the way kids are taught now in many poor countries.

Our teachers may not have helped us to understand the importance of what they were teaching because they didn't know. They may simply have taught the facts and skills they were instructed to teach. Are teachers in today's high schools repeating the same mistakes as those of the past? Ask the teachers. "No, things are much better now," they will say. Ask the students. "School is boring. My teacher is boring," may be the reply.

A famous old saying goes this way: those who do not learn the lessons of mistakes made in history are destined to repeat them. Heard that? Probably. Didn't mean anything, right? Why? Maybe because no one told us the significance of it. There wasn't going to be a test. So, we go ahead and repeat the mistakes of the past.

But there may be a test soon. Not on paper. This one will be real life. Ignorance comes at a terrible price.

If the sum of human knowledge is increasingly on computers, and it is, and decreasingly on paper, what happens when the power goes out? A lack of resource books while computers are becoming available in classrooms is making the Internet a critical part of the curriculum. What happens if a supervirus invades the Internet and destroys every computer that is connected online? In Afghanistan, following the war, Internet connection was non-existent.

Big computer databases are brought to their knees frequently. Repairs cost a fortune, money that is seldom budgeted fully, especially for schools. Fortunately the interruptions to school computer networks have been small so far. It would be better if human knowledge were in the brains of people and it were well known who these people are.

We live in a world of ignorance. It is inevitable, as the world is too complex for us to know much about any one subject. That is a reality we must face. It will not change. We can improve literacy skills, but each brain will only hold so much. We must accommodate ourselves to that. It will require adjustments on our part. There is too much for any one person to know. We need to have the skills to find out what we need when we need it.

This is not to scare, but to inform. Maybe we have been leaving the important stuff to someone else. Trouble is, everyone else has been leaving it to someone else too. Whose responsibility is it? Everyone's answer is "not mine."

If not us, then who? It has been well said that indifference is a sin.

Will someone accept the responsibility to be a repository of knowledge on our behalf? It may not be to our best advantage to sacrifice this responsibility unless we have a way to access that knowledge when we need it. First we have to accept that we have a responsibility for the continuation and advancement of the human species. Then someone might be prepared to take on that responsibility for us. But if we don't participate, why should anyone else care about our problems?

The sum of human knowledge is increasing rapidly. How can we accommodate that? We can't know everything. It takes considerable planning. It's not something our governments can appoint a committee to study and report back in six months.

It requires serious planning over a very long term. Decades.

Will this require a lifetime commitment for us to help? No. If everyone does a little, together, things can be changed for the better. It won't happen overnight. The sooner we begin, the better for everyone.

Violence 9

Humans are violent. We have been both aggressors-perpetrators and victims of violence throughout our history as a species. Violence has been a factor in each life in the history of humans. So it has been with each member of the animal kingdom.

Every animal and human lives by eating other living things. Most of this eating is done by microscopic life that eat both plants and other animals that have died. Larger animals eat other animals or living plants, from which they get nutrients. Rarely do animals kill other animals for any reason other than food, mates or territory.

With a few rare exceptions, only humans kill for other reasons. Bullying occurs in all social primates where there is a need for an order of dominance. However, gratuitous bullying for other reasons happens only among humans.

Along with this distinction for unnecessary killing and bullying comes another, which involves harming others, sometimes with twisted rationale, sometimes without any reason at all. We react to this hurt or the threat of it with fear. In some people this fear is active. In most of us it is suppressed. This fear is unproductive, damaging and restrictive in that it affects how we conduct our lives, sometimes in ways we do not realize.

This kind of unnecessary violence is something we would like to rid from ourselves. It's not natural. It is learned. What is learned can be unlearned. Better still, we should act to avoid having it learned in the first place.

Violence rages within us every day as our immune systems do battle with invading microbes. We are the hosts of that violence and, most times, the beneficiaries of its results. This is an animal-versus-animal kind of warfare, at the microscopic level. Violence external to our bodies varies in form, duration and intensity from one instance to another. Most of the external violence is of the psychological variety, including arguments, office or factory bullying, road rage and television dramas. Then there's the real-life personal, physical violence we read about in newspapers and see on television newscasts.

All of us experience psychological violence. Sadly, too many of us experience physical violence in our personal lives. While we concern ourselves with punishing the perpetrator and comforting the victim of such physical violence, we do little as a society to correct the causes that made the aggressor act out his sick behavior or to prepare potential victims to be able to cope with abuse against her or him.

Humans have had violence cast upon them by nature. In our distant past, large animals preyed upon us. Hurricanes and cyclones have taken thousands of lives each year. Volcanoes, twisters and tsunamis (a.k.a. tidal waves) have taken fewer lives, but in a much more certain, swift and frightening manner. Disease has taken more lives than all of the human wars and natural disasters put together. These are kinds of violence of which we have been victims, but over which we have little control.

Even as more cures for diseases and debilitating conditions are coming forward now than ever before with the dawn of this new millennium, new diseases are breaching the horizon and marching upon us. Well-known bacteria and viruses that were thought to be defeated or at least well under control are gaining new life with the new nickname "superbugs".

True or not, our media capitalize on our fears that still more terrifying diseases and destructive conditions could be in our future due to genetically altered foods, cattle with possibly dangerous diseases that may or may not be communicable to humans (but no one wants to take the chance), drinking water that was safe by old standards for people who lived an average life span of forty years but might not be safe over twice that length of time, life-giving air that could be filled with who knows what and overcome us in a matter of seconds, saturated fats that plug our blood vessels, too much vitamin C, too many prescribed drugs, and so on. This fear mongering is a form of psychological violence against each of us that few even understand and fewer acknowledge.

The media also eagerly report every incident of violence by one person against another. In a sense, this is double jeopardy, as we hear about real physical violence against others in grisly detail, making us uncomfortable about our home communities and causing us to fear potential violence against ourselves.

Despite the fact that invasion by aliens from space or collision with an asteroid remains a remote possibility, we will find every possible hint of them played up in the mass media. Is it our hunger for fear and violence, as they claim, or the love of the media for fear mongering that sells advertising?

Unlike the past where acts of ethnic cleansing and genocide in foreign countries were not reported much in North American news reports, now the news services send correspondents to the scene for live reports and video footage of every act of destruction and mayhem they can find, can afford and will sell.

Everyone who was beyond the age of puberty at the time remembers the day that U.S. President John F. Kennedy was shot in Dallas. The explosion of the space shuttle *Challenger* has long past, but will not soon be forgotten. The image of half a building that blew apart in an explosion in Oklahoma City, killing many people, remains with most of us. Everyone can recall the image of one or more scenes of hurricane damage. The names Columbine and Littleton instantly bring the school-shooting story to mind. No one will forget the World Trade Center buildings crashing to the ground.

Entire industries have been created to satisfy our ever-increasing need to worry about our health. As worry and fear are the most self-destructive forces we have in our arsenal, should we consider these industries as health risks in themselves? The media claim they are satisfying our craving for news of violence and threats to our health. In fact, they are playing on our fears that unknown destructive forces may be at work against us. This is psychological violence. The media create a market for this just as they create market needs for products through advertising.

The kind of violence that most concerns North Americans is the kind that should be within human control, the kind for which we have made laws to protect us, the kind that one human being commits against another. It frightens us when we hear that one of our community members has been hurt or killed by another. We hate it when someone even raises his voice, as it suggests that physical violence might follow.

There are people all over the world suffering from post-traumatic stress disorder. For some, involvement in a violent event such as a war, severe accident or death of someone significant to them has caused this tragedy. For others, violence against us personally or someone close to us has caused us mental anguish. Violence in our society, in our community, is something which distresses us. We suppress our concern to carry on with our lives as if it didn't matter. The effects on us of violence vary. No one other than those with a death wish likes violence.

No one is completely certain of the extent that media reported violence, real and fictional, and video and computer game violence have on the health of our people.

While we normally think of violence as those acts that do harm to the physical body, it is equally true that psychological violence may be wreaked upon us from many quarters, including the media, our fellow workers, our neighbors and even our own family members. Some claim that certain types of television advertising are forms of psychological violence. Unless we knowingly choose to embrace such advertising and have the skill to sort through it, our conscious mind is being assaulted in a way that is not of our choosing.

If we can accept that, then we must accept that some programming is also assaulting the minds of viewers, whether or not they appreciate what is being imposed upon them. Remember, just as standards of acceptable levels of physical violence vary from one country to another, acceptable levels of effects of psychological violence may vary from one adult to another in our own country.

Our thresholds for violence vary from one person to another. What does not significantly affect one person may impact heavily on another. The problem is not with the large majority of adults in our communities, only with a tiny minority that may not have the skills that most of us have. The people with twisted values don't go away because a majority of us are balanced. The more prisons we build, the more people we find to fill them.

For those who have more physical interests, there are wars. An average of thirty wars rage in the world at any given time, even now in these enlightened modern times. Historically, people in most parts of the world have been free of war for only an average of twenty to thirty years.

The young men of most countries have been invited to fight on behalf of their country's interests in at least one war for centuries. The most notable of these would be two world wars in the past century. Many living persons will remember commitments their countries made to wars in the former Yugoslavia, the Persian Gulf, Vietnam, Korea, Spain, South America, all within the span of one lifetime. These were major conflicts, with many fewer soldiers returning from them than left to fight in them, although few North American lives were lost in the first two.

In addition to that, we have had major incidents of genocide, including what we call the Holocaust, the slaughter of millions in Stalin's Russia, Cambodia, Rwanda, Costa Rica and other countries with fewer innocent people murdered in the same century.

While we won't debate the details of the Holocaust or condone its atrocities in any way, we should note that this kind of reaction by Germans during those years does not make sense out of context. There is no way that people of any nationality would normally act that way. But they did.

The explanation is that Hitler's deputy Goebbels had put on such a convincing campaign of false and carefully edited information that millions of people were persuaded to act in a way which was completely opposed to their natural inclinations. German people are not naturally violent, any more than any other people. The Goebbels propaganda campaign leading to the Holocaust was the single most effective mind-altering effort in human history.

Fortunately, the second most effective campaign has been that following World War II, the campaign to ensure that such a tragedy does not happen again.

In wartime, we call a campaign to alter people's thinking and actions propaganda. In peacetime we call it advertising, training or socialization. Or teaching.

Can people mount a campaign for good with the effectiveness of a propaganda campaign? It worked so successfully for evil, why not for good? Perhaps that is what has driven the International Criminal Court, the United Nations and NATO (North Atlantic Treaty Organization) to stop acts of genocide and to punish the psychopathic perpetrators. We don't want to send our young men to these war scenes to risk death, but we have been convinced that it is the right thing to do.

Since World War II, the number of wars that have involved huge numbers of fighting soldiers have been relatively few. In fact, a large majority of adult males living in North America today have not seen action in any fighting situation.

What, then, has taken the place of a war to satisfy the aggressive urges of young males? Hockey and football are the two most prominent candidates. Professional hockey not only condones some forms of violent aggression, but in some ways encourages it. American style football is war with padding. Even professional basketball and soccer have their share of violence.

Amateur leagues often have tighter rules against violent behavior than professional sports, though they are equally aggressive in their style of play. Participants in other team and individual athletic endeavors, such as those that culminate in the Olympics, world championships or World Cup events technically qualify as amateur. These tend to be non-violent. However, most still require each participant to be active and aggressive enough in his or her performance that anything less than the maximum energy output is unacceptable.

Some people seek physically and mentally strenuous activities but avoid violence elsewhere in their lives. They condition and train themselves to be aggressive to achieve a goal, but they stop short of the violence outside of that controlled context, the kind that characterized earlier generations of humans.

Athletic activities with aggressive play that does not succumb to violence may be regarded as positive, socially acceptable events.

What about the rest of the young males and females of the species who do not participate in sports or athletics? How do they find outlets for their natural aggressive tendencies? First of all, that natural need for aggressive or violent activity tends to decrease considerably after the age of forty. That leaves us with a large number of younger people, mostly males, that need some kind of outlet for their aggression that older males and most females do not, to the same extent.

Three significant questions jump to the fore. What outlets for physical aggression do these non-athletic young males use? What, if anything, motivates them the way team leaders, managers and coaches motivate athletes? How do most non-athletic males manage to restrict their expression of violence to socially acceptable outlets? One need only look at the number of males under the age of forty in North American prisons to know that we have problems. The answers to all three questions are discouraging.

For years people have been crying out that there is too much violence on television, in movies, on the streets. Kids get experience with violence with hand-held computerized games. Think about how physically close that game screen is to their brain. Media guru Marshall McLuhan said the medium is the message. This message is violent and is plugged almost directly into the brains of the players.

How much harm can this do? The evidence is rolling in and it is not good. In 2000, a group of professional medical organizations, including the American Medical Association, the American Academy of Pediatrics, the American Psychological Association and The American Academy of Child and Adolescent Psychiatry, issued a joint statement condemning entertainment violence. It pointed to children as the group most likely to be influenced by violence in entertainment, leading to aggressive attitudes, values and behavior.

This doesn't mean that all children will be influenced by violent entertainment. Then again, most children do not grow to become social problems in our society either. It's always the most susceptible minority that must concern us.

The statement claims that studies of large numbers of children show that young people have become desensitized to violence. They have come to accept that it is a part of their lives. They have seen so much of it that they don't consider it as anti-social as their parents and grandparents do. This is not to suggest that they like violence, only that they accept it more readily.

These medical groups do not make such statements lightly, as they know the opposition they will face from those who benefit from selling violent forms of entertainment: people with deeper pockets than the medical associations.

Young people see themselves as victims of the society in which they live. They feel they can't control it. Many believe that violence is an acceptable way of settling conflicts. Violence is, they believe, sometimes the only way they have of settling disputes. They don't have access to other acceptable methods of conflict resolution. The don't know how to avoid violence.

What motivates some young people to channel their aggressive tendencies into activities that we do not as a society consider to be overly violent or unsociable? Some young people do not need motivation from others, as they are able to find acceptable outlets for their aggression on their own. We need to study what works for some and spread the news around.

What happens to the young people who do not involve themselves with sports and do not get involved with other forms of socially acceptable release for their aggression? These are prime candidates for socially unacceptable kinds of behavior. If they suffer from enough anxieties and alienation from their peers and parents, they are the ones who cause the kinds of problems that worry us most as a society. They are the ones who commit what we call personal violence.

A few decades ago, around the time that the post-baby boomers were being born, there was a movement to somehow equalize the sexes. Girls, it was said, should be given the opportunity to play with traditional boys' toys, play traditional boys' games, and be encouraged as boys were to believe that they could handle themselves well in traditional male jobs and roles. And boys should be encouraged to explore their more gentle and creative inclinations, characteristics historically considered to be more feminine than masculine.

Generally speaking, this program has been successful. Women now occupy greater than ever proportions of positions in formerly male-dominated professions such as engineering, law, medicine, and they virtually control many office roles. They are even breaking into traditional male bastions such as the military, although only a limited few North American women see action when the guns are being fired. More men than ever are involved in teaching and nursing and many fathers are the parents who stay at home when the children are young while mother works full time.

When the movement first began, little boys still wanted to play with G.I. Joe dolls and girls with Barbies. Now how do both genders occupy their time? In their preschool years, they watch a lot of television. For decades now, North American televisions have been on for five hours or more each day; some studies say it's eight hours a day for preschoolers. Television has become the babysitter of choice in North America.

What are these little people watching on television? Anyone who hasn't watched some children's programs lately should invest a little time to find out what our children, the most impressionable minds in our society, are being offered. With some notable and marvelous exceptions, our children are being shown acts of violence at a rate that is almost beyond the comprehension of most adults.

It's interesting to note how many adult North Americans claim they hate the children's television character Barney. This character, which embodies almost everything good and decent in our society, tries to make children happy and teach them how to get along with others. These same adults who hate this peaceful, lovable character are role models for our children.

We can't teach our younger generation to be less violent, to be more peaceful and tolerant, while practicing the opposite ourselves.

Some television stations have grouped together to demand less violence in children's programming. As commendable as this is and as successful as they have been in reducing the amount of violence shown to children, consider this. Has a reduction of ten deaths or fights in a half hour down to one or two been a big improvement? Do our children learn less about violence that way? For certain it has eased the consciences of many adults and resulted in much back-patting among station owners. It hasn't made an improvement in the amount of violence in our society.

Consider this too: given how many hours each preschool and school aged child watches violence each half hour, will that reduction be enough to ensure that no child will ever act out in a similar way when he gets into his teen years? Think Columbine? Those of us who recognize that school name have the answer.

It only takes one alienated teen with anti-social ideas about violence and power to become a force for evil in a country years later. Adolf Hitler was such a teen. They have abundant role models to follow in their various forms of entertainment. Perhaps we are fortunate that our violent teens kill only a few others rather than becoming war-mongering political leaders.

These young, impressionable minds do not stay young forever. Once they get to school age they play video games, go to movies and watch endless hours of television.

Is this right? In our heads, our hearts, in our guts, is there anything that tells us that this is the right kind of activity for young people to involve themselves in? If there were a choice, in an ideal world, would we want our children or grandchildren to watch this kind of thing?

Evidence is building that these activities have a negative effect on young people who have experienced them, after they reach adulthood. Full proof cannot be presented until the damage is too horrific, perhaps past the point of correction.

Mass media news sources frequently show us that violence has become a way of life among some groups of young people. They may not become mass murderers, rapists or other dangerous criminals. But that constant barrage of violence must affect their attitudes in some way. That way can't be good. A price is being paid each day as acts of violence tally in their minds. We may not become fully aware of its impact until it becomes intolerable.

Keep in mind that the high schools of today might not be like those we grew up in. There are more weapons than most of us even want to think about being carried by students now. In those schools where weapons are forbidden, there are armed guards patrolling the halls and scanners at entranceways. Drugs appear for sale in most high schools. Alcoholism has become a regular fact of life in a startling number of students. Drug use, including designer drugs and cheaper methods such as glue sniffing, is common. Teen suicide rates are shocking.

Are these the minds we want to be constantly assaulted with visual acts of violence and death? Why take the chance? It might only take one vulnerable mind in a crowd to create a sniper or a rapist.

If a large majority of young males who are not involved in sports or athletics can confine their natural aggressiveness to socially acceptable alternatives, we should be able to channel the remaining minority in the same or some other manner. We need to have all children raised from birth with the same values, values that we all agree do not include personal violence. And we need to have outlets for aggressive tendencies that help each child to get exercise of mind and body, gain in self-esteem and avoid thoughts of committing violence of any kind.

North American children were historically taught a great respect for life. Movies, books, magazines and stories galore tell of the heroism of some people who risked their own lives to save another's life. A human life is the most valuable thing we have. At one time it was illegal to even attempt suicide. A human life was sacrosanct.

Think about what an adolescent is taught about his or her future. The 1990s was a decade where young people learned that few employers wanted to hire even qualified graduates of colleges, unless they had been in Information Technology courses. As a society we have been pounding into the heads of young people for decades that they won't get a good job unless they have a good education. Those without a degree will be lucky to find a dead-end job, a drudge job, a flunky job, if they have any employment at all.

Guess what, folks, kids believe what they have been taught. Many of them also know that they will be unable to go to college, for a variety of reasons. College is expensive, for one. We have unintentionally convinced these young people that they have no hope for a bright future. Surely we can't be surprised if they engage in behaviors that are dangerous to either themselves or others. We can't be surprised if they do things where they are living on the edge of safety and well beyond the grasp of security.

Without a future, what do they have for themselves? They know that, at best, a dead end job is ahead of them for over forty years of their adult working lives. For some, this is more than they can bear.

At this time, out of large numbers of young people who believe that they may not be able to find happiness and success in their lives, there are a few who commit violent acts. If that number grows to more than a few, these young people will find each other and form gangs whose primary activities will be organized crime and violence. There are many such gangs in the major cities of North America today.

If the situation of hopelessness about the future is allowed to continue and gang mentality proliferates, pockets of hate violence will develop. These are evident now in Northern Ireland, Kosovo, several parts of Africa, the Middle East, south Asia, southeast Asia, parts of South America and several of the Pacific islands. There is clear evidence of it now in the inner city areas of large metropolitan centers in every country.

Movies and plays have been warning us for decades about what will hap-pen when hopelessness about the future becomes more common. There are abundant examples of what will happen. We haven't paid attention. Life imitates art.

We have done a marvelous job of teaching some young people that they are worthless to the society in which they live. We didn't mean to do that. But that's the net effect of what we have accomplished with our heavy-handed way of threatening kids that they had better go to college after high school or they will lose in life.

That kind of threatening had the effect we wanted for the young people who did go on to college, especially in the early part of the last century. We convinced those who could not that they could have self-esteem by fighting in a war. That kind of teaching is out of date now. The ones who won't succumb to it become problems to themselves and others. There are many who will not accept this threatening because they believe it violates their rights. Sadly, they believe the message we teach without thinking.

We need some new ways before we destroy more lives with our well meaning threats. Heavy-handed ways do not work on young people now, especially on the ones who have emotional baggage to carry, who have learning disabilities of some sort or who are behind in some form of their development.

Going by past performance, learning difficulties are not readily evident to either parents or teachers without careful testing. Some are missed, they "fall through the cracks." We had better find some new ways before we carelessly destroy more lives.

For one thing, we need to give some evidence to young people that they will have a good place in the world, not that all they have to look forward to is a worthless, reject job. We used to teach respect for work and respect for our jobs. Now we give all sorts of examples that neither is of value, that what really counts with a good job is the income it brings. We teach that a job with a low income is for losers. We must again teach the value and importance of all work and the effort that goes into it.

Whatever changes we make, they had better be soon and they had better be positive. If not, we will continue to breed waves of young people who are frustrated with their lives, who believe that we have cheated them by bringing them into a world that is so bad for them. We may not want to believe that we are teaching kids that their lives are dead ends. But that does not change the fact that many think that way. And some of them will take out their anxieties in violent ways.

We are violent as a species. It's part of our nature. The process of civilization of a society includes training of its citizens to find ways to avoid violence, to live together in some measure of peace and harmony, to work together for our mutual benefit. This kind of training or socialization must take place when children are very young. Everything a person is and has the potential to be has its roots in a child's first decade. Whatever works must have taken hold before a child is ten if the training is to have a meaningful and lasting effect for a lifetime.

Are we becoming more civilized? The debate is on. We can make changes for the better. They must be wide ranging, simple to understand and be agreed upon by a large majority of the population. That may not have been possible or practical in past centuries. Technology and education today give us the ability to make changes happen.

We can influence the amount of personal violence in our lives and our communities. What we need now is to resolve to help make it come about.

We can make a difference.

---

* Christopher Stern, "FTC concludes entertainment industry ignores own warnings," *The Washington Post*, Washington, August 27, 2000, and Archives of Pediatrics and Adolescent Medicine 2000;154:366-369

10
Fear

Fear, the driving force of life. Fear influences much of what we do as a society.

If fear is a major factor in people's lives, then we should know more about it than we do. If the goal of this book is to improve the quality of our lives, then we must understand the factors that influence us in significant ways. Fear is a big one.

We can have a society that is the way a majority of us wish it to be. We don't have to suffer fear to the extent most of us do. We suffer because we are unprepared to cope with the unfortunate and tragic events of our lives. Worse, we are not prepared for what might happen as a result, so we fear that part as the unknown.

September 11, 2001 (9/11) was a shock to all US citizens and millions of people around the world. The "war on terrorism" and the publicity surrounding it have caused more anxiety than the risk of further terrorist attacks would warrant. We're afraid because we've been told that terrorism could strike any of us at any time.

Understanding fear as an integral component of our lives, rather than as an unreasonable, excessive and accessory emotion, is a good place to begin.

As personal survival is a basic instinct, fear of death keeps us busy for most of our lives. Fear of starvation drives us each day of our lives. These are hardwired into our brain systems. They are instinctive.

We may be afraid of heights, open spaces or closed spaces. We continue to have fears that influence our lives even if we do not think of them constantly or consciously.

We work to earn an income to avoid the consequences of not working. We fear such consequences as major lifestyle changes, eating smaller and poorer meals, displacement from our homes into lesser-quality accommodation. We see or read about homeless people and try to avoid imagining ourselves in that situation.

At this time in North America, nearly half the work force is comprised of women. With men and women competing for the same jobs and two adults working in many families, marital problems and other emotional disruptions may result.

According to this line of thinking, the increase in the divorce rate was caused by women entering the work force in greater numbers. But this is no more valid than claiming that immigrants have stolen jobs from people who were born in North America. Men fear that women and immigrants have taken jobs that they might need one day.

Picture a woman who has lived for twenty years as homemaker, wife and mother to her children, supported financially by her husband's income. If there is a family breakup, there is statistically a very good chance that the children will remain with the mother and that this group will live near or below the poverty level. This is an incentive for other women to continue to hold jobs while raising a family. This is an incentive for other women to become trained in skills that will benefit them in future jobs. This is, in turn, an incentive for all women to continually be on the search for some source of income that is derived from themselves, rather than from their husbands. They fear poverty.

This is what is driving the creation of home-based businesses which are dominated to a great extent by women. Home-based small businesses operated by women constitute a large majority of new businesses being created in North America.

It may also drive the divorce rate to around fifty percent. The fear of being left with nothing, of having our children taken away, of being alone drives everyone into the job market.

Our fear of helplessness to control our future is not only natural to us, it is one characteristic which separates us from other primates. Fear is integral to our being. We learn to live with it. But we don't necessarily learn how to use it to our own advantage.

Some adults live together as couples because they have a fear of living alone. Some people prefer to live alone because they fear the problems of living with someone else. This fear does not have to be on a conscious level. Nor does it have to be rational.

Nothing about fear is rational.

Our whole lives are surrounded by fear-producing situations. This is part of the natural world. Spend some time quietly observing nature to see this in action. When several varieties of birds eat seeds near each other at a feeder, the scrappiest among them are often the blue jays. The jays seldom bother with other species of birds, but they fight among themselves. No matter how much food is available, there is fighting among them. When their appetites are all satisfied, there is always plenty of seed left for the other birds. Every day there could be more food there than they can eat. Yet they fight. They naturally fear not having enough food.

The stronger and more aggressive among them scare away the weaker and less aggressive. Why do some bully others? We call it a natural pecking order, a drive to establish one's place in a hierarchy. While most of the bullying is nothing more than posturing, put on for show without the intent to injure, they know that their stronger flock-mates could inflict serious injury if they did not move away.

With little effort the blue jay squabbles could be compared to the more subtle squabbles among humans vying for relative positions in our society. People like to feel that they are better than someone else. We fear losing, or at least being labeled a "loser." Why do some of us lack self-esteem? They have given in to the fear that they are not as good as others.

Beginning in the 1950s, North Americans became acquisitors and accumulators as never before. We became a consumer society beyond anything previous generations had. We collected stuff. We bought it, we received it as gifts, we gave it as gifts. Why? For some, stuff is an adult security blanket. They need it to show how successful they are at their jobs, in their families, with their friends. They are afraid that others will think they are not successful.

Even the clothes we wear have significance to others. We dress one way because we don't want to look like the others. We are afraid to be thought of as being "like them."

Many of us were taught by our mothers to always wear clean underwear when we went out in a car, so that if we were in an accident and had to go to the hospital, the hospital staff would not think badly of us. That was taught fear. Would the doctor in Emergency say, "Uh-oh, this person has ripped underpants. Send him to the end of the line."? We don't even know why we have this fear. We just have it. Remember: we were taught to fear.

These fears do not include the group of fears known as phobias, which occur on an individual basis. Each of us has several phobia-like fears, but fears that are not severe enough to seriously affect our daily lives. These might include a fear of heights, of crowds, of spiders, of flying, of driving on high speed highways or of catching sexually transmitted diseases. As these are in-our-face fears that we hear about often, there is no need to elaborate on them here. Although they may not cause us severe emotional or psychological problems, they do affect our behavior in many ways. We act to minimize the effects these fears have. We pretend we are not afraid.

Fear affects our behavior as individuals. Fear also affects our behavior in groups. In a sense, each behavior of an individual within a group situation is still individual behavior. But that behavior could be influenced by association with a group.

We might behave differently as a member of a group than we would as an individual, for fear of suffering reprisals of our fellow group members if we do not. The behavior of gang members, as individuals and as part of the group, would be a perfect example of this.

Many of us would find it easy to accept a claim that each member of a biker gang acts very much like each other member, following the patterns and values set by and for the group and the rules established for group members. Members of such an organization would almost certainly disagree with the statement. Each group member would sees themselves as having a distinct position and personality within the group, saying different things, doing different things, driving a different machine, dressing differently, having a different mate and pals within the group from the others.

We tend to see our differences within a group in a more pronounced way than we see our similarities. Let's look at some examples that may be closer to our own group.

Teens in North America tend to associate themselves in groups and these groups distinguish themselves by their clothing. Some wear black clothing exclusively. Others, no matter what else they may wear, always wear at least one piece of clothing that distinctly identifies them as part of their group. Within their group they go to extremes to show that they dress and accessorize differently from each other member of their group. Jewelry, especially the kind that pierces some body part, stresses that individuality. Tattoos take that emphasis a step further.

Why do they wear black clothing and wear their hair in ways that are strange and objectionable to their parents? And pierce their bodies and dye their skin with tattoos in ways that they might regret a few years afterwards? For some, the black is an act and color of defiance: of authority, of parents, of society as they understand it. The body piercing and tattoos serve both as statements of individuality within the group and commitment to it. Wear black, have a strange hair style, pierce the body in at least one uncomfortable place, get at least one tattoo and they are confirmed as one of the group.

Others outside of the group, especially adults, look at these young people and think how alike they look. The ultimate insult. Tell them how terrible we think they look and they take it as praise. Tell them how much they look like everyone else in the group and they will hate it. Refuse them the cash to indulge themselves in these excesses, thus denying them acceptability within their group, and we alienate them completely, often to the extent that they will leave home and live on the streets.

That is a no-win, never-win scenario. Everyone is afraid here. As fear is inherently irrational, agreement is highly unlikely. There is no possibility for a win-win situation. In this case, the respective fears of each party create very unpleasant situations.

There are other sub-groups within this adolescent set. Each identifies itself by its clothing and accessories. Each has its own internal rules which are never written down but are widely known by everyone in the group. Each has its own behavior code. Each has its own code of ethics for group members. Although none of it is written down, everyone within the group knows because of peer pressure. Offenders are punished or ostracized. They learn quickly.

What if these groups meet, have a disagreement, have a conflict of interests? Differences are settled in ways quite similar to inter-tribal disagreements of primitive societies. There may be total alienation and mutual ostracization of the groups, there may be angry words exchanged or there may be violence. In each case, the punishment inflicted on the other group fits the perceived violation.

Why do young people put themselves into situations which are potentially harmful? Truly a subject for a series of books. But the simple answer is acceptance, a need for love by one's peers. Stated differently, a fear of not belonging.

Are teens the only age group that undergoes such rigorous orientation and group influence? Hardly. Watch three or more children in a sandbox. The study of socialization in the sandbox is a study of the beginnings of group behavior. It's the best opportunity we will ever have of being able to see the formation of group behavior in humans at its most basic level.

Rules develop. A hierarchy that forms, with leaders, followers and demi-bosses (middle management). There is a dress code, although violation of this code is not punished severely as everyone in the group knows that it was those big people who were to blame. Wrongly dressed toddlers know they are dressed differently, even if their blissfully ignorant parents do not.

Service clubs, church groups, professional organizations and inner-office bar meets are all groups that have structure, rules and a hierarchy. Each of us can understand that, especially if we are not part of one of those groups.

Other kinds of groups are less well-recognized. Take shoppers in a ladies clothing store as an example. A few individuals always receive more attention than all others put together. A few shoppers can walk into a discussion and interrupt the flow of conversation between a sales clerk and a customer without fear of reprisal. Why? There are no penalties for violating one of these situations.

Consider a line jumper at the supermarket. We have all experienced them. We didn't likely speak to them about the unfairness of their act, about the need for taking their turn, about how we are in a hurry too. If we did, the more often we have done it in the past, the less likely we are to do it again. The line jumper will almost always manage to embarrass us. We have been socialized to accept this small injustice. We have been taught that, even in that relatively random situation, the line jumpers are leaders and we must accept our condition as followers. To do otherwise might find us in court.

Do these people jump from their natural position in the line ahead of someone who is obviously a member of a biker gang, someone with long hair, a beard, black leather clothing with the group insignia on the back? Only the blind or the terminally stupid.

We are members of other groups. How about as taxpayers? Almost everyone in every country claims that they are charged too much in taxes. There's a group behavior associated with this, such as cheating on taxes. Almost everyone will cheat on their taxes in a small way, if they have the chance to get away with it. Almost everyone avoids cheating in a big way because of the risk (fear) associated with living part of our life in prison. Although we cheat individually, we do so because we believe that everyone does it.

Almost everyone has examples of how the governments that collect their taxes should be using those monies differently. We complain, sometimes silently, sometimes to others, about how our governments should act differently, about how inefficient they are, about how they are not working in our best interests. We believe that our governments may be "of the people" and "by the people", but few believe that any government is "for the people".

Do we fear that at some time our tax money will be used against us? Perhaps we have never been tried for a criminal offence. Some day we may be accused of a crime we did not commit. We might have the weight of the judicial system against us as we fight to prove our innocence. Most people have a fear of that happening. Our taxes, in action against us. And we would have to pay a lawyer to defend our innocence.

That is part of the fear that taxpayers have. So the group known as taxpayers do influence each other. The media and other powerful parties play a role in that influence.

The citizen voter is part of a group. Think about it. Most of the time that we complain about the government, we are discussing either taxes or a decision. Seldom is the subject of taxes mixed with other topics. When we talk about government, we are part of a separate group, the citizen voter.

If we are not aware of our status in this group, politicians are. At one time they hired advertising people to cast their campaign in a good light to appeal to specific people at election time. Now there's a scary thought. But wait! It gets better. Now they hire people who specialize in voter manipulation. That's right—there are people who know our ways so well as a member of the citizen voter group that they make a living hiring themselves out to politicians to win our vote.

They are very successful. During an election campaign, we have no way of knowing whether what we hear from a politician will have any bearing on his actions after the election. What he says is carefully managed for effect. For that matter, they also hire professional publicists to manage what we learn about them between elections. It isn't a high school student with a part-time job that puts together that material we receive from our elected officials between elections.

If enough voters feel the same way about any particular issue, these professionals will know it and advise their employers accordingly. Remember that.

We are, generally speaking, afraid of our politicians. Not afraid of how they could harm us directly, but what they collectively could do to us with political power that is only accountable to the electorate once every few years. If we claim we aren't afraid, then we may be suppressing our fear. If we complain about our government, then we are expressing some degree of fear. Fear expresses itself as discontent.

We are each part of other groups too. How about elevator riders? Unless the elevator is empty, we walk in, turn around, press the button for our floor, then either watch the numbers light up above the door, stare at the door as if in anticipation of a marvelous revelation, stare at the back of someone ahead of us, or adjust something on our person.

The rule for elevator behavior in North America is that we must never speak to anyone in the elevator unless we know the person well. A person who asks another elevator rider what floor something is on may be tolerated, even helped in a friendly way. Then the box falls silent again. Anyone who speaks in a friendly manner is, well, never mind. Those ignorant few who do speak soon learn to keep quiet. We justify this fear by claiming that elevators do not provide us sufficient personal space to be comfortable up close with others.

A possible theory is that most people are conditioned to believe that anyone else who speaks to them on an elevator either intends to rob them or rape them, or some such violent act.

Think about it. In any other such circumstance, it is to everyone's advantage to be friendly and share conversation on an elevator. We have been taught to behave that way.

There are exceptions to the silent elevator rule, just as with any practice. Some people overcome their fear and speak to others anyway.

Group influence shows us how to act cool and detached in an elevator, to act as if we really don't want to speak to anyone, to act like the proverbial rock. To act as if we are not afraid.

It's group behavior of sorts when we are reluctant to open the door of our home at night to a stranger. We are part of the homeowner group. As a homeowner (not house owner, as this homeowner group could include residents of a rental apartment, for example) we learn proper behavior for answering the door in the evening. We may be afraid of something. We have been taught to believe that there could be something dangerous on the other side of the door.

When we have a child attending school in grade three, we may fear that she will not receive the education she needs? We are part of the "parents of young children attending primary grades" group. We know that this is something we should be concerned about. We have learned our lessons as parents. Do we really know what a child should be accumulating and assimilating to prepare her for her life as an adult in the world of the future? Not really. We may be concerned that she won't learn enough. That is what the parent of a grade three student is supposed to do. We learned that behavior when our child was in grade two.

Many of us may be concerned about how our neighborhood is changing. We may be afraid that some nut will launch a nuclear bomb or "dirty bomb" in our direction. That the moral code we grew up with has been lost on the modern generation. Of losing our job. Of being destitute when we are old. We may be afraid of living our final years in an incapacitated state. That humans are destroying our planet. That our species will annihilate itself along with many others before our life would come to a natural end. These are all group fears. We learn these from others in our group, whatever that group may be. These are learned fears, not something we were born with.

Remember that: learned. We learn all sorts of things that affect how we behave.

We may be afraid of the unknown. Everyone is to some extent. Caution can be healthy. Fear creates such horrible tragedies in our world as hate, prejudice and ethnic cleansing.

We may be afraid of progress. Most people say they aren't, they just don't want things to change. We know the world is moving quickly, but we have no idea where it is going. We don't know if progress is out of control because we don't understand it. Most people have a natural reluctance to change. That is really a fear of change. Fear of change could be healthy or destructive in an individual. A healthy skepticism about a new industry or new venture of an existing industry may help to uncover environmental risks, for example.

A fear of change is unhealthy in some people, unhealthy for them as individuals and unhealthy for the community in which they live, if they express this fear loudly and inappropriately. By the same token, too little fear of progress, complacency, would result in companies taking advantage of people, animals and nature at a disgraceful rate.

We may be afraid of the future. Afraid that we might make a slip and our whole life will be worth nothing. Some of us look at people who live on the streets and turn away because we fear that one day we could be among them. That is a fear of the future.

All of these are group fears. We suffer them alone, but they impose themselves on us when we are part of a group. Discussion of these fears in group situations, such as over coffee or at a club or at church, actually makes these fears more pronounced. It validates them. That is what makes them group fears.

Our lives are filled with fears. We are so accustomed to them that we do not even think of them as fear in most cases. Fear so fills our lives that we suppress it lest it overcome us and we break down. Breakdown! What is that? We fear that too. Is that someone who has not been able to cope with the fears of his or her life? Oh yes, we have a fear of showing fear. Stiff upper lip and all that. Big boys don't cry.

There is something we could do to lessen that fear, both for ourselves and for future generations. We could make a difference, with a little effort. We could lessen the load of our own fears by joining with others to set conditions in such a way that we would not need to fear them.

It would help us all if we were taught how to cope with fear, how to manage fear effectively, even to use it to our advantage. It can be done. We can learn. We will.

Fear is an integral part of our lives. It is a part of our being. We can use it to our advantage and to the advantage of our society. Fear can be used positively, for the benefit of our whole society.

Fear can be positive when it shows itself as a healthy level of apprehension or caution. Beyond that, fear is destructive. We need to be taught how to make that distinction and how to cope with fear that passes beyond the level of caution or apprehension. We need to be taught what to do when fear reaches a level where it unduly influences other parts of our lives.

We need to know that help is available when necessary. We need to be certain that we can count on support when fear becomes a major factor in our lives.

We need to believe that asking for help is what we should do when we need it. It's not a sign that we are weak, defective or a failure. It's a sign that we are wise enough to shore up our needs to keep our lives in balance.

The Fight (or Flight) of Our Lives

Humans fight. The very nature of our species is such that we will, under certain circumstances, fight. We might fight to defend ourselves or members of our families or friends. This chapter will consider only defensive fighting, as offensive fighting such as bullying was covered in a previous chapter.

A mechanism in the brain will assess each fight or flight situation and determine if it would be wiser to escape or to fight. In a sense, each time the fight or flight mechanism is activated there is a conflict within us, as we want to defend ourselves though it might be safer to get away.

The kind of fighting in which we engage varies greatly from one person to another. If there is an option, an individual may choose to run rather than fight if the chances of winning a fight or surviving it are low.

"Fight or flight" is a phrase used to describe human reaction to violent or threatening stimulation. When the adrenaline gets flowing, we will either fight the opponent or run from him. The threat may be either physical (e.g. engaging in some form of violent act or running from it) or psychological (e.g.

arguing or retreating into silence), depending on which offers the best chance of success and security.

The majority of us do not go out looking for a fight, but we all have the fight or flight mechanism to cope with potential violence. In this chapter we will consider the "fight" part of that inbred part of our nature.

Like others in the natural world, our species has the will to survive as a primary instinct. It's built into our genetic make-up, although the exact source of the genetic code and process by which it works are not yet fully understood. The debate about just how many characteristics of humans are instinctive has been waged for many decades. Few will dispute that our will to survive is built into us.

Biologists believe that the drive to survive and to have our families survive has to do with the perpetuation of our genes through our offspring. As mothers are historically the primary caregivers to our children, their survival is next in importance. Fathers and unmarried people are next down the hierarchy. Nature works to protect those at the top of the hierarchy. Those lower down the scale protect those above them.

Nature provides us with the chemical mix and the physical strength between the onset of puberty and age forty to fight when we must. These have been, through the prehistory and most of the history of the human species, the prime physical years.

Historically, these are years when we have the ability to do the most good for our families, be that as protectors of the family or as killers of large game animals for food.

The chemical mix that makes this possible is ready for use whether we have need for it or not, although it is not constantly activated in most people. For some people, all they require to set off their fight reflex is some form of stimulus. For some, that stimulus need only be minor, what would be insignificant for most of us. What we call a drive for power is sufficient motivation to stimulate the chemical mix in some people, such that they demonstrate this in the form of bullying, fighting or intimidation of others. Alcohol or other mind-altering substances tend to lower the fight threshold, except in the cases of people who tend to get "high" when drinking, causing them to act out and become aggressive.

More important to us than our own survival, instinctively, is our children, the survival of our DNA, the genetic code that makes each of us who we are.

Genetic code is passed on through our children. One of the values we still hold dear is to enable women and children to escape danger before men. Note that this does not necessarily mean that fathers have less influence on the characters of their children than do mothers.

In times of war, the men go into battle while the women stay with their families and mind home, hearth and sometimes keep our industries going, as they did in World War II. While there are females among the fighting troops of many countries around the world, their numbers are still significantly fewer than those of men. Only in the case of a culture being in danger of disappearing entirely do the numbers of men and women in battle come near to equal. In those cases even children are recruited to fight.

On a personal level, one of the most endearing and loving statements that a young man can make to his beloved is that he would give his life for her. In most cases, in most marriages, the male would die to save the female and children. Men also will fight to save the families of their siblings, as the genetic code is close enough to warrant the risk.

In times of war, media propaganda is all that is needed to prompt many young men to sign up to fight for their country. It is unclear whether they fight to save those who have a similar culture and language, or those that they perceive have a close genetic code to their own, or even a mix of the two. The fact is that they are prepared to fight with minimum motivation.

Males are prepared to sacrifice their own lives to save as many females as possible, to give our species (our cultural, racial, ethnic, or language group) the best possible chance of survival. That is, a man will fight and, if necessary, die to save not only the genetic code that is borne by his children and the mother who bore them, but also for other women and children who could continue the human race.

If males must die to save future generations, they will. Otherwise they will fight to save their own lives and those closest to them. A man will risk death to save a child in a burning house. A father will risk his safety to save his family from muggers or invaders of his home. He will go off to war to save his country. The trigger that stimulates this fight or flight mechanism can be tripped very quickly and surely in most men.

Given the success of humans on this planet compared to other animals, the forces we have been able to mount toward this goal of aggression have been enormous.

There has never been a shortage of wars for aggressive males to involve themselves in. Historically, there has been a major war in which a young male could involve himself every twenty to thirty years, at least one major war per generation. When there were no wars at home, there was always service as a mercenary in someone else's army. Each male has been able to join an army and fight in a war during his lifetime.

In peacetime, we fight our way up the corporate ladder. Some people still refer to their returning home after a day at work as "returning from the wars." We enquire of someone's health by asking "How goes the battle?"

In our leisure time, some men engage in gentlemanly wars such as tennis, badminton, racquetball and squash. Note that these are considerably more popular in terms of numbers of participants than similar games where the combatants do not carry some form of club in their hands. Granted, the club or weapon used in these games is used to hit a ball rather than one's opponent.

The more aggressive among us participate in team sports such as football, hockey, basketball, volleyball, boxing, wrestling or the ultimate in non-contact, non-team, "team" sports, golf. We can include golf in this list because it is rare to find a golfer playing alone. Even in a non-competitive round of golf, the players enjoy the benefits of team play as they walk together, while the enemy is their respective golf balls. The objective, after all, is to strike that ball as hard as we can. It's difficult to know whether golfers get more benefit from exercise by chasing a little white golf ball or from whacking it as hard as they can about one hundred times per round of eighteen holes.

The popularity of competitions in these sports and athletic competitions on television testifies to the ability of many to release their aggressiveness by watching others exercise theirs. Riots or riotous behavior following some team sport events, either wins or losses, results among those who cannot fulfill their need to express their aggression fully through other means, or those whose aggression threshold has been sufficiently lowered by alcohol that they feel the need to see action.

Most of these sports involve hitting, sometimes of each other and sometimes of an object such as a ball. Even basketball, ever purported to be a non-contact sport, can get rough as some "accidental" shoving has become accepted as part of the game. Many more males than females find these sports exhilarating. Women seem to enjoy being spectators more than participating in these games, going by numbers of participants. Only in recent years have women taken an active interest in such contact sports as hockey, wrestling, boxing, even football.

Some males do not enjoy these active contact games. They prefer their war games to be more mental than physical, such as chess, cards, computer or video games, shouting at the driver ahead of them on the road, arguing with their wives, or complaining to their friends about their employers or their governments. These war games are more intellectual or emotional.

These men, in good ways or bad, have outlets for their aggression. Most are socially acceptable. For many of the past decades, men would gather at a bar for a drink and conversation after work where they would release their tensions of the day. With the campaigns against drinking and driving, this practice is dying out. Coincidental to this was the increase in road rage and speeding.

What happens to people who do not have safe and acceptable outlets for their aggressive tendencies? These are the subjects of front-page newspaper and television news stories. Enough has been written and spoken about these cases, so we need not relate them again. Remember that non-typical aggressive behavior, such as getting angry around other people, is discouraged in our society. Ironically anger, although once virtually forbidden in office situations and still socially unacceptable in most situations, is becoming more common. Some North American office workers report experiencing anger from others once a month or more.

What happens to adolescents and young adults who do not have socially acceptable outlets for their aggression? The built-in need is there, but they have no way to let it out safely. If a young person is not doing well in school, but is not of legal age to drop out, the law insists that he must attend school each day.

If he believes that he will not be able to complete enough of the education necessary to get himself a "decent" job, he will suffer from anxiety. Our society has promised him he will be a failure for the rest of his life. If he believes that he will not find a "good job," with or without enough education, he will live daily with reminders that he will be a reject, a loser, a nobody. Getting a "good job" has become a mantra in our society. What we neglect to stress is that not having a good job does not mean a person is a failure as a person. That neglect can have a devastating impact on some people.

Imagine attending school with one of these perpetually rebellious young people. If we knew that our son or daughter was in a class with one of them, one who wears black every day, who has pierced body parts, tattoos and who has access to a gun, we might feel very uncomfortable. We might want to remove our child from that class or school or have the child who is "different" moved to another school. Sometimes neither of these options is possible. Sometimes no corrective measures are taken. Sometimes no one is aware of the potential for problems.

There may be nothing wrong with the "different" child in the example, but most parents would not want to subject their child to a risk. Separating our child from the risk is an action we would seriously consider. Would we also want to bring the "different" one back into the mainstream? That is, would we be prepared to give our school board the resources to change this person? If not, "different" students will remain and their numbers increase. The potential for trouble remains when the cause is not addressed and cured.

There were students like that when we were of high school age. The numbers are greater now than then. There were events similar to Columbine when we were in high school. We would not necessarily have heard of them because news, especially bad news like that, may not have been spread as far from its source. It was kept quiet as a community disgrace.

Most young people have ways of channeling their aggressive tendencies in a manner that is acceptable to their communities. Some don't. These young people still have the fight in them, but they do not have the coping skills to know how to express it in a positive and acceptable manner. They also may not have the will to be socially acceptable. These young people are society's failures.

Most people want to do something about troubles in their community, their society, their country, but they don't know what to do. Unreleased aggression is a danger to our society. We're not addressing the causes of the problems now, only building new prisons to remove the worst offenders from our presence.

It isn't working. Our society is getting worse in some ways.

The time has come to put the future of our species ahead of the next sitcom on television. Or the next game of golf. Or the next web site on our computer. Our community will not improve on its own, no matter how long we ignore the problems.

We left solutions to others in the past. The problems just got worse. When people don't have the knowledge and skills to know what to do in a crisis situation, their behavior is unpredictable.

Staring Into the Future

THE faint of heart cringe at the thought of predicting the future. No one knows for certain what the future will be like in, say, fifty years. The future doesn't matter so much to us until it becomes the present. When people or governments don't care about the future, what they are doing is not caring about a present that will happen at some future date. Unless we die in the meantime, the future we don't care about now will inevitably become our present—if not our present, then the present of our children or grandchildren.

What we do or don't do now will influence how our country is in the future. We countrymen are the architects of the future.

We spend most of our lives working toward a future that will be better for us and our loved ones. If we don't give attention to the future, it will take its own careless course. If governments don't have a plan for the future of their communities and their country, the futures of their citizens will be chaotic.

As late as the mid-1900s, life was much different from the way it is now. People traveled long distances mostly by train, with only the well-heeled being able to afford private rooms in the rail car, while the moderately affluent could afford pull-down beds or "closets with screens," and the ordinary folk slept on wooden seats propped up straight.

Aeroplanes (later to become airplanes) were mostly for military or business use, and were relatively slow, small, noisy, draughty, bumpy and ran on uncertain schedules.

Automobiles had become more stylish, with colors other than black, regular equipment such as AM radios, windshield wipers with motors, interior lights, and they were built to last a long time.

Houses were mostly small, with most covering about eight hundred to a thousand square feet. Brick homes, more common before World War II, would reappear again in new homes once the wartime shortages were past.

Many young people got jobs with companies that would keep them employed for their entire working lives. The common concept of a family was mother, father and two to four children. Families were larger then than now, as memory of high infant mortality caused parents to ensure that several of their children reached adulthood by having several children.

Communities were relatively homogeneous, although new ethnic communities were sprouting up within cities as immigrants from former wartime allied countries came to North America, mostly to do factory, construction and domestic jobs.

African-Americans in the United States rode in the rear of buses and attended churches and schools populated only by African-Americans. Asian people were interned in camps in Canada and the United States during World War II. No options were offered.

In Canada, children grew up knowing that immigrant people with different clothes, different habits, different food preferences and different languages and customs were likely "DPs", a shortened form of the derogatory term "Displaced Persons". They were not taught why these were DPs or even what the letters represented. Native-born Canadians were taught that they would be wise to stay away from them. "Don't make friends with them, as you never know what could happen if they get you into their houses. And, whatever you do, don't date one of them."

Marrying outside of "your own kind" was considered taboo. Best just not learn about them, just stay away from them. They are probably dangerous people, even if they sound pleasant when we speak with them.

Discrimination, prejudice and bigotry were a way of life. They were everywhere. White children were not taught that they were WASPs (White Anglo-Saxon Protestants), since they didn't need a name for themselves within their own cultural communities. They were a majority. It was a given in their communities (a belief shared only among themselves, we now understand) that they were superior (in what way was never stated), and their grandparents and some parents reminded them when they blundered. It was not unusual for a parent or grandparent to punish a child who played with a child from a different cultural background or of a different skin color.

It was the objective of most red-blooded Canadian boys to get out of school as soon as possible, which would be at age sixteen for most, to get a job, earn some money, buy a car and cruise the streets for those ever-waiting girls. Brains, browners and other assorted strange people continued on in school to become professionals and politicians. Girls seldom stayed in school beyond high school, as they were expected to work for a few years to get worldly experience, find Mr. Right, marry, quit their jobs and raise children, never to work again. Education was not considered beneficial or even proper for girls, by the standards of many families.

The preceding may not be our view of how the world should be. It could be our impression of how the world was at the time, at least in North America. In those times, some young women were forcefully told that they did not need to finish high school, that they should be out of school by age seventeen or eighteen, perhaps having taken a short course in office skills, teaching or nursing, if the family could afford it.

The fact that those times were so different from the way life is now emphasizes the magnitude of changes that can happen in fifty years. Remember, things changed slowly in those days. Other than the Korean War, the coming of television to almost every home in North America, Ozzie and Harriet, Friday night wrestling and rock 'n' roll, nothing much happened in the 1950s. After half a century of war and deprivation, North America slept late when it could.

We can easily see the changes that occurred over the past fifty years. The pace of change increased rapidly.

What can we expect in the way of changes during the coming half century? While playing the role of futurist is risky, we might project what are likely developments, based on what is happening now. For the most part, let's concentrate on North America. Since the first human space tourist spent time at the international space station in 2001, we know that big changes are ahead.

First, few people who were born after 1960, who live a full life, will die with the same body parts they were born with. While organ donation is progressing well now, despite great shortages in some areas, organ regeneration will be much more popular in the future. When we need a new body part, it will be grown from our DNA, either inside or attached to our body or by getting its start in a laboratory. This will include arms and legs and even some brain parts. Only body parts that cannot be regrown will be replaced with artificial ones.

Three score and ten, the traditional Biblical length of the ideal human life for centuries past, will become the age at which only people who have abused their bodies will die. Babies with genetic predispositions for common diseases will have this corrected before birth. That is happening now in some cases.

Tissue regeneration of all sorts will be commonplace. New limbs will be grown for those who lose arms or legs to disease or accident. Whether these will be grown in the laboratory or on our body will depend upon which method currently under development is more successful.

Brain parts will be able to be regenerated on location. While conventional wisdom held that this was impossible in the past, recent research with mice has been very positive.* Brain transplants will only be necessary where there has been irreversible and irreparable damage.

Those who are now scornfully called "tree huggers" will likely become mainstream by mid-century as research shows that the life forces of plants have more in common with us than we thought. In fact, it is entirely possible that the life forces that drive plants will be discovered to rank well up in the comparison scale with the brains and instincts of animal life. In other words, plants are smarter than we give them credit for. We have some learning to do to catch up with them. We will learn to communicate with some animals and a few plants.

Life will be dominated more by economics than by governments. As megagiant multinational corporations control large portions of the economies of many countries of the world, they will be forced to preserve the standard of living of their customer base, rather than destroying it. It would be counterproductive of them to create more jobless people who could not afford their products and who would form anarchistic gangs bent on destruction of what they perceive as the evil empires of business. This is what terrorist and anarchist groups are doing now. This is why terrorism will never work on a large scale. The big corporations will control the flow of money, thus the behavior of a majority of the populations of most countries.

Corporations will have their own internal family culture among their employees and their families. In some cases, this structure will be extended to entire communities. This is, in effect, what happened in new mining communities along railway lines a century and more ago.

Women will play a prominent role in both government and business. Men have proven that they are inherently better with the hunter-gatherer/warrior scenario than they are at controlling a world at peace. Women in prominent government leadership roles meeting around the world will eschew the firing of weapons, insist upon child care facilities at all world conferences, allow time for social exchange about family life and balancing budgets, provide computer films for showing off pictures or holographs of their grandchildren or children and bring cultural information to share from their last trade mission abroad.

Should world leaders be comfortable enough with each other that they could consider themselves friends and feel at ease in each other's presence? Imagine the possibilities for world peace if such conditions existed. World leaders who consider what they have in common rather than their differences. Quite different.

This is not to suggest that female leaders of business and governments cannot be sound negotiators. They can be as firm and as wily as men. They have a different outlook on negotiations and critical discussions than men, in general. These differences will become more appreciated as the century progresses and as women voters vote for women candidates in elections.

Is that an overrated ideal? Perhaps, to some men or someone who is ingrained with traditional male-patterned thinking. Those people will become cultural dinosaurs in the near future.

Every major trend leading into this century suggests that women will be better equipped to take leadership roles in government than men. That is not to suggest that men will be squeezed out of major roles in government. It is to say that men must make more changes to prepare themselves for government positions of the future than women.

These changes will involve negotiations between people rather than between foes in battle.

Women, in general, are more nurturing than men. They give birth and they want peace and prosperity, structure and guidance, morals and principles in the family in order to see their progeny succeed as they grow and mature. These are the same things that male political candidates have been promising for the past century, but have failed to deliver.

Women make up a slight majority of the population of North America. Few of us trust politicians now. Politicians are mostly male. In the next fifty years, women will make the necessary connection and step forward. Women have a greater chance to be considered for political positions because they do not carry the baggage of past failure and political embarrassments and shame.

Politicians can be honest.

Politicians can have feelings for others that are greater than for themselves.

Politicians can put the good of their country and its people ahead of the good of their respective parties.

Politicians can have good moral standards.

Politicians can provide places for homeless, poor and elderly people to live with dignity.

Politicians can take action to relieve the causes of violence, rather than building more prisons.

Politicians can hold worthy beliefs and stand for just causes.

Politicians can help people be proud of their country without taking it into war.

Politicians can make people feel good about themselves.

Politicians can give hope to a people in troubled times.

Politicians can tell the truth, the whole truth, not an edited or partisan version.

Politicians can explain government activities to people so they understand what is happening.

Politicians can educate the people that elect them.

Look at the possibilities for the future. Our future, the future of our children, grandchildren and great-grandchildren. The future of our respective countries. The future of the society in which we live. The future of civilization itself.

Can our present politicians do what we want them to do for the future? If not, something must change. If we don't speak up, then we become part of the problem.

Apathy is a great concern. People stop caring when they lose hope. People will care, will vote, will express their opinions and their thoughts to their representatives when they know someone will listen.

Not all political parties will change at once. The successful ones will move first. The others will have to follow or become insignificant. The more successful political parties will be those that stress what most people have in common, not how voters can be alienated from their governments.

The time has come. Let's make the necessary changes now, while we have the chance.

---

* Josie Glausiusz, "Brain, Heal Thyself," *Discover*, August 1996

13
Governments

GOVERNMENTS don't pay attention to the people who elect them. Almost everyone in the world, no matter what country they live in, language they speak, culture they practice or station in life, feels that their government does not care what its citizens think. People may be proud of their country, their heritage, their language, their culture, but they are unhappy with their governments. It is a worldwide phenomenon. Billions of people can't be wrong.

Let's make a distinction here between elected politicians and government. Government is made up of the people who run a country, province/state or city. The leaders of the government (Prime Minister, Premier, Governor, President, Mayor, Congressional party leaders) and their respective deputies actually have the power of government. The rest of the elected politicians either support their leaders or oppose those who represent the opposition parties. Most elected politicians try to help the voters who elected them in their constituencies, but they are almost powerless when it comes to governing the country, state or city itself.

Political leaders claim they spend many hours each week listening to their constituents and their colleagues present proposals about how to make improvements. The proverbial squeaky wheels take up the time of the elected representatives. Regular folks don't come together the way the special interest groups do, so they feel there is no point in investing their time in approaching deaf politicians. In the long term, it is the will of the political leaders that prevails, whether or not that represents the thoughts and beliefs of the majority of citizens.

Governments, even in democracies, have reputations for not listening to the people they represent, to the opposing parties, even to the backbenchers in their own parties. The leaders have their own cadres, their cliques that they satisfy. They only turn to their constituents at election time. This must change in this century or people will find faster and more effective ways of ousting governments they don't like. There have been some excellent examples of this in Canada during the past decade as a few ruling parties almost ceased to exist after being thrown out of power in the next election.

Many people believe that politicians and bureaucrats only work in their own best interests. Some blame corruption among government officials. While those accusations may have truth in some countries, it is no more true of politicians or government employees than it is of any of the rest of us. The more often citizens level that charge against them, the more politicians tend to turn off, tune out, stop paying attention.

Legislators have two main functions: the passing of laws and the provision of services. Instead of treating these as two separate arms of the same body, able to work together for the benefit of the whole, they tend to treat these functions completely separately. Laws are intended to provide guides for behavior, to set limits of acceptability in society. Instead, laws are used to govern behavior, to control many of the things we do during our lives.

As behavior can never be controlled by legislation, this method is doomed to failure and bound to create the overwhelming weight of laws that we now think of as "too much government." As a reaction against the claims of too much government, legislators reduce the government-paid workforce, thus making the laws they have passed unenforceable and the laws themselves and the people who passed them laughing stocks.

The way to change the attitudes and behavior of a people is through the provision of services of government, beginning with education. People behave as adults the way they were trained to behave as children. Changing the nature of education is a long-term solution to everything. This is difficult for anyone elected for three or four years to contemplate. Politicians want quick solutions, in order to be able to take advantage of their success before the next election. It doesn't work.

A look at changes in the education system in any local jurisdiction will likely reveal few major shifts over the period of a century. This is unacceptable in the modern world. Life now is much different in industrial and post-industrial countries than it has ever been. It will not change back. Education must adjust to prepare people to cope with the requirements of the new conditions in which we find ourselves.

Further rationale for changing our education systems and a methodology for doing so will be discussed in later chapters. For now, let's look at the mechanism of government in order to understand how it works. To change government other than by revolution, we must first understand the system we have in place.

Politicians may claim that they have no direct control over education. However, in each country one level of government has the legal responsibility for the education of each child. Elected boards of trustees follow the guidelines and curriculum put forward by the government.

In democratic countries, the people we elect to represent us act in ways we resent and disapprove of. They do not seem to clearly represent the values that a majority of us hold. In some countries there are so many differing opinions that literally dozens of parties develop to accommodate each opinion set. In others, the United States, for example, two major parties duke it out, with many of the differences of opinion being dealt with behind closed doors before the public presentation begins. Opinions on methods of implementation differ greatly. Values within a culture do not. The governments concentrate on differences, though most parties agree on general objectives.

So many forms and ways of dealing with differences of opinion have developed. Almost none begin with the common goals and objectives of the people and work forward from there.

In countries with multiple parties, alliances, associations and various handshake arrangements are made in order to keep the wheels of government moving and the bills being paid. The number of actively participating political forces reduces by one means or another, in order to avoid chaos or anarchy.

Do different parties have equally valid opinions about how governments should operate or are they more interested in tearing down the opposition so they can take power themselves? It is true that there are differing theories about which is the most effective, efficient and equitable form of government. But these seldom show themselves in distinct forms as parties adopt each other's policies in order to gain a larger share of the voting marketplace. The name of the game for political parties is power and longevity. It's rarely about the education of our children, our future.

If opinions about how governments should operate are so different, how can parties combine to create effective vote majorities and how can they justify stealing each other's policies, whether they be regarding foreign affairs, economic reform or social programs? The simple answer is that multiple political parties exist as a result of the ignorance of the electorate about their similarities of policies and thought. They tend to be personality-based rather than policy-based. Each exists for its own survival, rather than for the good of the people it was created to serve. Political parties often form to benefit their creators and leaders more than their voter constituents.

Perhaps we have wondered why the post-election actions don't match with the pre-election advertising. We wonder how these people in government could act so differently after an election from the way they did before the election. Are they all corrupt liars, or do they become party-bound automatons? The answer is no to both, but there is great confusion. It's hard to tell them apart, the honest ones from the bad ones. The line blurs so badly that all politicians are considered careless of the values of their constituents and corrupt, no matter how good each may be.

The media in North America have led us to believe that there is no such thing as an honest and pure politician. When they face a candidate with a lily-white reputation, the media know they have to dig to find the "dirt" on this person. They know that any candidate or elected official can be brought to his knees if they work hard enough at it. They can often count on assistance from the candidate's opponents or the opponents' supporters.

This is not to say that there is no such thing as an honest politician. The media would have us believe that. The media play a large role in the formation of our understanding and our thoughts about and our attitudes toward politicians, government and our society. We may not believe most of the stories that we read or see, but the constant barrage of negativity affects our beliefs and attitudes about politicians and governments. Good politicians are tarred with the same brush as the bad ones.

Whether on television, in the newspapers or on the Internet, a successful politician, one that has the potential to win an election, may be the subject of public critique. There is no such thing as an elected official with enduring and unimpeachable respect from his electorate. Every one may be subject to the destructive forces of the media. That means that each of us citizens can be victimized by a mass medium with a hidden agenda.

Politicians run our cities, our states and provinces, our countries. Can a politician be effective after predatory media have tasted his flesh? We have difficulty respecting either politicians or the media for a long while after such assaults.

Another key problem with governments is their long-standing custom of keeping their electorate in the dark. They claim that the affairs of government are too complex and involved to keep everyone informed of everything. They claim that if people want to know what is going on they should follow the affairs of government through the media. As if the media are unbiased.

In fact, as things stand, it is nearly impossible for an average person in North America to objectively keep up with the workings of any level of government that represents him or her.

Because most matters of government require a person to attend sittings of legislatures and committees full time to gain a reasonable understanding of them, the amount of information available is enormous. The tradition has been to tell voters nothing other than what is available through the media. Their excuse is that each topic is simply too complex. In truth, many politicians and parties have avoided telling their electorate about matters under consideration because they find it inconvenient to have to deal with people who have opinions that differ.

The politicians consider these topics too complex to convey them to their constituents. They expect the media who attend meetings only part time to educate the public about the activities of their government. Assuming that the media must get their information from the politicians, it follows that the media may be fed editorialized and slanted information, if any.

We should have some say in the way our country, state/province and municipality are run. Yet our opportunities to learn about what is going on are limited. We could learn the facts that would help us to be more properly informed through the media, if we were given the chance. This would matter if we were given a voice and someone to listen. Technology of the 21st century makes that possible.

As there come to be more and more well-educated people in our society, the discrepancy between those in government who know and those of us citizens who should know (and have the desire to learn) becomes ever greater. Let us consider the democratic form of government.

The word *democracy* means "government by the people." The word began in ancient Greece, Mesopotamia or India, where each man had a vote on important issues of the day. Setting aside the fact that there was no place in this scheme for women and slaves, the system worked fairly well. It is true that a sort of verbal gang warfare developed, where the weak would be outshouted by the more vociferous and occasionally the wine of peace was spiked with a substance designed to end an argument permanently. We now call this "party politics."

When there got to be too many people for everyone to be able to hear discussions, have the opportunity to speak and to vote, regular attendance became more sporadic and the seating arrangements decidedly crowded for important discussions. Rules for speaking developed whereby the better orators were heard in full, while poorer speakers (in all senses) were actively discouraged from participating in debates. Representative government evolved when it became obvious that voting citizens no longer knew enough facts to be able to cast a vote in a knowledgeable fashion.

With representative government came the belief that citizens were no longer required to learn the facts relating to each issue of the government. They would simply be informed of what had taken place, the decisions made, the laws passed. Elected officials came to believe that their electorate was better off kept in ignorance, as a knowledgeable electorate was a dangerous thing to them. People who know what they are talking about have opinions and people with knowledge and opinions are a threat to politicians.

As issues became more complex, even elected officials were not able to stay fully versed on every matter. The elected people then had to somehow make up for what they did not know. They depended on their parties to tell them how to vote. As keeping track of various issues became more difficult, elected representatives hired others to keep the stories flowing out from their offices, carefully edited to place the representative in the best possible light.

So it happened that an ignorant population of mushrooms (kept in the dark and fed "fertilizer") trooped to the polls on election day to vote in the way that the most effective political propagandists that money can buy told them to vote. Some, of course, stopped voting entirely because their political acumen shriveled from atrophy and they forgot what voting meant. Too many people don't know the candidates or the issues.

The more ignorant about the stuff of government that people became, the more they despaired and the more apathetic they became. In turn, the more their representatives believed that their constituents should not be kept apprised of the facts of government. Politicians were able to fulfill their greatest wish, to be able to avoid discussion of important issues with the people that elected them.

Think about this. If a new law affecting our driving habits is passed in our province or state, how do we learn about it? Newspapers? What if we miss that item? As the courts say that ignorance of the law is no excuse, we are then responsible for adhering to a law we know nothing about. The government that passed the law has not taken any responsibility for informing us of a law that will affect us. We are innocents waiting to become victims of our own ignorance. Most of us learn about new laws by word of mouth. We all know how accurate that is. Many of us learn about laws from television. However, as laws differ from one jurisdiction to another, our perception of laws that apply to us may be inaccurate.

We have an ignorant, partly despairing, largely apathetic electorate charged with the responsibility for voting for its representatives to government. These representatives believe that the people who elected them do not have either the sense or the interest to understand the affairs of their government.

Politicians pride themselves when fifty percent or more of eligible voters cast their ballots in any election. What they don't realize is how few of those voters understand the history of the government over the previous term, the policies of each party and what influence (if any) the representatives they elect will have on the affairs of government.

Picture a husband and wife who have been arguing, shouting at each other for so many years that they no longer hear each other and no longer care how the other feels. Divorce is believed to be the only way. How can we divorce our government? This is a problem that we can't walk away from, as we can a spouse. The problem will not leave, will not lessen over time, and may even turn into anarchy, rule by gangs, or a dictatorship. Couldn't happen? Germans in the 1930s didn't think so either.

The technology and the methodologies exist now to permit each person to participate in a vote on any matter which affects us, either directly or indirectly. This is one possibility that should come to pass. Are we ready for it as a nation? Hardly.

How can we prepare for the coming century of government so that democracy can adapt and survive? To prepare for the future, we must learn from the past and understand the present.

The forms of democracy that are in place in the world's most powerful nations today took form and established themselves in the eighteenth and nineteenth centuries. They began with the signing of the Magna Carta in England in 1215 CE when the king of England acknowledged that the will of the people must be heard.

The Declaration of Independence of the United States of America, separating it from Great Britain, and the subsequent Constitution a few years later, set the standard in the Western World. It gave notice to older forms of democracy that a new form of representative government was in order. While democratic forms of government existed before that, they gained in effective power from that time on. Monarchies either disappeared or kings and queens became more figureheads than political leaders. This is not to take anything away from Great Britain or any other kingdom with a democratic government. Only to recognize that the United States set standards for this new form of democracy that others followed.

During the past century, the right to vote was granted to every citizen and, with some limitations, every resident in a democracy. With the mechanisms to do so in place today, it now becomes necessary in the near future to put the potential people-power of the system to good use.

It is time for citizens to learn about the affairs of their governments. It is time that people learned the facts about decisions that will affect them. It is time that people took action rather than sitting back and counting on others to do it, others who will only look after their own best interests. More than any other time in the past two hundred years, our participation in the political process is needed to help it prepare for the future.

The standards have been set for us in the past few decades. Special interest groups have shown that collective voices can be heard and can have an impact on government. The aboriginal peoples of Canada learned about their history, learned about their past, then proceeded to force their governments to negotiate new agreements that will empower them far beyond the wildest dreams of their grandfathers and fathers. The Canadian government listened, but only after these people spoke with a single, large voice.

The time has come for us to act in our own best interests and those of future generations. Technology will provide us with the means and the methods to do the right thing. We need to have the will to make it happen.

We have heard ourselves referred to as a knowledge-based society. Yet when it comes to how our country is operated, we don't know much about it. We must become more knowledgeable about who in government is making the choices that affect the lives we live and what they are deciding.

We must use our knowledge to help govern ourselves so that we can take pride in ourselves and our country, and to pass along to future generations a nation that has the ability to survive within the framework of principles and values that we set for it.

We have the power to destroy our world. We also have the power to save ourselves and to build a truly great nation. Cash flow is important and essential to the economy and the standard of living of each of us. But people must come first. Education is the key to the power of people.

There are things about our governments that we know need to be changed. We know that we have little effective voice in government right now. We can see that some others are making their voices known and are having an influence on our governments.

Too many people before us have left it to others to speak. We are all suffering for it.

Democracy is our birthright. It's time to declare ownership of that birthright.

The Rudderless Ship of State

A NATION on the road to chaos. People on their way to grief. Government without long-term plans that reflect the values of its constituents. So big a problem that we force ourselves to avoid thinking about it. We ignore it so much that people don't even recognize it as a problem any more. A government without long-term plans flags and founders like a lame ship lost in a storm at sea.

Governments without long-term objectives for their country and no clear connection to the values of the people they represent make managing other problems, including special interest groups and social problems, an impossible challenge. Political parties claim to represent the will of the people, but they rarely ask those people what values they want represented. Politicians say they talk with their constituents frequently and those constituents make their views known clearly.

They do speak with their constituents. If the actions of our governments reflect the views of those constituents, then our representatives have been chatting with miscreants, special interest groups and people with personal agendas.

We should all ask ourselves what we will be like ten years from now. It's bound to be a little vague. Where would we like to be? What would we like to be doing? What kind of person would we like to be? Given that amount of time to put a plan into effect, we could surely make major changes to ourselves. We could make almost anything we wanted of ourselves with that amount of time to prepare. It would require a decision and commitment.

Now try twenty-five years from now. It's getting fuzzier, isn't it? We could be hit by a bus before then. Maybe tomorrow. But maybe not in twenty-five years. Maybe busses will be different then. Remember, it took less than a decade of determined effort from the time the commitment was made to put a man on the moon until it was a fact. Maybe busses will have devices to protect people from being hit by them in less than a generation. They may not even travel on today's roads, but above them. Those who don't believe that could happen are not keeping up with developments in technology.

How about fifty years from now? Half-way through this new century? We may not even be around, right? There are those futurists who believe that most of those who were born after 1950 will live to see the turn of the next century. The latest advancements in medical research show that rapid progress is being made on many fronts towards removing barriers to the maximum age to which humans can live. This includes creating new body cells in the brain and growing new limbs, for example.*

Can we imagine ourselves in fifty years? Never mind the biological aging process. The wiser among us are already trying to do what we can to slow that down. Our bodies will be able to make new cells with perfect DNA by then, as opposed to the damaged DNA our new cells have now. We need to think young, but act our age. We should treat ourselves with respect, not abuse. Our maturity will be an advantage in the coming century when medical science finds ways of making our bodies younger.

We should have a wish list of what we would like the world to be like in fifty years. What we would like life to be like for our grandchildren and great grandchildren.

If we could make the world better, how would we change it? Go ahead, give it a try.

Hang on to those thoughts. We will need them later. All of us will need those thoughts later. Our descendants are an important part of our plan, so consider what kind of a country we want them to have.

Corporations make long term plans. Three- and five-year plans are a must. Ten- and twenty-year plans are common. The leaders of companies and their boards of directors sit together and consider not just where the company should be going for the coming few years, but how they can distance themselves from the competition in the future. For one thing, it helps them to assign figures for their research and development projects.

New pharmaceuticals often take ten to fifteen years to bring to market. Even some food products, especially unusual ones, require extraordinary commitments to research and testing. Sometimes ethical questions enter the picture to complicate the process. This slows down the progress too. So corporations need to plan years, even decades in advance. At the least, companies want to know how to position themselves in the marketplace that far into the future because they want to hold prominent places in the minds of their consumers.

The ideal situation for a big company is to develop a new product, patent it, then hold exclusive rights to it for many years to come. Some companies can't maintain exclusivity, but they can make plans. Ever wonder if there will be a burger joint in the first community on the moon? Couldn't happen? There are already multiple McDonald's restaurants, stores and banks on some military ships. There are vacation companies planning adventure vacations to the moon. We can reserve tickets now. Why not the other amenities that go with a vacation?

This kind of long-term thinking is absolutely essential for companies in the future. Without it, present companies could fall behind or disappear as others surge ahead with their superior planning and preparation. Global marketing, rare for most North American companies more than ten years ago, is a reality now in most postindustrial countries. Can off-planet marketing be that far off?

Let's bring ourselves back to our own environment for a bit. Most of us wonder why our governments don't do things the way we think they should. The people who have special interests and specific agendas get out there to talk up their views, lobby legislators and vote. They vote for the people they want and they encourage others who think the same way to vote too. They lobby their elected officials after the elections. They write letters, hold meetings, make phone calls. The active people are getting their way, often unchallenged by the majority of eligible voters.

What is the government in power right now interested in? Chances are, its primary objective is to maintain its hold on power. That's a given in any country. It should have other objectives stated in annual pronouncements of its plans. Those plans seldom go beyond a few years at most.

Our governments may have plans for the coming five years. Trade agreements, closer economic ties with some countries, military alliances, political arrangements in some cases. It's not likely that these matters involve the quality of life much. Yet quality-of-life matters are exactly what concern us about the world around us. Quality-of-life is what political parties talk about before elections but forget about after them.

For ten years from now, what have our governments planned? What will life be like in ten years because of what our governments have planned today? We may have a few predictions, but almost no one can base them on the long-term plans of a government.

Twenty-five years from now. How are our governments planning and preparing for what they want life to be like in our countries in twenty-five years? Chances are they haven't given life a generation from now a thought, except in a general sense. Maybe we haven't either. Someone should, unless we intend to let life evolve the way it has in the past few decades. A generation from now, our children will be roughly the same age as we are now.

What about the kinds of work that will be available a generation from now? If someone doesn't plan it, then it will develop by accident. We should not be satisfied to have the world evolve according to the forces at work today. That's the way it has happened for the past fifty years and look at the results.

A country, a government, a people can plan that far ahead. Think of it this way: a child born today will likely be a parent in twenty-five years. She won't be intellectually mature enough to become president of the United States, but then she will have to be a little older before that is legally possible anyway. This child will only be ready to begin her adult life in twenty-five years. What she learns in the coming years from her parents, her schools and other sources she will be able to put to use after that with her own children, through her own vote, with her own toil.

What will that child be able to accomplish in a generation after that if she has been prepared properly and fully during the coming few years? Most people won't have a clear idea.

Fifty years isn't really that long in the history of a country. Think about twenty-five years ago. It doesn't seem that long ago, does it? Time does pass that quickly.

Let's do a little history check. In the early 1700s, many of the British colonists in North America were unhappy with the way the mother country was treating them: sucking them dry, treating them like slaves. By the 1730s, they were putting their heads together and planning to break from the tyrannical mother country across the Atlantic. It took a while to put the whole plan together and to raise sentiment to take some serious action. It happened because people worked together.

In 1776, with the Declaration of Independence, thirteen colonies were ready to revolt. They knew what they had to do and why they had to do it. The Declaration spelled it out. Freedom and a new life in a new country were in their future. They would not be held back.

The Declaration of Independence, planned and approved by all thirteen states, gave the colonies the direction they needed to get them through the war to follow and the few years after that.

Once the war for independence was over, something more permanent was needed. A few years later the first constitution of the United States of America was produced. A few years after that it was approved by all of the colonies and became the law of the land.

It didn't take long to require amendments, to be sure. But they clarified the constitution rather than changing it. The constitution became a blueprint for how the country would operate for the future. Remember, the composition and values of the society had basically been formed. People knew what they believed in and what they wanted. Everyone knew what was right and wrong and what the country stood for. It was there in print. The Constitution represented the beliefs and values of the people.

The whole process of separation of the United States from Britain, assembling the colonies into a country, establishing a constitution and having it ratified took about fifty years.

Canada's constitution was an act of the British parliament, the British North America Act, until it was repatriated from the U.K. two decades ago. With a few significant additions, such as the Charter of Rights and Freedoms, Canada had what it needed to take it to the end of the twentieth century. Canada, a huge country with a population of just over thirty million, has taken its place on the world stage among the G8 nations, is a founding member of NATO and a provider of peacekeepers to the world's trouble spots through the United Nations.

Canada's constitution was enough to give it strength and guidance in a world that did not change much. From the time that Canada began to stand on its own as a nation, taking its place in the world community as an identifiably independent country, rather than as a colony, until it repatriated its constitution in the early 1980s took a little over fifty years.

We should be seeing a pattern here where major changes in a country require about two generations to take full effect.

But what of the next century? Two nations, India and Pakistan, tested nuclear weapons of their own design recently and several others have such weapons that they have never used, from among the nations that did not have them previously. Europe has formed itself into an economic partnership that could become a political power partnership within a few years. It already has its own currency and parliament.

The two most populous nations on Earth, China and India, are rousing themselves from their long sleep and planning to become economic superpowers in the years to come. Imagine what else they could afford to do then. They might exercise military influence using the threat of their military might over other countries the way the United States does now. The United States is, by historical standards, an honest policeman, a country with integrity and standards. We must be certain what to expect of countries that have five or six times the population of the United States, but less political stability. Planning can help with that.

Depending on how major countries of the world negotiate the use and storage of nuclear weapons, the world could be considerably different in two generations than it is now.

The Internet has made neighbors of everyone with a computer. Some of us exchange greetings and do business on a daily basis with people on every continent except Antarctica. We can chat with them as if we were on a telephone. Some have cameras on their computers, so that we can see each other as well as talk. Better than a telephone. And cheaper. Where will it go from here?

That's the good news. Terrorists have access to these same systems. They can recruit and make purchases much easier and faster than ever. Nuclear and biological weapons are being dismantled in cash-strapped Russia. Parts could be reassembled elsewhere by some rich, well-connected madman with delusions of world domination.

The world might be a different place now if Hitler had atomic weapons. Think about how life would be different today.

That was just a little over fifty years ago. But the stories are still fresh, the memories all too clear.

What plans do our governments have for our future? In most countries, not much. No one is interested. Politicians claim they can't get any support for long-term planning.

Our governments promote the commercial and tourist benefits of our countries to the world, yet they have little idea of what the coming few decades will bring to us. Are they doing the right thing? At the moment they believe that international trade (read: exports and ownership of industries in developing countries) is good because it brings hard currency into the country. This hard currency, in turn, gives the government bargaining power in international forums.

What is the plan for the future? A government, even more than an individual, needs a long-term plan. A country does not evolve into a position of strength by accident. It can lose power and endure economic and moral collapse through lack of attention to its future.

The ship of state should be steered where we and people like we believe it should go, not where it drifts on the wind or with the guidance of those with personal agendas.

Unless we take action, our countries will be governed in the future by the owners of the megagiant multinational corporations. They may even be controlled by a foreign dictator. We have seen in recent history how large countries can be controlled by strong men who control the military. Many countries are now effectively in the hands of multinational underground organizations. That may be in store for a country without long-term plans.

One voice, added with those of enough others, can make a big difference. The important thing is to speak together.

It's a new democracy. It will work if we want it to happen, and if we will add our voices to those of others in our countries.

---

* Josie Glausiusz, "Brain, Heal Thyself," *Discover*, August 1996

Loss of Innocence, Embrace of Guilt

TIME to look closer to home, into our own mirrors. Whether we like it or not, what we do and say impacts on our community and our country. We can't be part of a solution unless we clarify the extent of the problem and our involvement in it, and unless we endorse change.

When did we stop having *accidents* and start being *negligent*? No one is said to have an accident any more, an event that resulted despite reasonable diligence. Instead, someone is always at fault. Cut our finger? It was our own fault for not being more careful. Run over a tricycle in the driveway? It was our son's fault for leaving it there. Tax increase? Our municipal representatives are at fault for being fiscally irresponsible. When something goes wrong, no one is assumed to be innocent.

Cars used to be involved in "accidents." Now cars are considered to be the victims of negligence by careless people. When a police officer is called to the scene of a collision, he or she must issue a citation, at the very least. It is up to the officer to determine at least one person who can be labeled as being "at fault." Someone must always be wrong. There is no room left for the possibility that two drivers were doing their best and something unforeseen just happened, unless the charged person wants to fight the case in court. If we believe we are innocent of wrongdoing, we must prove it to a judge.

A police officer's written report was always used by insurance companies as the basis to determine which party should pay, in the case of a two-vehicle collision, should there be a difference of opinion about which vehicle caused a mishap. Now, the written report is one factor in a civil case, but a citation is given by the police as well. It has become somehow important to determine the guilt of someone, no matter what the situation. Compensation for damage is no longer sufficient. In many jurisdictions in North America, police officers must lay a charge when they attend an accident. There may not be room for an officer to determine that the drivers involved were doing their best and circumstances took the situation beyond their control.

Someone must suffer, other than an innocent victim. Someone must be guilty. Someone must be wrong. Someone must pay, if at all possible, when something unpleasant happens. We seem to function under laws that do not allow for the possibility of "accident." In court, good effort and intent don't matter; guilt does.

Why must someone always be at fault? We now expect that we mere humans must be perfect behind the wheel. That's not realistic.

Consider this: when we are driving, we must give one hundred percent of our concentration to our driving, no matter how many hours that might be at a stretch.

Can a person talk on a cell phone and give a hundred percent of their concentration to their driving? Police and other emergency vehicle drivers do. By that reasoning, we couldn't even have a conversation with anyone else in the car and be innocent if there were an accident.

We shouldn't listen to a radio either. All vehicles come with radios, use of cell phones is permitted in moving vehicles in most jurisdictions and conversations among driver and passengers are considered a matter of course. In fact, we might be considered anti-social if we, as drivers, do not converse with our passengers.

Consider this possibility. In days past, it was common for boys to break their arms by falling out of trees. Let's say a boy falls out of an apple tree on his neighbor's yard while trying to steal an apple. In the past, that boy would be considered to be guilty of trespassing and theft and, if he did not have his arm in a cast or at least a sling, he would be punished by his parents for being on someone else's property. Maybe both.

Now, after the fall, the situation would be reversed. First, the owner of the tree could be charged with negligence for allowing a dangerous condition to exist on his property (a tree that can be climbed by anyone tall enough and strong enough to do so).

Second, the boy may not even be accused of trespassing because all property that is not protected on all sides by high fences is considered to be freely available to anyone who wishes to access it. Unless a non-owner has been warned by the owner at least once to stay off the property, in some cases in writing, then the non-owner cannot be charged with trespassing. At least that is how the law is practiced in many municipalities now.

Third, there could be a civil suit against the owner of the tree for pain and suffering by the boy.

Fourth, the municipality could force the landowner to place a fence around the tree, high enough that it could not be climbed easily, and place one or more signs on the fence warning people to stay off the fence.

Do these sound like impossible outcomes of a fall from a tree? If so, then a review of recent happenings in the court systems and municipal councils should correct the situation. They may sound ridiculous, but similar decisions are being handed down in courts daily in North America.

No one has an accident any more. We just have events in which someone must be the guilty party. When there is a problem no one is assumed to be innocent except the victim. Even the victim must provide sufficient evidence of innocence.

When did we stop seeking excellence for ourselves and start demanding perfection of others? To a person, we seem to excuse ourselves for any action we make, no matter if it is illegal, immoral or harmful to others. When some of us are guilty of something and actually admit it, we rarely apologize or ask to be forgiven. We don't hear someone apologize or admit guilt for something very often. Many people will deny having done the deed, even when there is ironclad evidence that they committed it. Lying to avoid the penalties of guilt has become a way of life for many of us.

Can one lead a perfect or virtuous life? Not likely. Perfection means not getting caught when we have done something wrong, either by deed or by neglect. Eventually our misdeeds catch up with us.

Yet we expect perfection of others, especially our leaders. They are expected to live exemplary lives, despite the fact that few of us are able to do this ourselves. Even our religions do not expect us to lead completely pure lives.

Political and military leaders throughout history have led dual lives, with a dark side being accepted as a cost of having that person in the leadership role. This is no longer accepted, even if the transgressions do not harm others. The personal lives of our leaders, especially political leaders, are open for public scrutiny.

This should not be the case. Our leaders should have a private life as well as a public one. It's not necessary for the public to "own" the personal life of each leader and hold him or her accountable for any personal action we don't like.

Prominent figures in the entertainment industry parade their lives before everyone to gain media attention and prolong their time in the spotlight. It works for them. We no longer expect entertainment figures to be real people anyway. Publicity, good or bad, works to their benefit in most cases, as it keeps their names in the limelight.

That should not be the case with our political leaders. Through the media, we judge the success and effectiveness of a president or prime minister more by his private life than by what he accomplishes. A president may save the world from a terrible fate, but he is bad if he commits an indiscretion that most of us take for granted or would at least excuse in ourselves. Most of us know more about the personal lives of our national leaders than we do about the effectiveness of their work in office.

Differences between their transgressions and ours could be minor. We don't like to acknowledge that a celebrity has accomplished something that we could not, even though we might never try.

It's hypocrisy to condemn others for doing the same things as we do ourselves. We don't acknowledge our own guilt. Hypocrisy has somehow become acceptable.

Look around. Look at the double standards among people. Do they expect more of others and excuse behavior in themselves that they will not in others? Think carefully.

We certainly do not admire the success of others. We search for the faults of prominent people, then dwell on them until they suffer complete humiliation or leave their position of prominence. The mighty must be brought down to our level.

Hypocrisy may not yet be considered a virtue, but it has become a characteristic of our lives. We expect goodness and perfection in others that we do not expect of ourselves.

When did we stop respecting the traditional professions, such as law and medicine, begin heaping scorn on them and seeing them as possible sources of income from litigation? Include skilled tradespeople with that group.

It's not about taking the sides of the lawyers, doctors and plumbers here. We just need to think about what we have done to ourselves. Lawyers represent our judicial system and doctors represent our medical system, two of the most important functions in our civilization. Yet these professionals can't get through their careers without at least one case of malpractice. That is the expectation for current graduates of these professions.

New graduates to each of these professions can expect to be in court at least once in their careers. People see the rich insurance policies of these professionals as a source of potential wealth for themselves. "Make a mistake with me and I will sue you."

What good is served by the profusion of cases of litigation? Someone gets rich while the rest of us pay, one way or another. Ironically, it is often other lawyers that benefit most from litigation.

We may wonder why it's necessary for these professionals to make so much money. Let's consider just one of the costs, litigation insurance, for one of the medical specialties, obstetricians. A Canadian obstetrician, a qualified expert who brings new Canadian citizens into the world, may be required to pay up to fifty thousand dollars per year in litigation insurance premiums. Count the zeroes.

These professionals work endless hours for the benefit of their clients or patients. True, they benefit financially for their hard work and years of study, including regular updating of their skills. But they can't make a mistake without being sued.

Perhaps if we are in a position to benefit from litigation, now or in the future, we might believe it's right. If so, the point is made.

Greed and the desire to bring down the famous and wealthy have become hallmarks of our civilization. What is important to citizens of our respective countries? Can we name one thing that is important to us that does not relate directly to us, will not benefit us in some way?

When did we start believing that life had to be fair?

"That's not fair!" We hear it all the time. It used to come mostly from young children. But now it comes from adults as well.

What is fair? "Anything I like is fair and anything I dislike is not fair. Anything that anyone does to me that is not to my advantage is unfair."

What would qualify as being fair? Who judges this? If we judge something to be unfair, is there an equivalent party on the other side that considers it fair?

When we were children, anything that another child did, especially a brother or sister, that went against what mommy said was "not fair". We could threaten to tell mommy. Usually that would be sufficient to rectify the situation and help us to get our way. If threatening didn't help, it was especially unfair and we were then justified in shouting for mommy's attention at the top of our lungs.

We have moved that concept into our adult world. Who takes the place of mommy now? The courts. The establishment of the community or state. The police. The local bartender or café server. Our spouse. Our lover. "Yes" and "no" to each of the above. Some have the power and ability to enforce what is fair, in their judgment, under the guise of determining what is right. Others do it informally.

Why do we believe that life has to be fair? We believe that good people should live longer than the bad. They don't, and we say it's not fair. We believe that the young have a right to live more years than the elderly. Sometimes they don't, and we say it's not fair.

Life is not fair. It never has been. There is no evidence in existence to suggest that life should be fair or that it has ever been fair or that it ever could be fair. Yet we insist on fair treatment. We want to punish people who do not treat us fairly. This is not part of nature. Are we trying to change these standards of right and wrong? Who is to be the judge of this? Are we adopting godlike abilities to decide who is right and who is wrong?

Some people carry guns, for example, in order to even the score (make it fair) in their own way. It doesn't work. Life is still not fair and it never will be.

When did the three categories of matter (animal, vegetable and mineral) become four, adding humans? We have intellectually separated ourselves from the animal kingdom.

We do this to excuse us from being responsible for the exhaustion, extinction and decimation of members of the other three kingdoms. We artificially created an "us versus them" situation to ease our guilt of responsibility. When we stopped thinking of ourselves as being a part of nature, we began to take advantage of it.

When did people stop looking for things they have in common with a new acquaintance and begin to look for differences and faults with the person? When we look for things we have in common with a new acquaintance, we see if there is a possibility of establishing a friendship. When we look for differences, we look for a possible enemy.

When we think of an acquaintance, we might think about how different she is from us or how much we have in common. Chances are we think more about differences. We won't even know the person well enough to know the things we share. It takes time to learn common interests. Differences can be seen much more quickly.

We can't make friends with a person we think of first and foremost as being different.

Is it really possible to like ourselves? Some people seem to have a grudge against the world. They are pleasant when they must be, such as at work in the presence of their boss, but they frequently grouse about other people when they have the opportunity. They have no difficulty finding fault with others.

These people don't really like themselves. Since finding fault with themselves is not much fun, they look for the weaknesses and mistakes of others.

Happiness in this life begins with accepting that we must be our own best friend. For many people, they are their own worst enemies. They don't like themselves, so how can they ever like others? They can't accept themselves for what they are. They can't forgive themselves.

There is hope for these people. We could change them. It would take a while and a determined effort. It's important to prevent our younger generations from growing up the way these people are now.

People who don't like themselves probably do not like others. They are also the breeding ground for hate.

Hate is the breeding ground for violence and abuse. It's what many of us most dislike about the world we live in.

People who dislike and disrespect themselves don't know how to change.

When did communities begin to identify themselves with sports teams and shopping facilities rather than other values and virtues?

Think of a well-known city. What is the first thing that comes to mind about that city? A sports team? Shopping? If so, lots of others think the same way.

What does this tell us about the way that our cities present themselves to the world as being home to a sports team? Vacation destinations are, for the most part, sold by advertising. Given our choice, would we like our city to be known to the world only for its sports teams and its shopping?

What would we like our home city to be known for? Just wish for a moment. How would we like our city to be thought of by people around the world, if we could have our wish come true? Should sports and shopping at the top of our list? Maybe our cities should advertise themselves for the strengths we believe they have, not just what visitors can purchase in them.

When did it become necessary that we consider all people as being equal, in the sense of having equal skills, potential, attitude, drive and desire for the same goals?

One of the greatest speeches in the English language, the Gettysburg Address, delivered by President Abraham Lincoln from the battlefield in Gettysburg during the Civil War, declared that the United States of America was "dedicated to the proposition that all men are created equal." Thus began one of the most misunderstood and misinterpreted concepts in North American history.

Lincoln's meaning was clear to him. He had engaged in a war with southern landowners who wanted to keep slaves. As with most wars, it was one of propaganda as well as physical conflict. He and his northern supporters maintained that people should have equal access to freedom, which was not possible under the ownership system of slavery.

He did not mean that this equality only applied to men, but not women. In Lincoln's time, the words man and men were generic terms that referred to all people, of both genders.

He was not referring specifically to racial equality, although there was definitely a strong element of racial distinction to slavery.

He was not saying that all people were created equal intellectually or physically or emotionally. He was not saying that they should all have one eye color or hair color, or even any hair at all.

He was not saying that everyone should be able to reach the same level of wealth.

He was not saying that all people should have the same values or religion.

He was not saying that each person should have the same level of education.

He was not saying that each person should have the same knowledge of different subjects.

Yet each of these has been an interpretation of Lincoln's statement by at least some people, whether consciously or not, over the ensuing century and a half. What many people want is for everyone to be the same as they are, preferably while holding values that they personally hold dear. Not equal in Lincoln's sense of the word. This will never happen and should never happen. Such a society would stagnate and die.

If we believe that any interpretation of the above should be values that we hold dear or changes we should make in the attitudes of people, then we must agree and take action to ensure that they come about. If we believe that any values that we hold collectively, in sufficient numbers, should be taught to our young people and should become values for which our country stands proud, then we should take action to see that it comes about.

Can we do it? Not by keeping quiet and sitting on our hands.

We have to find a way of coming together, of finding agreement among us. That is where the rest of this book is going.

We will be looking for what we have in common, not differences among us. It's only through finding how much we have in common and working together to advance beliefs and interests that we will build a better nation.

And a better world. A more peaceful and less fear-ridden world.

16

Education

"SCHOOLS are failing our young people." "Schools are not giving our children what they need to succeed in the world as adults." These have been said so often in recent years that they're almost clichés, mantras, motherhood statements. Is there truth here?

A vast majority of people other than leaders of school boards, departments and ministries of education believe it. This is not to say that adult citizens believe their schools are not teaching what they should. On the contrary, most people support each part of the curriculum that is being taught. Schools are not teaching enough of what they should, parents believe. Yet teachers can't cram any more into their already overloaded school day.

Confusion and uncertainty haunt most schools. As curriculum size increases, educators must also take into account the capacity of their students to learn more than is presented now. Some students can't manage as much as they must at present. Social problems, correction and discipline, completely separate from curriculum, impact on the ability to learn of every child.

By the end of high school, the finished product of education is somehow less than the sum of its parts. Many young adults are not equipped to function fully, properly and responsibly as employees, parents and citizens. Even if our young people have learned everything their schools have taught, they lack some life skills they need.

In a desperate attempt to grasp at someone or something to blame, parents fault teachers. Teachers, in turn, claim lack of support and resources from their school boards. In a magnificent and unprecedented nation-wide show of mutual agreement that something is missing from our schools, we all fail to identify the cause of the problems.

Administrators furiously add more paperwork to the workload of each teacher. More stuff to teach. Students write more standardized tests to prove that they have all memorized the same minimum of what was taught. Teachers work longer hours than ever to prepare lessons and cram a huge amount of added curriculum into the school day. Students manage to assimilate more information than ever before in history. The problems get worse. More young adults leave school not being able to read as well as they should. More students take drugs and alcohol. More shootings shock the nation. More young people live on the streets of our cities.

No one admits that their own part of the education system fails to meet the needs of the students. Everyone agrees that something is wrong, that there could be improvements and that improvements are not likely to happen in the foreseeable future. Except the politicians. They force education systems to do more work with fewer resources, causing more anxiety, exhaustion, breakdowns and dropouts among teachers. Teachers entered the profession because they wanted to help kids. They bail out when they accept that the system isn't working and that the stress is too much.

As the amount of work done at all levels increases, fundamental problems remain. One critical difficulty is that no one at senior levels of education is prepared or allowed to address the causes of the fundamental problems. That would require too much change, too much listening and acting. Politicians believe that voters do not want change. Everyone wants improvement, but no one wants change. They pass laws, make policy and curriculum changes, pat themselves on the back. The troubles increase.

It doesn't get any more fundamental than that. Something is wrong and no one is looking at it, no one is addressing it.

As there are no quick and easy solutions to this problem, we will take it one step at a time. One difficulty is that there are problem students that the school system does not seem to know what to do with. Some get into trouble through sex, some with drugs or weapons and some with the law for other reasons. In a few rare cases, a student will bring a gun to school and shoot other students and teachers.

Carrying some form of weapon is considered a necessity by students in some parts of North America. In some high schools armed guards patrol the halls and airport-style body scanners check each student for weapons as they enter the school. This does not help much if the student brings a gun into school to fire at whomever he sees.

People believe that schools should be able to see problems in their students and divert them away from disaster. It isn't happening. Teachers don't have the skills, the authority or the resources to deal with these problems. Taxpayers want the problem solved, but not by raising their taxes. The most common response is to hire armed staff to patrol halls, making schools seem more like prisons than ever before. Lucky schools have psychologists. But psychologists only enter the picture when the problem becomes full-blown.

Guards, psychologists and the most dedicated teachers can only contain a problem. They can't correct anything by themselves.

Some people have no opinion because they have no idea of what is going on in the schools in their neighborhood. All they can see is a situation in their community, their city, their country, that they don't like. In fact, they are afraid. So they don't want to think about it. Because of their fear, they block out the subject and pretend it doesn't exist.

Students are unhappy, at least at the secondary school level. In the elementary grades, most children have not had the opportunity to think for themselves and make choices that affect their own future. That is, the younger kids don't know any better. Until we know that something is wrong in our world, we adjust to whatever we experience in it. We think our lives are normal.

Young children learn about their world by experience. Their understanding of the world depends on their experiences. Experiences give them the framework for their concept of how the world works. If children in elementary grades are taught by their peers that there is something wrong in their lives, that school has problems. If not, the school will have fewer of the kind of problems that worry adult citizens of the community.

At the high school level, adolescents are realizing that adulthood is ahead of them. They want to be like adults, they are given some of the responsibilities of adults, but they have many restrictions that make them feel as if adulthood is being held away from them. Many are unhappy because they don't like the look of their future, as practiced by the adults they know. They fear what is ahead. They don't understand it. They know they are not prepared for it.

The nature and causes of this fear are difficult to define. Sometimes the way in which they show themselves is difficult to explain or understand by adults. Adults have few analytical tools for understanding fear, even in themselves. Most people instinctively suppress their fears and find other ways to relieve their anxieties. It is more difficult for a younger generation that has different values from adults.

Everyone has ways of disguising their fear. Often this is done by attacking others, either physically or orally, such as bullying.

Teachers express discontent with the attitudes, behavior and work habits of their students. Administrators and support staff complain because of their hands being tied by school boards that fear litigation by disgruntled parents. Parents are unhappy because their children are going through a traumatic adolescent period that seems unnecessary. Each one of these interested parties believes that one of the others is responsible for the problems.

Yet when each of these parties with vested interests is asked how to improve the state of education, no one has any concrete answers. Unless it's to teach more basics: more reading and math. Or they have answers that can't find favor with the other groups. Zero tolerance, a system of tight and inflexible rules of behavior and often of dress codes, has received mixed results and limited support. This answer creates a police state within our education systems. Some, out of desperation, believe it may be the only way at their disposal.

The reality is that education is at the threshold of a major shift in emphasis. Either that or more frequent disasters. Perhaps we don't understand or appreciate the degree to which the problem has developed. To those of us who do, it causes concern.

In ancient times, education of the young was the responsibility of parents. Parents knew what their children needed because they were not much past that age and stage themselves. People mated younger than they do now in order to raise their children while they were still young themselves. Death came extraordinarily early by today's standards, often in their thirties or younger.

Throughout human history, there have been wars in most societies at least every twenty years. This, coupled with disease, a high infant mortality rate and death rate of mothers in childbirth made it essential that a society that wanted to stay healthy and vibrant produced as many children as possible while parents were of child bearing and rearing age.

It was relatively easy for parents to teach their children, as most children were expected to follow in the footsteps of their parents. The son of a carpenter was expected to become a carpenter, for example. Parents taught moral behavior, a common knowledge base, job skills, social skills, a religion and the ways of adults right in the home or workshop area. These were supported and enhanced by churches and eventually by schools.

At some point, the diversity and location of jobs, the means of support for families and individuals became more diversified and more distant from the family home. This was when schools came into their own as major providers of education for children.

At this time, there was a common understanding of what was required of a basic school education. This is when the three Rs (reading, writing and arithmetic) became the necessities for everyone who went to school. While there were varying degrees of proficiencies in these subjects among common people, it was agreed that these basics should be learned by everyone. Further education consisted of advancement of these basic skills into related areas, such as literature, composition and the sciences, for example.

A young person of school age learned the skills, values and moral behavior that would be important in his or her future as an adult. Schools and parents supported each other in this task.

Furthering one's education usually meant apprenticing with someone in a specialized vocational field, with a view to gaining expertise that would make one more valuable to an employer. The masters who taught these apprentices knew the skills that needed to be taught, as they used these skills themselves daily.

As the Industrial Revolution brought about the need for additional new skills and trades, there was further diversity in the world of work. Many of the new jobs were in new fields, in factories and in businesses that supplied goods or services to factories. There were not enough experienced masters to train the new people. This is when colleges arose to teach the needed skills to larger numbers of young people. The objectives of these colleges were straightforward, as they were training people to fill jobs with well-defined skill requirements.

At the same time, universities were expanding into the liberal arts. These courses were filled by children of the new middle class, whose parents believed that they should have a broader educational spectrum than previous generations. As history, literature, drama and so on were already written, the universities knew what they should be teaching. It was already in book form. If it was already in print, it was easier to teach than something the teacher had to create.

In the past few decades, the emphasis of post-secondary school institutions turned to more practical courses again, as it became necessary for the middle classes to learn post-industrial skills that would serve them well. Post-secondary schools knew exactly what they should be teaching, as their courses were directed towards skills needed by specific trades and professions.

It was left up to the secondary schools to do what they could to prepare students for the colleges and universities. Post-secondary institutions competed with each other for tuition funds from students, as their growth and continuity depended upon their being able to attract an ever-increasing number of students who brought tuition money with them. Colleges were focused on what the students wanted, which was training for future jobs.

Secondary schools took form in the nineteenth century and their function was firmed up in the early part of the twentieth century. They found themselves increasingly out of touch with the needs of their students. Rather, they believed that they could dictate student needs through curriculum. As funding for secondary schools came from public tax monies, a safe source, they didn't worry much about this; school attendance was mandatory, so funding was guaranteed. Post-secondary institutions insisted that the high schools not teach subjects that were specifically being taught at the higher level. This, they claimed, would provide competition for their own services.

The more that high schools lost their purpose and focus, the more disenchanted their students became. The more disenchanted secondary school students became, the less prepared they were to attend post-secondary schools, the less prepared they were to fill skilled jobs, the less prepared they were to cope with the rigors of adulthood, and the more inclined they were to wear black, have strange hair-styles, puncture and tattoo their bodies and carry weapons into school.

Disaffection became rebellion, which turned in some cases to more severe forms of anti-social behavior.

Conventional wisdom among high school students taught that they could get good jobs when they left school with a high school diploma alone. It became a student mantra that the curriculum was irrelevant and that most of their teachers didn't care about them.

Children are not taught to expect high school to be their first major trial of life and to learn to use it for their own benefit. They don't know how to cope with it. They suffer a detachment, an alienation, from the world they knew as young children. They have no idea about how to approach an adulthood they see as being filled with people who have values they don't understand. They know the world has changed and they don't know where it's going.

As young children they were taught that childhood should be fun. They generalized from that experience that life should be fun. Their primary objective should be to be happy as often as possible. Any activity or place that prevented them from being happy was wrong and should be avoided. No one told them anything different.

As they entered adolescence, their parents were imposing more and more rules on them, rules that didn't exist for them as children. They looked forward to being older, with more freedom, more opportunities to be happy. They were relieved to be free of the restrictions of childhood, but confused by new restrictions at home, school and elsewhere that they didn't expect. Getting older meant more restrictions, not less, as they had expected.

They didn't know that the world of adults is one of restrictions, responsibilities and commitment to everything they associate with. They didn't know that life is a whole lot more work than fun. They didn't know that we have to give our best to our work as adults or we will lose our employment, our source of income. They didn't know that they must make a huge commitment of love and devotion to family in order to make the family relationship work. Some didn't even know clearly what's right and what's wrong, how to treat others with respect, or how to make friends.

They didn't know because no one taught them. Fewer families attended church where some of this could be taught. Schools avoided anything that could be equated with religion for fear that someone could be offended. The closest that school got to morality was that covered by the judicial system and local laws and bylaws. The United States Supreme Court mandated that there should be no suggestion of religion in public schools, for example. Anything related to religion was politically incorrect, in fact illegal. The values taught for millennia by religions were lost when prayers and religious teachings were removed from schools.

With human knowledge increasing at an overwhelming rate now, school boards and departments and ministries of education have laid on more curriculum material, more required testing and more paperwork for the teachers. Teachers became little more than fact-spewing employees and were treated with all of the warmth and caring by the boards that would be accorded to automatons or machines. They turned the very grindstone that the school boards were holding to their noses.

What would happen to the good teachers that took a sincere interest in their students, teachers that really cared about them? They burned out. For the others, there was no time for caring.

There were plenty of examples of where caring teachers got into trouble with parents and even the courts, even if they were innocent. There was no room for caring and values in the curriculum. Burnout became a career path for teachers. They were unable to care for their students safely. If they did, they risked censure by fellow teachers and school administrators for getting a little too close to their young charges.

Good teachers have more to fear than mediocre teachers. Some parents literally don't want teachers to care for their children. They say that it's not the responsibility of teachers to care, only to teach facts and skills. They insist that teachers mind their own business, that teaching should not be personal.

We have today what can only be described as a dysfunctional education system. Everyone is trying to do their best. No one really knows what they are doing, in the sense that they don't know the effect their work is having on the students. Curriculum change is implemented in systems where there are sometimes no support materials at all. Funding and resources do not follow the introduction of new curriculum, let alone precede it to allow for proper preparation time.

Our school systems are not teaching people any coping skills and mechanisms for when they lose their spouse, or their job, have a serious medical problem or lose a parent. Students leaving high schools today don't have much of an idea of what to expect in their working adult lives. Some know what to expect when things are going well at work, but most have no idea what to do if things at work go wrong or if there are problems at home. These problems can result in disaster for several people in a family when one of them can't cope.

If a student can survive his or her years of formal education before entering the work force, he or she should be ready to face the world as an adult, we might think. To those who can survive the chaos of the education system, an organized employer company should be easy. Not exactly. Some of today's students have been so tuned out during their high school years that they are not prepared for the working world. The ones who are prepared may not have jobs for a few years anyway. Even the jobs they get may be temporary, unskilled and low paying.

At one time, a student who graduated from high school could look forward to a career of his or her choice. "You can be anything you want to be" went the chant of upbeat parents in the 1950s and 1960s. Choose a career that will last a lifetime.

Then it changed as employment conditions changed. A young person was told in high school to be prepared to attend college and to be involved in three careers in his or her lifetime. Three complete career changes, not just job changes within the same field. This was in the progressive years of the 1950s and 1960s.

Today students are told to expect to have as many as ten careers during their working lives. Young people are not prepared for that. Schools are not teaching toward that end. The chaos and dysfunction of high school now is going to become a situation bordering on anarchy in the working world of the future. Kids are not being taught coping skills for the problems they will face in their future.

Is this really what our young people are facing today?

Yes.

Is this the kind of uncertainty that they can expect in their futures?

Yes.

Are high schools still expecting adolescents to be calm, dress properly, behave and do well with their studies while the kids know better than their teachers the kind of life that lies ahead for them?

Yes.

Is there any realistic hope that can be given to young people today?

Yes. But not the way the system is set up at present.

Is there any real hope that can be offered to good teachers to entice them to stay in the profession and bring others into it?

Not the way the system is set up.

Is there any hope that departments and ministries of education will ever know what is happening in the world outside of their ivory towers?

No comment. We have this book.

Is there any hope for the future of our society, our civilization, if each young life experiences this confusion during its growing years, its formative years?

Yes, and that hope is based on our making up our collective minds to accept that the system must change to meet the needs and demands and the conditions of our people today.

The fact that we now have this book is a start. The solutions are not so difficult to understand. Just hard to find. The problem is that we're not looking in the right places, at the right things. A hopeful future is ahead of us. We'll find it before the end of the book.

Education 2100

WHERE WE ARE TODAY

MANY of the major social programs, such as the provision of education services and the exercise of government responsibilities, are severely behind the realities of our times. They are out of date with the lives of the people who voted their leaders into power. In some cases, the provision of education services has not changed much since the early part of the last century.

Education must change, and soon, to meet today's challenges. Much has changed over the past decade in the way people in communities, countries and societies conduct their lives. Many ways of the recent past are obsolete, ancient history. Backward communities tend to fall behind in the quality of life of their residents. Only education can keep a country abreast of the times.

The twentieth century style of classroom education in North America, only moderately successful in the early part of the century, fell severely behind the pace and needs of life in the last four decades. New computers in classrooms make those adults who know little about education curricula and resources feel that schools are keeping up. Computers did not change education.

We citizens have been led to believe that computers will be enough to make our classrooms modern. What most of us don't know is that there are many factors that work against modernization of our education systems, factors that can't be overcome by the placement of technology in classrooms. Even educators may be unaware of this.

Students often know more about how to use computers in their classrooms than their teachers. Put a student and a teacher in front of a new video game and watch the teacher struggle to learn the new rules while the student works to better his high score from the previous ten games. The thinking and learning curves are the same for video games as for computer learning in general. We can guess, then, what students will be doing with their computers while the teacher is busy with others.

While teachers and curriculum writers stick with their belief in the intellectual immaturity of children and their inability to grasp concepts, these same children are using the Internet and video games to satisfy their hunger for the brain activity that is being withheld from their classrooms.

We recovered from the need for bomb shelters of the 1950s and the age of protests began in the 1960s. The 1970s were dark days of despair as the quality of life worsened while there were few signs of optimism for the future. People turned inward in the 1980s as the "me generation" realized that they had better look after themselves since the rest of the world seemed to be looking more and more like the enemy. Very little changed in the way education services were offered over those decades.

The 1990s was the decade of successful special interest groups. People took their futures into their own hands and lobbied governments who otherwise would have paid little attention to them.

They were successful because politicians were unprepared to counter their polished and well-prepared presentations, their slick form of networking and lobbying, and their threats. Politicians didn't stand up to these groups, didn't know how.

Many voters would not voice their opinions either in opposition to or in support of any alternative in debates of possible new laws, mostly because they were unaware of what was going on. Those that were may have complained to their spouses or friends. There was very little organized public opposition to the lobbying of special interest groups, so their causes earned unfettered air time in the broadcast media and print space in newspapers.

If the majority of voters would express their opinions in a coordinated manner now, about subjects they agree on, there is every reason to believe that governments would go along with their wishes with less resistance than they gave to special interest groups. It's a given that such an expression of collective opinion must be done in a manner that is appropriate. Democracy today means rule by the majority of those who speak up, not rule by uncommitted people past the age of majority. Running a country involves more than voting once every few years.

During the latter part of the 1900s, education systems made minor changes which secured the positions of administrators, made citizens believe that something was happening in education but did little to improve the lives and skills of students. Politicians regularly reported that education was improving. Meanwhile, social problems escalated.

In terms of helping children cope with adulthood and preparing them for the realities of their fifty-plus years as full-fledged working adult citizens, there was little real progress after the 1950s. While the lives of North Americans altered dramatically over those decades, the provision of education services for most young people became increasingly inadequate.

Education systems are notoriously bureaucratic and resistant to change, despite their claims to the contrary. Education systems do not change until either a brave political leader forces it upon the bureaucrats or a large majority of citizens demand it and insist with their voting power.

An uphill struggle will lie ahead for disorganized groups or individuals who propose changes to education. Change begins with suggested solutions, not with complaints.

Brave political leaders with foresight and conviction are scarce at this time, especially when it comes to education. What is needed is an unpurchasable leader, someone with conviction, courage and the will to design the necessary changes and ensure that they are implemented thoroughly and properly. A leader who knows what children need, not what facts adults think kids should know. A leader who believes that children are not little computers who need to be fed data and exercised, then sent home.

This requires a government leader with a majority and the support of a dedicated electorate who are devoted to democracy in its broadest sense. People participating. It requires a leader who is committed to the nurture and education of children, who knows what children need, not what he or she as an adult brought up in an antiquated system several decades before thinks they need.

This scenario is unlikely to happen on its own. Politicians do not come blessed with such experience and gifts of insight. The alternative, a large group of citizens requesting that their government update the process regarding delivery of education services, may seem unlikely. However, that's perception, not reality. A large majority of the voting citizens of each country now agree that changes must be made. Majorities rule elections and governments. Let's see if we all agree.

This book will provide guidance about new methods that will improve the system of educating our young people. When the two are put together, people with ideas, changes will happen, if people clearly state what they want and have the numbers of voters for support that they need.

Education systems (boards, ministries and departments) as they exist now are products of the past. True, they have been updated, sometimes dramatically, to meet perceived needs. But the fact remains that they are playing catch-up, always following a crying need in their respective communities, and never getting ahead.

Each community searches for ways to overcome social problems. It would be comforting if a blanket system designed to compensate for the unfulfilled social needs of our communities could be applied to everyone who is directly or indirectly affected by the education system—that is everyone in the country. But this is impossible as a short-term solution, as our lives do not permit us time to accomplish this.

Education must be revised so that it foresees the needs of the community, the country and the world in the coming century and prepares everyone to meet these needs. Curriculum must be designed to teach to these needs, not just give lip service.

Where We Need To Be

In order to provide a reasonable basis for community discussion of what is needed, let's consider some factors which will influence education and require changes in the present systems.

- Education must hereafter be considered a lifelong activity and pursuit. Only those in the terminal phases of a fatal disease can afford to stop learning.

- Education should begin only a few weeks after conception. Mother must provide a stimulating environment of sound and light for the developing fetus. Meanwhile, parents should be learning parenting skills and techniques that will help them to provide a productive learning environment during the first few years at home. Parents must be encouraged to take training courses before the birth of their first child. These will be courses in parenting in the full sense, not just in diaper changing, feeding and babysitting techniques. Education begins at home.
- Education in pre-adult years must prepare children to live and work in environments other than those in their home town, country or even continent.
- Education must prepare people to be able to adapt quickly and effectively to new environments, be they job-related or personal. (Most employers seek experienced people, despite the fact that inexperienced new employees do not come burdened with bad habits. To be employable, one must be able and ready to make the necessary moves to get the needed experience or training.)
- Education must prepare people to cope with conditions which have been devastating to adults and students in the past, such as the death of a loved one, the break-up of a relationship, the loss of employment, financial wipeout, retraining, relearning and re-educating.
- Education must prepare small children for what they will face in future years of their formal education and life as adolescents and as adults. They must learn that growing up is a process of adopting responsibilities and making commitments.
- Education must prepare teens to be able to cope with a world they do not understand and may fear. Worry is unproductive. Fear is destructive. Each young person must have the ability to direct his energy to productive use for the benefit of himself and those with whom he chooses to share his efforts, caring and life.
- Education must include lifestyle choices, moral training, values training and long term objectives training, the form of which would be determined by national or state/provincial governments, through plebiscites of their citizens. Voters must be convinced that the changes are necessary and they must understand why.

- The main goal of education must be to model students toward the role of ideal citizens of the nation. That is, every young person should be taught the role that is required and expected of them and the responsibilities that are required for a citizen of their country.

A QUICK REVIEW OF THE PROCESS

Let's start at the beginning of the education process. An unborn child only a few months after conception will respond to music and light stimulation. Just as plants grow healthier with stimulation from certain kinds of music, so does a fetus. A light, such as a flashlight, passed over the mother's growing baby-cocoon stimulates both the eyes and the brain of the fetus. The more prepared a fetus is to accept new learning, the better prepared the new-born baby will be to learn in its new environment.

Newborn human babies, it is generally acknowledged, have little in the way of instincts. Sucking and a will toward learning and survival are argued as being built-in, or hardwired, as the current terminology goes. That fact is, we don't know much more than that for certain.

Babies, even fetuses, have a tendency toward appreciating certain sensory things such as light, movement and music. No doubt much more will be learned about children of this age over the next century. At this stage, we have problems learning about them due to their inability to communicate with us using our language. Maybe we should say that we have the communication problem, as we don't know how they perceive and learn.

As the century progresses, we will learn more about non-verbal language, perhaps allowing us to finally communicate more fully with babies. We now know, for example, that newborn babies can infallibly distinguish their mothers and even their fathers from other large people. Studies will soon reveal how this happens. Early results suggest that it is likely by smell. Perhaps our sense of smell is much more acute before we learn language than it is afterwards, or maybe we don't use it as much after we develop skills with our other senses.

In the meantime, we will consider that babies begin their lives with an intellectual base nearing tabula rasa. It's believed that babies learn as much in their first few years, before going to school, as they do in the entire rest of their lives. Whether we question that or not, beginning from a knowledge base near zero to a child ready to attend classes in school requires a great deal of learning and mental exercise.

Learning slowly in a formal school classroom setting follows a period of rapid learning in pre-school years. This is a shock to both the child and the system. Professional teachers take over teaching a child after untrained parents have been responsible for half of what the child will ever know. The education system must make an attitude and lifestyle adjustment to the child in order to administer to it the prescribed school curriculum.

It's important to realize that this major adjustment in the child's approach to life is necessary because the adult world (school) is not giving the child what it wants and needs, which is knowledge about how the bigger world outside of the child's home works. Instead, it forces facts on the child, information and skills for which it has no immediate need and will not have a pressing need for a few years. No wonder there's reluctance on the part of primary school children to adjust to this new regimen.

Parents hold the main responsibility for the education of the child during the first precious and critically important few years. There is very little training available for new parents, other than for the birthing process. Most soon-to-be-parents who want to learn as much as they can about how to care for their precious new child have no formal source for such information, even less than was available a thousand years ago.

At least in ancient times adults actually taught children what they would need to know and how they should behave as parents and as adults. Parents learned from their parents. Today the teaching is more by example of our own parents, less by teaching.

Parenting does not come with a training manual. Most parents try their best to be good parents, but they may make mistakes because they have not been taught what to do. We have a habit of learning parenting skills on the job. We learn as we go through the process of raising our own children. We learn the hard way, while we also busy ourselves with other pursuits in life.

A training manual should be provided for new parents. We have been parenting modern homo sapiens for thousands of years, yet we still do not have any common guidelines for parents. In fact, the most primitive tribes that have been discovered in the past few decades, ones that have had no contact with modern society until recently, have a more highly developed system of raising (teaching) children than we do in the developed world. They have fewer problems with young people in their adolescent years. The rebellious teen period is unknown to them, for example.

Young babies, less than one year, have little else to do with their time than to learn from their parents, the people they see the most. Yet these adults have no training in how to be good parents and what children of that age require. They assume that the child of less than a year has no ability to learn from them. How very mistaken they are.

Parents of these young babies are role models. Are they good role models? Do they project the kind of image of our world that we would want these children to learn? We have reason to doubt.

Learning in the critical first year of life is left entirely to chance, to the abilities of new parents who are the sole teachers of a subject they know little about. Most parents act as if nothing they do other than what they do directly with their babies (playing) will be learned by the children. How extraordinarily wrong they are.

As a personal experiment, watch parents of young children on a downtown city street for a while. Observe their behavior and think about what kinds of role models they are for their impressionable young children. They cross the road in the middle of the block. They cross an intersection against a red light. They may commit other offences they don't consider important as adults, yet they will (ineffectively) try to teach their children a few years later to avoid such behaviors for their own safety.

These parents often have no idea that they are teaching their young children every moment that they are together. They teach their children by example. They think that all the learning their children will ever need will be provided when the kids get to school, whereas most of what the children learn in those critically important years they learn at home.

How does that make us feel about the future, that around half of all learning by children is taught by people who have only a vague idea of what they are doing? Many of us will feel very uncomfortable.

As children move beyond their first birthday, they learn more from others, although their parents are still the primary role models. They watch television. They go for walks in their community. They visit the shopping mall, restaurants, doctor's office, parks, homes of family friends and anywhere else their parents take them for the next few years before going to school. They play with other kids and quickly learn their habits.

These are the years we should be teaching these children the values and moral code that we would like them to hold for the rest of their lives. Values and moral codes of behavior are reflected in our laws and ways of life in our respective countries. Most parents do set a pretty good example, if only by accident; but not good enough for some kids. Look at the results in our communities.

Young children are at an extremely impressionable age. Their parents should always present themselves as good role models. The children learn much from television, so this should be guided, not just monitored or ignored. If they go to day-care or nursery school, these facilities should provide the kind of healthy learning environment that our children need.

If any of the above sources of learning for a child are questionable or are not as positive as we would like, then some changes are in order. These changes are manageable and do-able. But they must be undertaken on a large scale, to ensure that support is provided by all members of our society.

This requires agreement on a mass scale on how to go about it. At this time there is no encompassing plan to accommodate the social and developmental needs of children of this age and no formal support is provided for these needs. Their development is left to chance and the skills of their untrained parents and child-care facilities that concentrate more on behavior modification than on values. Given those conditions, we should be thankful our country is not in worse shape than it is.

Look at the young people (teens) we see who will be parents within a few years. Are we confident that they will be able to provide the kind of love and guidance to their children that they deserve? If not, we should add our voices to those of others who want to make the changes that are needed.

Love is an essential element to the life of a child. As many adults do not have a clear idea of what love is and how to show it, or even how to feel it, as parents they will be unable to provide for one of the critical needs of their children.

When children first go to school, we immediately begin to treat them as small adults. While we do not expect adult behavior from them, we encourage them toward self-discipline in their behavior, so as not to interfere with the learning of others. And we begin to formally teach them what we believe they will need to know as adults. That is, we teach them number skills, reading skills and encourage them in the arts.

This is done in a formal teaching environment, the classroom. The content of the curriculum has been fairly constant for decades, although the teaching methods have changed considerably. That is, we want these children to learn to read, write and do arithmetic, even if the methods of teaching these are different now from how they were in the past. We teach more facts and skills than in previous centuries, but the process is basically the same as it was in the nineteenth century.

Young children learn these skills slowly. It takes a long time to teach these skills, as most of the kids have only limited experience, at best, with the concepts. It can take three weeks for a child in grade one to learn what a child in grade four could learn in a couple of hours. But the teachers are patient and the time is allowed in the curriculum, as these skills are believed to be important.

Here's a question that might be considered radical by the education establishment: how important is it for a child to learn one particular skill in grade one rather than in grade four? What are the benefits of spending so much time in grade one when a tiny fraction of the time needed to teach the same thing could be taken in grade four? Okay, that was two questions.

The same child in grade four has a crammed curriculum, so not much time is available for learning other things, such as things he or she will need to know about life as an older person.

For example, in grade four a child is learning about the evils of smoking, why it should be avoided. At this age, the child has been exposed to smoking for a few years and will have developed a concept and an attitude about it already.

The main reason the curriculum is so crowded is that so much time was wasted in earlier grades teaching things that were not essential, far too slowly.

Why not teach the child about smoking at the age of six, in grade one, before he or she has had much exposure to it from others in the community? A child of six may not be capable of learning to read or add quickly, but he or she is able to understand the values of life. Learning the values of life is a small step for a child of six, as it follows the same cognitive patterns as the child has been using to learn for the past several years. Arithmetic, on the other hand, requires the learning of new cognitive skills for most children this age.

For the past century, we have been formally teaching children of six to do arithmetic skills they find difficult to learn at that age and will not have much use for immediately. Meanwhile we cram life skills and values into children of ten, through a crowded curriculum. The values of these children have already been set through examples and role models of the people around them in their daily lives in previous years.

This is not to suggest that children have no use for arithmetic skills from ages six through ten. It is intended to suggest, however, that these skills should be taught when the child can cope with a steeper learning curve and the needed time for learning is much shorter. More importantly, these skills should be learned just before they will be needed.

For most children, the need they have for arithmetic skills begins when they need to understand the exchange of money. The urgency of this need varies from one child to another. It's controlled mostly by activities kids do with their parents. A child who has trouble understanding the exchange of money will also have difficulty understanding simple arithmetic skills.

Why force either when there are more important things to teach young children?

Children need most to be able to understand their world. They need love and caring. These vary greatly from one family to another. A child of six may be loved but not know it because he does not understand how his parents show their love.

The understanding of love between a mother and baby may be easy, but after that a child must learn what love is, how to show it and how to recognize it being shown to them by others.

A child who does not believe he is loved is likely to have difficulty learning in school. A child who is loved and understands that he is loved, but that his parents express their love differently from other parents, will have a better chance to learn his academic lessons faster. A child is capable of understanding and accepting this difficult concept.

What should our priorities be? Should we provide the child with experiences that will help him to understand his world and feel better about how he fits into it first, then give him the academic skills he will be able to use and learn quicker later? Or should we first teach the unnecessary, to be followed later by social skills and information that come too late to be believed or appreciated?

Which sequence will likely produce the better child? Which will more likely create a child that has a healthy outlook on life, more positive attitudes toward life, more eagerness to learn the skills that he will need and be able to use in his life? We have a right to hold opinions on these subjects. We have a right to have our opinions heard.

We should be satisfying the needs of the child first, before satisfying the needs of his parents to know that he is on his way to learning the facts and skills he will need as an adult. Older children and adults can learn in a few months the same skills that take children several years to accomplish. This shows that a mind that is prepared to learn can do so quickly. However, a person who has other needs that interfere with learning and are not covered in school will require a much longer learning period and will not be capable of steep learning curves.

Children with emotional problems have trouble learning. We accept that children with recognizable problems will have trouble learning. What we don't recognize is that all children have emotional and social needs that take priority in their young lives, even if they don't realize it. They just think that school is hard, that others learn easier than they do. They don't understand themselves. Some kids think they are dumb because they can't learn as easily as other kids, while the truth is that they may have unrecognized and unaddressed social or emotional needs.

All children need to know they are loved. They need to be able to recognize the love that their parents and siblings have for them and how they express this love.

They need to be able to express their own love in ways that these other family members understand. They need to be able to tell others that they need a show of affection. This is extremely important. Our education systems do not make any provisions to accommodate those needs, the need to understand significant other people in their small world. Few parents teach these to their children. Most were not taught themselves.

Children with underdeveloped social skills have trouble learning. Children who are socially immature for the dozen years or more of their formal education understand the feelings of isolation, of alienation and of just not being "with it." They know what it's like to feel different from everyone else, to believe that they would never catch up with their peers.

Social immaturity is not something commonly addressed in schools today. Teachers don't know what to do about it, and often can't even recognize it in children. A child who is a discipline problem, for example, may be allowed to leave school at the age of fifteen because he is socially immature compared to others his age and because the school just wants to get rid of their problem. This child may live a life of poverty, even of functional illiteracy, because his teachers, his school and his school system don't know how to address social immaturity among children.

Socially immature children need to be given the experiences that will help them adjust. In many cases, we offer that in schools as a side benefit of group work and joint projects. It is seldom offered as a goal in itself. We offer little to promote social growth to kids who have greater needs than most but are not recognized as having addressable problems.

A reordering of priorities of our education systems is necessary. We need to develop new curriculum that meets the needs of children, not the desires of well-meaning but misguided adults. And especially not the whims of ivory tower bureaucrats who have their own temple of power to preserve. In order to do that, the adults that demand changes in curriculum need to become informed themselves. The adults must learn about the real needs of children before the children of our future will have a chance. Those needs go far beyond arithmetic and reading.

We also must consider the fact that the knowledge base of humanity is growing faster than anyone can keep up with. No matter how much our school trustees and education bureaucrats add to the curriculum, no one, child or adult, will be able to keep up with advancements in knowledge. No one of any age can learn enough, fast enough, to keep even with the advancements of human knowledge.

We will have more experts in the future than we had in the past. We will have, indeed we have now, many people who are experts in one field but who know no more than a high school dropout about most other areas of life. Experts who know a great deal about one very confined field, but nothing much about any others. If that field now were computers, we might describe them as geeks or nerds.

Hubris makes some people believe that because they have expertise in one area, they are experts in all areas. The simple, ugly truth is that we are all falling behind. We are all becoming ignorant about the developments in most fields of human endeavor.

As much as we may read or watch television, we are only catching the headlines, at best.

The only way we can cope is to learn as quickly as possible what we need to know in order to do what we need to do. We need to accept that learning is a way of life, something that will be part of us our whole lives. We need to know how to cope with a situation in our lives when we know nothing about the subject, but have to learn quickly or risk hurting ourselves in some way. We need the skills to know what steps to take to learn what we need quickly, such as where to find information.

We need to be able to ask for help from others without feeling deficient or ignorant. We need to know that others will help us when we ask.

We joke that men do not ask for directions when they get lost in a strange community. But why? What did the male half of our species learn in their growing-up years that would discourage them from asking a stranger about where they are?

This is a learned behavior. Where was it learned? At home.

The need for the Golden Rule has never been more important than it is now. We must help others and we must be able to ask others to help us. Education is about helping others to become what they can be. It's also about welcoming the help offered by others and asking for it when we need it.

Wisdom is knowing enough to offer help to others when they need it and to ask for help from others when we need it.

Packets of Education Objectives

Let's consider in more depth the factors that we listed at the beginning of the second part of this chapter. Each will have a major impact on life in the coming century.

- **Education must hereafter be considered a lifelong activity and pursuit. Only those in the terminal phases of a fatal disease can afford to stop learning new things.**

Life in the millennia prior to this was relatively static. People lived close to where they worked and died not far from where they were born. Life did not change significantly, in general, during one's lifetime. Of course wars, famine, political upheaval and natural disasters played their roles, but life as a standard remained pretty much the same from the beginning of each century to its end.

People learned what they needed to know on the job. They learned about life as they lived it. What they needed to know was taught to them by our parents or relatives.

Through the century just past, there were great similarities up to 1960. Two world wars, the popularization of industry throughout the continent, the struggle of the unions, the rise of a large middle class all had common elements to them. People mostly had one job through their entire careers.

They learned what they needed to know on the job. The nuclear family was intact, with father, mother and children all living together.

From the middle of the century to 1990, technology took the fore. Large machines made large projects possible. Cheap power became plentiful and industry responded accordingly. Computers allowed trips to the Moon and the use of space for hundreds of other purposes. The technology of weaponry developed to the point that the targets became facilities and weaponry, not people. Life in this part of the century was significantly different from the first half. People often had two or more jobs through their careers.

In the last decade of the twentieth century, the pace of life increased with the pace of developments in the computer industry. While the pace ratcheted up and the global marketplace became a reality, many people still were able to avoid becoming caught up in what they thought of as the computer generation. For others it became possible to be employed by a large corporation, yet work at home. New home-based businesses arose at an unprecedented rate. Some people found they had to change jobs, even change careers, every few years. Some people prepare now almost constantly for a new career.

At the dawn of this new century, it's no longer possible for people to avoid the influence of the computer. Even retired people are learning to use it, both for self-development and for communicating with their grandchildren by email and voice messaging. Those who are shut-ins are now able to make new friends, not just near home but anywhere in the world. This has become important for families too as so many are spread not just around one geographical area or one country, but around the planet.

People must continue to learn in order to keep pace with developments in their own fields, to keep up with other competitors who would take their jobs. Some find themselves in occupations that are downsizing or about to disappear, so they must learn new skills to prepare for career changes.

The general level of knowledge must increase in our population as the amount of knowledge increases. That means it is necessary to stay up with the news. The news now is not just about minorities, murders and mergers. It is about developments in any and every field of human endeavor.

Knowledge is wealth; the poorest are those who don't know what is happening in their world.

Even retired people are attending college to complete the degrees they missed when they were younger.

Education has become a cradle-to-grave affair. Education systems must adapt to accommodate the needs of information rich people of all ages who are hungry to learn more.

- **Education in pre-adult years must prepare people to live and work in environments other than those in their home town, country or even continent.**

Education systems in North America now generally prepare young people to fill jobs that are available in their own local area, province or state. In some cases, young people are learning job skills that will allow them to find jobs in other areas of the country. These opportunities are limited by education systems as the system administrators want the payoff for their efforts to benefit their own local area, not some city a considerable distance away. They don't even consider jobs available in another country.

In other words, self-interest of the controlling bodies is a factor. No one in education will admit this. Each education system trains its young charges to take jobs it hopes will be available in the same general tax jurisdiction. Failing that, it hopes that they will find jobs in neighboring communities. Few consciously train young people for jobs that will take them to distant places, out of the local tax base.

While this may sound inflammatory to some, it is entirely understandable and reasonable given the historical interest in maintaining the survival of the community by ensuring that young people stay near where they were born. There are ghost towns all over the country that testify mutely to the failure of their former inhabitants to provide jobs and skilled people to fill them locally.

How can a small province or state train its young people for jobs elsewhere? Does it want to do this? Could this be justified to taxpayers if it did?

This raises the problem of revising the tax system, which in turn raises the problem of equalization of tax funds for education purposes. If one area can afford more for education per student than another, due to a different tax base, then the students of the first area will have an unfair advantage over the students from the second area upon completion of their formal education. This even applies for entering costly post-secondary institutions where preferential treatment applies.

This problem can only be overcome by national will. We preach equality as a value we hold dear. Do we have the will to put it into practice in the most important area in which tax dollars are spent, education?

True, changes would be needed and these would require time to work out. But it could be done if the nation had the will to make it happen. Otherwise, the country could be eaten apart from within by petty jealousies more fitting in the past than now.

We can see the progress that is happening in other nations of the world along this line if we study their records. They have national policies, nationally administered education systems and, fittingly, national pride in them. What outcome of the total education process can we say that we take pride in?

Some countries are training their young people to take jobs in other countries. As strange as this may sound, there is good reasoning behind it. It is true that graduates will leave their home country to take jobs elsewhere. But a program of national pride is carried on simultaneously with the rest of their education.

The graduates go to another country, often on work visas, where they gain experience and job skills, then return a few years later when the economy of their home country has improved and their visas have expired. Continued emphasis on improvement in the education systems of the home countries raises the economic potential of these nations, thus making them more attractive to expatriates who want to come home. This requires a national plan covering many years and the foresight and determination of many people to make it happen. It is happening in many countries of Asia, for example, and it is working for them.

As unlikely as it would seem in North America that a young person would want to leave to take a job on another continent, it is happening and will happen to a greater extent as expansion of the global economy requires employers from other countries to hire away our brightest graduates to drive their own industries. In short, citizens of these other countries want what we enjoy in North America now and they are willing to pay what they must to get it. They pay well.

We must have the national will to prepare our own country before our position at the top of the hill has been taken away by other countries.

To prepare our young people, we must institute a program of national pride in education, the kind of pride that made our country great in the first place. At the same time we must prepare these young people to live, work and thrive in other countries, cultures and climates, with different languages and customs.

The ones who leave will learn first-hand about what is happening in these forward thinking countries and bring their experiences back with them a few years later. The ones who stay will gain a better understanding of cultures that are foreign to them, giving them a better chance to compete on a global scale for business. Speaking English alone is just not good enough to compete in today's world.

- **Education must prepare people to be able to adapt quickly and effectively to new environments, be they job-related or personal.**

The easiest person to train for a new job should be one who has not had any previous training from another job that would interfere with or conflict with the new training. This is not what is happening in the marketplace. Employers want new employees with experience. The problem is either that employers do not understand the advantages of having an eager new mind to prepare for fulfilling tasks on a new job or that employers know the attitudes and work habits of recent graduates and would rather re-train over old habits than try to change attitudes. If the latter is the case, then schools have been misdirecting their efforts for decades.

Most employers know the quality of graduate that is coming from schools on the North American continent. They also know that it is easier to retrain a person to new habits than to change the attitude of a recent graduate.

In other words, a recent graduate is not a diamond in the rough, but another mineral that must be changed into a diamond by some magic of alchemy. Employers have learned that from experience.

A young graduate faces the dilemma that employers want experienced people, but no employer will hire the recent graduate to allow him to acquire the experience. The best graduates face this problem.

It's an old story. But how have schools adapted to this situation? Not at all. The simple but gruesome fact is that our public school systems are turning out graduates that no employer wants to hire. That's some graduates, certainly not all. But, needing their newly learned skills at less pay than for experienced people, some employers do take the plunge.

An attractively employable graduate is precisely what our school systems were designed to produce. At least they were in the past. This is not so true now.

Can this be changed? Not easily, nor quickly. But it can be done. It will require the will of many good people who have been too silent for too long. It will require a grand plan to be developed by some very special people and strategies to be implemented by people who have grown up in a world that has changed beyond their understanding.

It will require graduates with training in loyalty, dedication, a drive to learn and a work ethic that an employer will appreciate.

- **Education must prepare people to cope with conditions which have been devastating to people in the past, such as the death of a loved one, the break-up of a relationship, the loss of employment, financial wipeout, retraining, relearning and re-educating.**

We have social problems. They're in the newspapers every day. We hear about them in our workplaces. We see them in our shopping malls, churches, on highways, in governments, in police departments and so on. A home or family that is not badly affected, even at times devastated, by such tragedies is rare.

Tragedy is part of our existence in this world, part of life. But is it necessary that we be unprepared for it? So many lives are destroyed or badly impacted by such common events as the death of a loved one, divorce or loss of employment that we should be preparing people to know how to cope with such common events of life before they happen.

It's so common that we have come to accept that the tragedy and devastation are part of the bad luck of life. However, so long as it's not happening to us at the time, it's someone else's problem. We don't let it bother us. If it's our own fate, we are too busy suffering to be able to cope well.

Why are there deaths and injuries from shootings and stabbings in schools? Because the students (often self-described as "inmates") cannot cope with their lives, given the skills, resources and experiences they have had. We can't get rid of violence by forbidding the bringing of weapons onto school property. It hasn't worked. It may move the scenes of violence elsewhere, but the causes will still exist. So will the effects.

Drugs are sold illegally in and around schools. There is a market waiting. Can we eliminate the market by getting rid of young drug dealers? It hasn't happened. Anti-drug slogans and programs have not worked, in many cases. Drug use in schools is increasing on a national scale. We fuss over the effects, but we don't address the causes.

Alcohol abuse has become common among teenagers. See the previous two paragraphs.

A tragedy such as the shooting at the Columbine school in the United States brings our attention to it for a while. Then we forget it because we don't want to dwell on the negative for long. Nothing changes. We pass more laws, put more armed adult guards in high schools, tell the police, teachers and social workers to watch for problems. But it continues. It gets worse. Still we have no answers. Still we take no effective action.

Why? The simple answer is that, as individuals, we do not know what to do. More importantly, as a nation we do not have the will to do what we must to make the necessary changes. We continue to attack the symptoms but ignore the causes. The bandage-on-cancer approach fails again.

The place to prepare people for the tragedies of their future lives is in the schools, while they are young. This does not mean that we must teach them to be permanently depressed and morose or to suppress their emotions. It means that they need to be prepared for downturns in their lives and have the coping skills and tools to reverse their situation more quickly. We need to prepare them for real life, not just what we hope for them or what they see on television.

They need to know what to do to help themselves when crises happen in their lives. They need to know that they are not failures when these events happen. Tragedy plays a role in every life.

The school curriculum is becoming ever more crowded each year and teachers ever more harassed to do more and more until they want to leave the profession in unprecedented numbers. We can't just pile more work on. That doesn't work either. A new approach to the curriculum is required.

It definitely requires planning. It requires cooperation. It requires considerable changes to the present form of public education systems. It requires leaders to step forward. And it requires tremendous support for these efforts from the electorate, from us.

It can be done. We will discuss the possibilities in more detail later.

- **Education must prepare small children for what they will face in future years of their formal education and life as an adolescent and an adult.**

It's ironic that adults want to protect children from learning about the world they will face as adolescents and as adults. Then, when these young people reach their mid-teens, we wonder how they have so much trouble adapting and why so many of them have such problems with adult attitudes and understandings.

The choice of solution is fairly straight-forward. Either we pour huge amounts of money into social programs in the schools to help young people to adapt to the world in crisis that they are facing or we give young children the understanding of the world ahead of them and the skills and resources to cope with it. But then, can the curricula of high schools today set aside so much time for teaching such social skills? Not if they are to maintain any level of productivity in knowledge and other skills that these young people will need.

We can find time to do these programs in the early years of elementary school. We can if we have the will to make changes.

It will require a commitment of huge proportions. In other words, it will require a large number of people to support a program of change, so some can develop a new system that will accommodate what is needed.

We have come to expect that children in grade one will begin to get serious about the three R's. Because that's the way it has always been done? Actually, no. It is the way it has been done since our education systems first became organized. Before that, the world had other needs for children to learn and those were taught, mostly having to do with family and simple work skills.

In the past in North America, most young people were not expected to finish high school and fewer still were expected to complete college. Some children would not remain in school more than five years in total. What the world of that time needed was people who could read, write and do simple arithmetic. So the emphasis in schools changed, adapted to the new needs. Teach them the basics they need, and fast.

Now young people stay in school for at least a dozen years, most far longer than that. There is lots of time to teach the basic skills that they need.

It requires literally weeks for a child in grade one to learn and secure a few basic skills in addition. The same child in grade four can learn the same skills in an hour or so.

Consider this. How important is it during the three years between grade one and grade four for children to have specific skills in addition? Most children do not have much opportunity to use those skills outside of school until grade four anyway. In fact, the exact same skills are re-taught under the guise of review in each succeeding year between one and four. This should at least hint that there may be room for change.

Then how about the knowledge that is learned in the first three years of elementary school? How much do we remember of the knowledge that we gained during those years? We may be able to remember when we learned most of the knowledge and skills we retain now, but most people can't remember a significant amount of what they learned in those first few years of school. What they do remember of those years are the social things: good and bad times.

If there is a change such that some skills and knowledge are postponed from the earlier years of elementary school, this would make room for the much more important social skills that these young people will need during their lives.

Young children learn large concepts before they learn relatively small skills. Among the first and easiest for them to learn is how to understand their world. Remember, their world is small, limited by their experiences. If they are not taught directly, they learn from what they experience outside. They accept what they are told by those they trust. If they are not told, they learn from what they see in their lives and on television. Not good.

We should teach them about the experiences they will face in their lives and how to cope with them. We should teach them how to help each other in times of great need. We should teach them to ask for help, to ask about anything they want to know, to learn by asking. Now we teach them to suppress their emotions, to help themselves and not worry about the problems of others and to be quiet in class except to answer questions asked by the teacher. These are broad strokes and exceptions may be found in every classroom in the country on any given day, but the points remain.

We are trying to teach the right things at the wrong times. It is not until the early years of high school or at least the latter years of elementary school that social skills are covered, if at all. And even those are done poorly, in general, and much too late, as the children have already formed their opinions, concepts, understandings and attitudes about the world by then.

In the early years of school, children learn by direct instruction and by correction of their behavior by teachers, with considerable peer influence as well.

Give children the information they should know about the world and the social and coping skills they need before they need them. If we do it after their attitudes have already been formed (often incorrectly, we understand now), they reject their teachers, or hate them.

The leaders of education in this country will not make such huge changes in their programs without the support of a majority of the adult population in their areas. Indeed, they will not likely make such changes unless they know that other boards of education are making similar changes. That's where we come in, as we are part of the majority.

Such changes should be made on a local level. But there must be more. If they are only made on a local level without coordination between communities, then the results will be as bad as the situation we have now. There must be a national policy on major changes, new programs and initiatives, supported at the provincial or state level. The national policy must be agreed upon by all parties making the change, so that each area knows the level of mutual moral support they have elsewhere in the country.

Specifics and resources may be left to each local school district, but it would be better if these could be shared among larger and smaller districts so that the cost of developing them can be minimized.

- **Education must prepare teens to be able to cope with a world they do not understand and may fear. Worry is unproductive. Fear is destructive. Each young person must have the ability to direct his energy to productive use for the benefit of himself and those with whom he chooses to share his efforts, caring and life.**

We learn for our own benefit. If we refuse to learn, it's to our detriment. The lives of teachers and parents will not be affected so much by refusal of young people to learn as will the futures of those same young people. The need to learn must be taught.

Confused and fearful teens form a considerable portion of the student body of most high schools in North America. If we look at them and don't see that, then we are seeing what they use to cover their true feelings with. No one tries to show their fear.

If they had been prepared to understand the world they would face, when they were younger, then the confusion and fear would be much less as they come fully into their adolescent years.

We fear what we don't know, don't understand or don't expect.

Counseling programs can then deal with specific students and counseling classes will be able to have sharing sessions where experiences can be freely expressed so that all may benefit from them. All may offer suggestions, comments and help.

We may wonder if this does not sound suspiciously like group therapy. In fact there are similarities. The main difference with the student counseling groups is that they would not be filled with people with dysfunctional lives, as therapy sessions are. Even hearing their peers say that they are experiencing problems similar to their own will be helpful. This is what peer support groups do.

One of the biggest problems teens have is that they believe they are the only ones who are experiencing certain feelings and troubles. Problems seem to lessen in intensity when it becomes understood that "I am not alone." Sometimes just learning that others have similar problems is enough to lessen the anxiety of people. If they have been taught that they should seek positive solutions, then they will be able to do so together.

In this kind of school environment, a young person who is so messed up that he would carry a gun to school and shoot at students and teachers would stand out and be recognized long before he reached the crisis stage. When a social environment of sharing and helping each other is fostered in a school, his peers will help a troubled classmate. Help from peers is accepted by a teen far more readily than help from adults.

The trouble now is that those with problems are avoided in school. The very people that we need to help become isolated, ostracized by their peers. We don't consciously teach that, but we reinforce it by allowing it to continue without trying to avoid it earlier in the lives of the students.

For those who will object to teens without problems helping their peers with problems, keep in mind that the help always goes two ways. The helper learns while helping. That is how teachers, social workers, doctors, lawyers and others in helping professions gain their expertise, in most cases.

- **Education must include lifestyle choices, moral training, values training and long-term objectives training, the form of which would be determined by national or state/provincial governments, through plebiscites of their citizens. Voters must be convinced that the changes are necessary and they must be helped to understand why.**

This point practically stands on its own. The process by which each voting adult can participate in the program of developing these programs will be discussed in a later chapter.

For those who would disagree with this general point, try this: separate each part off and consider it individually to see what might be disagreeable about it.

There are those who will say that these should be taught in a different setting, such as in the home or the church. Many people would agree. But they are not being done this way, in general. Doing this in schools is better than not doing it anywhere, as is the situation at present. At least in schools there could be professional instructors.

We still have problems of critical importance on a national scale. Big problems require big solutions and a great deal of cooperation. Otherwise the country degenerates into the kind of mess that many underdeveloped countries are in now. No one can agree on anything, so tragedy prevails. That is where we are headed if we do not change soon.

There can be variation in specifics from one jurisdiction to another. We need to have agreement on the general policies among as many groups of people as possible.

A civilization can only be degraded just so far before it becomes impossible to put it back together again. Read the history. Look elsewhere in the world at countries where improvement is beyond hope. Most of the great civilizations of the past have slid beyond the grasp of any measure to help them. Beyond a critical threshold is chaos and anarchy. We may already see signs of it now.

There could be a risk of world war of unimagined proportions if our condition continues to deteriorate. In times of chaos, we would expect the military to prevail. It will, to be sure. We don't want that.

- **Education must begin when children are newborn infants. Parents must be encouraged to take training courses before the birth of their first child. These will be courses in parenting in the full sense, not just in diaper changing, feeding and babysitting techniques.**

We now know that children begin to experience their world before they are born. They begin to seriously learn about it shortly after they are born—maybe even before, but we are not developed enough to be able to manage that yet.

We also know that most children of school age spend more time with their teachers than they do with their parents. A child really needs three parents, two that nurture her when she is at home and one who fills that function when she is at school. If only one parent is available at home, then that at least will mean one at home and one at school.

This will require that teachers are taught how to fulfill their traditional and historical role as parents in the absence of the real parents while children are at school. *In loco parentae* is the legal term: in the place of parents. It will also be essential that nurturing teachers are recognized for the extremely positive and essential roles they play in the lives of young children, rather than being looked on suspiciously because they truly care for the children in their care. They must be encouraged, not discouraged.

The early years of schooling should be a nurturing environment for a child. They don't have to be overly protective, just secure. Ironically, although such conditions exist in most North American elementary schools today, many teens speak of their high schools as prisons. This could be because they have not been taught early what to expect in their later years of schooling. Not just told, but actually taught, complete with examples and explanations, like a regular classroom lesson.

Young children look forward to getting older and being able to do things on their own, things they could not do as children. Where do we let them down? When do they become disillusioned? Parents try to help them. Teachers try. Friends try. But the results are disappointing.

Change can only come in one of two places, home or school, the two places where they spend the most time. Shall we choose one of them?

Change should happen in both environments. When home and school work together, their combined efforts will produce a calmer, more productive child and a more settled young adult later.

The catch is that both home and school need to know their responsibilities and each needs to support the other as well as the child.

If one of these parties tries to dominate the relationship, the other will demure. But the party that gives reign to the other will blame the other for all errors and problems that the child has.

Think about the local situation. Education is the second biggest cause of finger-pointing (after governments) in the country. We love to find fault.

In the interests of our country and our children, we need to turn to the foundations of democracy and let the majority decide what should be done.

The majority needs to accept that a few complaining people should not be allowed to dominate the education system of the country. It can't be called a democracy if a minority of whiny people rule. A minority of noisy people voted the National Socialist Party into power in Germany in 1933. But it was a very active minority.

The majority must have faith in themselves. The majority must stand together. If that happens, the worst that can occur is that the nation will stay together and strong.

Imagine what the best could be.

- **The main goal of education must be to model students toward the role of an ideal citizen of the nation. That is, every person should be taught the role that is required and expected of them and the responsibilities that are required for a citizen of their country.**

"Education" in the sentence above must be considered to be the total learning of a child, the sum of all experiences of the generation that will run the country a few decades later. Education in this sense does not refer strictly to what a child learns in school. It refers to what the child learns and experiences at home, at school and in the community.

Just as no parent could be expected to be perfect with thirty of his offspring to look after, teachers cannot be held noses to the fire for problems of their charges either. Teachers need the support of their immediate administration and the board or district agency that administers the system. They also need the active support of parents.

Teachers try to help a troubled child. Administrators concern themselves mostly with punishment. Punishment has not worked as a deterrent in high schools, no more than it has in prisons. Punishment alone doesn't work. Punishment is a small price a young person pays after suffering through his own problems for many years.

The most important employees in the entire school system must be the teachers, as they are the people who directly supervise the education of each child for several hours each day. The purpose of the administration must be to assist with the teacher's functions, not to make them more difficult. Ivory tower administrators do not help children.

We must place our priorities in order. The Director, Minister or Secretary of Education is not the most important person in the education system. The most important person is the child. And the most important paid person is the one who directly supervises that child, the teacher. Any other arrangement makes children victims of political wrangling.

The purpose of a school board and administration is to facilitate the job of the teacher in as complete and wholesome a way as possible.

Yes, that is opposite to the way it is now. But what we have now is a bureaucratic nightmare that has resulted in unhappy teachers and confused and fearful young people.

School boards have become little kingdoms, in many cases, complete with autocratic leaders, aristocracies and peasants.

History is there to provide an abundance of examples for us to read. The primary aim of an autocratic leader is self-preservation. That's what we have now. Rather than having an education system that is designed to serve the child and his needs, we have an education system that functions to serve the desires of its leaders.

At the bottom of this hierarchy today is the child. The very person that the system is supposed to mold into a model citizen of our country. What we have taught that child about the hierarchy is not the message we wanted carried into adulthood.

Each child leaves that system eventually. What he has learned about the way the world operates through his experiences in school is not what most of us want.

It isn't any wonder that adolescent children are confused, self-centered, hateful.

In 1889, United States Commissioner of Education, William T. Harris, said, "Our schools have been scientifically designed to prevent over-education from happening. [...] The average American [should be] content with their humble role in life, because they're not tempted to think about any other role."*

At that time, few Americans would have believed him. To us, it sounds as if he were saying that there was a conspiracy to keep Americans ignorant. There was no conspiracy, of course. Just a plan to train kids to be cooperative adults.

Dr. Harris, an originator and prime mover to begin kindergartens in schools in the United States, believed that "the moral regeneration of the race" should begin at the kindergarten level.

Why would a respected person with such a significant role in education for his country make the statement about schools preventing over-education? He must have believed that he could see what few others could and still fewer would believe if they could see it. He must have been able to see impediments in the design of the system for provision of education services that prevented many young people from reaching their maximum level of intellectual competence.

Over a century later, we can see design flaws. While the flaws themselves are no more obvious now than then, the results in a much larger United States nearing three hundred million people are much more evident. Our education systems claim to provide child-centered education. Educators have learned how to teach children in ways to which they are receptive. What they teach is what they believe a child should learn. What they don't provide is the kind of education a child needs, when the child needs it most. The effects of this negligence are in our faces every day.

By continuing to approach the provision of education services the way they have been taught for two centuries, we admit we believe that nothing has changed in the way the world operates in the past two hundred years. The world has changed. Education has not kept pace. Our continued failure to adapt to a new world will ensure that the social problems of our country will continue and worsen.

We are each a voter with the power to change the system. We need not act alone. But we must act.

We can do it together.

---

[*] William Torrey Harris (1889), Quoted in John Gatto (1992) *The Tyranny of Government Schooling*

The Pyramid of Living System

THINK of a young child. For the sake of discussion, let's begin on the day of birth. Although there is a rapidly expanding body of knowledge about how a child learns in the fetus stage, we can afford to set that aside for now. Virtually everyone agrees that learning begins in a major way at birth.

This child's learning process has several important influences. Think of the child as being at the apex of what will become a pyramid, its pinnacle. On her day of birth, she is at what we will think of as base zero, in effect at the center point of a square, with the pyramid yet to rise. The learning process is two dimensional at this time, without height. Then the influences begin. Each major influence will become the side of her pyramid, as each helps to raise its particular side of the structure that will become her life.

A person can and does learn without external influences. That is, a person has the capability to learn in the absence of influences, such as by independent reading or research on the Internet. But the reality is that most of the time a young person learns within a set of circumstances (the environment) and with a set of influences acting on her. These influences may or may not be present at the actual time of learning. For example, what a parent has taught a child can influence how the child learns even when the parent is not present at the time of learning.

Learning is a very personal thing. It's done individually, even if there are others around at the time, either learning or influencing. No matter how many people may be around at the time of learning, exerting and accepting influences each in their own way, each person learns individually. That is, a person learns individually, even if she is in a group at the time.

Given the same set of circumstances and the same influences, two people might learn differently. With that in mind, it's important to make opportunities for children to learn what we most want them to learn, so that there is a common base of knowledge among children. Influences must be as positive, consistent and constant as possible.

One of the major influences in a child's young life is her parents. This is a no-brainer, someone is saying. But does each parent think, on the day of their child's birth, that he or she is influencing that child right away? Right there in the hospital or birthing place. Each father is a role model for his child from day one. Each mother will influence her child in many ways each day of that child's life for many years to come.

The fact is that most young parents are learning themselves. The child is, in effect, teaching the parents how to be parents, through experience. Perhaps parents who were better trained for their positions could better understand how much and how often their behavior influences their child. The trial and error method of learning to be a parent is not necessary. The trial and error method of a child's learning will always exist, but it should not be the case for parents learning about parenting.

A baby has nothing else to do with her waking hours than to learn. She will learn at an alarming rate. Knowing nothing to start, she will learn from every experience and everybody in her immediate environment, whether or not these people intend to teach her. She may not be able to focus her eyes yet, but she has visual impressions of her surroundings. She also has very sensitive hearing, extremely sensitive taste, the most acute sense of smell that she will have in her life and her best developed sense of all will be her sense of touch. This is the case because she has had experience with touch for several months before birth. Experience inevitably means development.

She will try to influence her environment in any way she can, but let's consider the influences that act on her. She learns when she tries to manipulate her environment to get food, be changed or get attention. She learns both by the actions and the reactions of those around her. She learns that certain behaviors will get her food and others will not, that some will bring her relief from a wet diaper and others will not, and that some things she does will get her picked up and cuddled.

If this child is in a hospital, most of the major influences in her life will be at hand. The parents may like to think that they are the only influence on their child. In fact, they are but one side of the base of a pyramid of influences. Others, including hospital staff and adult visitors such as relatives play a role in the young life. These people comprise a second side of the pyramid, what we will call the community.

Consider the time that the child is in the nursery. Are there any influences there from the other infants? It doesn't seem likely, does it? Anyone who believes this should walk into a nursery when one baby begins to cry and see how quickly others join the chorus.

No wonder nursery attendants rush to satisfy the needs of each child when it cries. They are not just trying to avoid a sound stampede, but also trying to influence each child away from what amounts to infant anarchy. That is, they are trying to avoid having a child think that collective (group) behavior can be more effective than individual behavior. They can learn that.

So we have the influence of the peer group, in this case other babies in the nursery, as the third side of the base of the learning pyramid.

Already we have a structure that could rise into three dimensions with three base sides. A three-sided pyramid, with the child at the apex. There are such structures as three-sided pyramids, but they are less common than the four-sided variety. Four-sided pyramids are generally thought of as being the most substantial and enduring.

The fourth side of our PLS pyramid is education. There are those parents who believe that education is best left to schools, as that is where their children will learn from professionals. Yet the child is influenced in half the learning she does in her lifetime before she sits at a desk full-time in a classroom.

In the case of a child of a few years or older, a strong case may be made for having the school teach some parts of the child's total education. But all of it? It won't happen that way. It can't. There are too many influences on the child when she is not in school. Experience means learning. And most experiences a child will have are outside of the influence of the school. Each experience will likely come about within the sphere of at least one of the four base influences.

Let's consider that education, our fourth side, is any kind of formal training of the child, no matter who offers it. At the age of three or four or five, depending on the area, the child will begin to attend a publicly funded institute of education. But even during those first years of school, the child is awake, out of school and learning for more hours each day than she is in class.

Some parents believe so wholeheartedly in a formalized form of education beginning with their children early that they begin to teach their children at home, even before the children reach school age.

The belief here is that a child will do better in school if she gets a good start with reading or arithmetic (the usual favorites) before her first year in a classroom. They want her to be at the top of her class academically, right from grade one.

Whether or not this is a well-founded belief is not important to this discussion. What's more important is that these same parents may not be aware of how they are influencing their children in other ways than they intend.

When we have a pyramid that is trying to rise with only one strong side for support, we have something unstable. A one- or two-dimensional child at the age of five will have severe problems in school. They go to school with children who have had five years of experience with all dimensions of life. They will not have the ability to function comfortably in school. That means that they will not be able to learn as well as other children with more complete backgrounds.

Other children do not understand how a child who is underdeveloped in some way feels. They don't understand how easy it was for that child to disappear into the background and be unnoticed. This makes such a child someone that other kids may not want to befriend. A child without friends has the potential to develop personal problems that may become social problems.

The school is ready to teach that child what they believe he needs to know, according to the curriculum. The child may be socially inept, emotionally twisted in knots, intellectually lacking in knowledge and experience and may have this nasty habit of becoming invisible to others. Can a person learn properly under those conditions?

By the age of five, the four sides of a child's pyramid are in evidence and ready to support the life of that child. But schools don't know what to do if the child is a misfit, if the child is underdeveloped in ways other than the intellectual. They are neither prepared nor equipped to deal with such a child-centered problem. In the absence of an equal and balanced support system, a partially underdeveloped child will miss out on too much of what he needs by that time of his life. The structure that is the life of that child resembles a lopsided pyramid.

Let's return to our discussion of parents who want to cram their children with reading and arithmetic lessons before they get to school. Perhaps now we can see how these children could have one side of their learning pyramid stronger than the others, even to the point of overpowering the others. These children might be academic powerhouses in elementary school. However, they might suffer for years because their other support systems are decidedly weaker. This could result in social misfits in elementary school and adolescents who lack coping skills when those tough teen years take their toll. They might be lopsided pyramids, unless there are other factors to compensate.

Some educators find it easier than others to see lopsided pyramids among their students and to help them to straighten. A teacher with a full curriculum can only help so much.

We must make provisions for all children so that as many pyramids as possible stand straight and tall. And proud. Supported by four equal and strong sides. It's our responsibility.

PLS is the Pyramid of Living System. Each life stands atop a pyramid of influences and experiences built from its past. We must ensure that our children have the support they need to become the adults we hope they will be. The child will grow as the apex of a pyramid. Wherever possible, all four sides of the pyramid must work together and be strong and supportive. If not, the pyramid (the life) will be lopsided.

A child needs the support of the community in the form of neighbors, family members, the staff of stores they enter, and other influences such as television and movies. Many children spend more time being influenced by television in their early years than they do by their parents. Television represents the community side of the pyramid, the only component of it for some children.

Never mind the rhetoric folks. Many children are learning, by watching television, more than they are learning from their parents. Is that what we want? Is the content of these programs what we want our children to be learning? Never mind scientific proof. Our young adults are acting like the role models they see on television. We can see that. There's nothing left to prove if the evidence is there for all to see.

Some adults make fun of children's programs that teach the basic values on which our society is formed. They make fun of "the purple dinosaur," a lovable character that teaches them how to be good people. These adults don't know what a child needs. We haven't taught them what a child needs. These same people are influencing the children and even other adults around them. Yet they speak and act from a position of relative ignorance of the responsibilities they hold toward children.

We can't increase our longevity as a developed species, one that has the ability to think rationally and act responsibly, if we don't even teach the basic lessons, skills and values that every other mammal in the animal kingdom learns from its parents and others of its kind.

A child needs the support of a responsible and knowledgeable community, in whatever form that community may take. It's our responsibility to provide for that need.

A child needs the support of her peers, other children the same age. A child will learn from her peers, no matter whether that support is good or bad as an influence. It's up to us to ensure that these other children have learned the same belief system as the rest of their community so there's no conflict of influences, giving the impression of a conflict of values. To do this there must be a common system of values and a common manner of providing experiences with them for each and every child.

All this requires some changes to our way of conducting our lives. This is not an overnight project. It will require many years, some major planning and the cooperation of a majority of the population of the country.

Can it happen without a majority of support from the adult population of our country? Yes. But it can only happen with a majority of voters who actually cast ballots supporting the program. Where there's an election with low voter turnout to cast ballots, a minority rules. Those who don't vote lose out.

We must ensure that we, as voters, are given the right subjects to consider, the facts and factors we must absorb, in order to choose wisely, and the political strength and wisdom to follow through on the choices we make.

This will require our participation.

Will the politicians follow through on our stated wishes? They will if we ask. If we don't ask, they'll follow the same path they have in the past. And that is? Think about it.

We need to ask together.

We need to ask soon.

A big project like this takes several years to put together, then many more to take full effect. It could take two generations, fifty years, before our country is the way we want it to be. Meanwhile we're doing nothing and things are getting worse.

When should we start?

Building the Pyramid 19

WHAT role should we play in building the pyramids of children in our lives?

Each pyramid becomes the foundation for the life of every person in our country. By looking around we can see the four forces exerting themselves without conscious intervention or participation by the majority of citizens in each community.

In the chapter entitled "The Pyramid of Living System," we established that children go through the years of their most significant learning period influenced by four basic factors: parents, education (teachers and curriculum), their community (including all media) and their peers. Each of these is so basic and essential to the development and maturation of a child that we likened them to the four sides of a pyramid, with the child at the apex, on top.

This is PLS: the Pyramid of Living System.

The extent and direction of influence of each of these factors for any one child is difficult to determine at any time. Like fingerprints, each child has a unique blend of effects of influences from these four basic factors. However, unlike fingerprints, a human's ability to assimilate, sort, prioritize and adopt some input while rejecting others of these influences is impossible to quantify.

With four bases for our pyramid, we have four sides. These are the effects of the four influences that form the personality and being of each adult human. As the pyramid rises and the child/adult matures, the four influences (four sides) have gradually less effect.

There is more to a pyramid than just its sides. It must have the infrastructure inside to support the child at the top. The "top" in this case meaning the individual that is experienced and influenced by others in the world. The infrastructure is what the child/adult builds herself, her experiences, given the four influences.

In what areas do these influences have their effect? In what ways do they affect the maturation process? There are four main areas: emotional, social, intellectual and physical.

The emotional health of a person is determined by her life experiences with each of the four main influences. Good and bad experiences both play vital roles in the emotional makeup of a person.

Due to the unique makeup of each person, the same experience for one person may be good, while for another it's bad. For example, an unfortunate experience can be a learning situation for one child, thus it is good in this sense. For another, it could be psychologically damaging and cause lasting harm. No childhood experiences can be clearly defined as good or bad. While behavior might change for the better as a result of a bad experience, it might build a fear for something that adults may not easily be able to account for. A fall, for example, might build a fear of heights.

The degree or depth of emotions of a person may be likened to the swing of a pendulum. Think of a pendulum on an old-style clock. A pendulum swings the same distance in each of two opposite directions. So too the emotions swing as far one way as they do in the other. A person who has experienced great sadness will have the ability to experience great happiness. A person whose experiences are shallow on one side will be shallow on the other. A person who has experienced a large degree of swing on one side but not so much on the other will have psychological problems.

An uneven swing pattern to each of the natural emotional extremes is cause for concern. For example, a person who can experience happiness but not sadness will have trouble keeping friends because he will not be able to sympathize with someone who experiences an emotion he doesn't understand. A person who experiences sadness but not happiness will be similarly difficult to befriend. Each situation holds the possibility for a psychological disorder.

The full range of emotional experiences may be controlled by external influences (such as parents and teachers) or by the individual herself. Whatever limitations or controls are placed on one side of the range of emotions will have a corresponding limit on the other side.

The four main influences of PLS help to determine the extremes of the swings of emotions. In school, for example, extremes of emotions are discouraged, even punished. A child who demonstrates extreme happiness in a classroom is as disruptive and distracting to her classmates as the child who demonstrates extreme sadness or anger, although the two cause concern in differing ways. It's easy for most of us to imagine how an angry child could affect others in a class, but not so easy to picture how an extremely sad child could influence others. Unlike adults who learn to suppress their emotions at work, children have their antennae out at all times. They detect the sadness of a classmate and this can have a very disturbing effect on the behavior of others.

If asked whether a child should be discouraged from demonstrating extreme happiness, most adults would say, no, the child should in fact be encouraged to be happy. However, some ways of demonstrating happiness may not be appropriate in a classroom, sometimes at home, frequently in public situations such as a church service or in a store. How can a child learn what is appropriate happy behavior for each circumstance? When should the child stifle that emotion? Is stifling healthy or wise?

Many adults long to experience the happiness they enjoyed as children. The control required of them on their happiness in some places became generalized for all circumstances. Many adults are unable to experience happiness the way children do.

Adults, especially parents and teachers, become especially upset when a child becomes sad or angry. Yet if the child is not allowed to express and experience sadness and anger, her ability to express and experience happiness and joy will be limited. We can't put limits on one side without affecting the other. What is acceptable?

Who determines what is acceptable? Parents? Yes. Teachers? Yes. Other kids? Yes. Community? Yes. Each has its own standards of acceptability and its punishments for exceeding those standards. The child learns by experiencing the boundaries of acceptability, either herself or by watching other children test their social envelope.

Is a child in a classroom given the opportunity to experience as much happiness as sadness? Yes, but very little of each. In fact, both are discouraged in our present system of public education. The acceptable range of emotions allowed of students in a classroom is extremely small. Children in school are expected to learn, not to be.

By early afternoon, a teacher of younger children may sometimes face a sea of squirming bodies, tired of the routine of their day, yet not close enough to home time to settle down and wait. That's when a teacher could take them for a walk, such as around the perimeter of schoolyard. The walk should be fun and relaxed. There should be no restriction on sound. The teacher could walk very slowly for a short distance, then increase the pace as fast as he could walk. Running would be against the rules. Children participate enthusiastically, finding it hilarious trying to walk as fast as they can to keep up with an adult. The teacher can alternate walking speed and sometimes abruptly change directions, causing more upheaval. By the time they have circled the schoolyard once, the kids would be exercised, happy and ready to settle down for some serious study. The whole event might take about seven minutes. In the process, the teacher would gain a good hour of work time from them, work that would otherwise have been nearly impossible. Children have fun walking when there is a different incentive to their regular routine. How many teachers think of that as a happy experience? They do when they see their children ready to work again.

The teacher, administration, school board and ministry/department of education all have a clear idea of exactly where each child should be going and the center line of acceptability of how to get there. They do not accept much variation to either side of that line. Straying too far from that line could be considered deviance, a problem for the system. Administrators will sometimes discipline teachers who either permit such deviance by children in their classrooms or demonstrate deviance themselves.

Within that small range of acceptable emotions, how can a teacher recognize when a child is sad? Sadness will inevitably affect a child's ability to learn. Children are actively discouraged from demonstrating emotions in school. Teachers should be taught how to encourage experiences with emotions and to recognize suppressed emotions in their charges.

Consider this. Many teachers (influenced strongly by their principals) have been drilled to believe that a good class is a quiet class or one that is actively pursuing the goals of the lesson of the day, but with a minimum of sound or kinetic expression (movement).

Does this further the emotional growth and maturity of a child? On the contrary, emotional growth is restricted, impaired by the requirement for uniformly quiet classrooms. Yet emotional growth is undeniably very important. Schools do not deny the need for emotional growth. They simply prevent its natural development within the confines of their influence. Remember, kids are in school more than they are anywhere else when they are awake.

Where do teachers think that children can freely express their emotions? Many teachers would say "somewhere other than in my classroom." The words used would not be these, but euphemisms of these thoughts.

Where do parents think that children can freely express their emotions? Sadly, in some cases the reply would be "somewhere away from me." Some parents censure their children who experience emotions and express their feelings. They claim can't stand "the noise" of laughter or "the fighting" sounds of children confronting each other. As it happens, what seems like fighting to parents may well be the learning and development of social skills for the kids.

Is it any wonder that people have problems with their emotions when they reach adolescence or adulthood? We don't even know what's right and what's wrong, what's good and what's bad, what's normal for a person and what's abnormal.

Where do we learn this? Where should we learn this? Think about this. Where did the person in the car behind us, who honks and gives us the finger while kissing our rear bumper, then races past us, learn his emotional control and expression? It was definitely learned, as emotions are not necessarily instinctive.

The second area of growth that is important to a person is the social. Where do we learn what is socially acceptable? When we are small, our parents teach us how they want us to behave when with others. But do they actually teach us what to do, or do they just teach us what not to do? Many of us learn what is socially acceptable from our parents more through correction of what we've done wrong than from teaching of the right ways.

Many of us can remember famous warnings (about behavior) that our mothers or fathers repeated so many times to us. Many children are socially inept when they reach the stage where they spend more time with their peers than with their parents. They know what not to do, but they don't know how to act in a positive way. Few children are taught these skills formally. Anywhere. Yet we all expect that they will know what is socially acceptable and what is not. And that they will know how to interact socially with their peers and adults. So they experiment.

The community, including family members other than parents, play some role in this, either by example or by demonstration. As children, we copy our parents but we also learn by watching others. Other people become role models, willingly or not. Our neighbors may not be good role models. The people our children see on television for several hours each day are frequently poor role models, teaching behavior we don't want our children to use themselves. All for laughs. These people don't even know what it means to be a role model, let alone a good role model. Why not? Television doesn't consider itself a teaching medium, with a few notable exceptions.

Where do we learn what is socially acceptable or unacceptable? As adults, we learn this from social service campaigns, such as those opposing smoking, driving while intoxicated and taking drugs. We also learn what's acceptable from advertising. When we watch a deodorant commercial, we're being socialized to believe that body odor is unpleasant and unacceptable to others.

The whole thrust of advertising is supposedly to teach us what is socially acceptable behavior. With advertising, this usually involves buying a commercial product. Buy our product and be socially acceptable, loved by all.

Children learn what is socially acceptable in similar ways. Television programs don't correct children, as a parent would. Rather television teaches kids by example. Persistent and effective examples they are too. Good examples they aren't, except for those for the very young where some values training is provided in children's programs.

We also must learn when new laws are passed that affect us. Consider this: ignorance of the law has never been an accepted defense in court. We are expected to know the laws by which we live, in our country, our state or province and our municipality. We can learn about new laws that are passed, as they may be discussed in newspapers and on television. But it's a lot of trouble to keep up.

Where do we learn about laws that were passed twenty years ago, forty years ago, a hundred years ago? Some are taught in school. Politicians will direct adults to a printer or a government library where they can read about them, if asked.

Our municipalities and senior levels of government continue to pass laws to control our social behavior. Yet no satisfactory mechanism is put into place to teach people what these new laws are and how they impact the very people whose behavior they are intended to affect.

Old laws are supposed to be learned by everyone. Again, no mechanism is in place to teach them. Most of us learn about these laws, if at all, the same way we learned about sex as children. Laws are designed to control behavior, set acceptable social norms. They would be more effective if we knew what they were.

How do we learn how to interact socially with other people? The hard way, by making mistakes and taking our lumps, or by watching others.

We learned to be quiet in school. To learn how effective this learning is, check out how pervasive the lecture style of teaching is in colleges and universities. Discipline and conformity are the two most important and consistently emphasized lessons taught throughout public schools in North America.

We learned to be quiet and not look at others in elevators, subway trains and buses. We learned not to make eye contact with people on the street. Then we find we have difficulty holding eye contact when in a job interview or on a first date. Our night-clubs play music so loud we don't have to show that our social skills of conversation are sadly lacking. We have trouble getting up close and personal with others. This should not come as a surprise.

We become experts at discussing the weather, bad government and sports. Can we discuss anything else with anyone other than those we work with? Sex, religion and politics are considered too risky and the common knowledge base for most other topics is too thin to be helpful. Some of us seldom have good conversations because others we want to talk with may have much to talk about.

Many marriages break down because the spouses have little in common to talk about after some period of time together. Many of us today have fewer close friends than our ancestors. Many of us have trouble communicating in a meaningful way with each other. We may not know what to say. We may not know how to act in certain situations. Some of us don't know how to or don't want to express our feelings. We may have trouble explaining to others what our personal limits are. Some of us don't know how to listen carefully. We may find it difficult to learn from others. Some people don't know how to accept help from others, if they are fortunate enough to find someone who is willing to help them.

Many popular magazines tell us that we don't know much about social interaction. Many of us didn't learn from our friends, neighbors, family members or co-workers how to interact well with others. We may have learned how to write computer software, become lawyers, teachers and dentists, but we may not know how to learn from each other, to accept each other, to teach others what we know.

Some people scorn the touchy-feely stuff of some support groups. But here we are talking about expressing to anyone how we feel and about listening to others talk about how they feel. Many of us don't want to express how we feel to others. They don't want to listen to others talk about their problems. Then they wonder why someone didn't know about something being dreadfully wrong after a person commits suicide or guns down a family member or work mates.

Is it absolutely necessary that we learn all this by accident of fate? If so, we are driving ourselves toward destruction. We need to have a place and a way to learn this.

We need to have the proper kinds of experiences in school. And we need them before we require these skills in real-life situations. As with other skills, such as mathematics and reading, we need to learn this before we have to use it. We need to learn the basics, at the latest in the early years of elementary school.

The third way that the four main influences affect our growth and maturation is the intellectual. This, after all, is where our schools should shine. This is what our schools were designed to teach. This is what we have been led to believe, but it is not really the case.

What do we do at school? In the early years of elementary school we learn skills we will not need for years to come. These skills take a long time to cover in school, because some children are not ready for them developmentally and have little immediate use for them anyway. This removes the key motivation to learning for the child. Other than approval of teacher and parents, the child feels little reward for learning these skills.

Some kids learn faster than others because they're intellectually ready for it. Then these quick learners have little to do while the rest of the class catches up with them. They are given separate, often non-social activities to do. Ironically, these are often the kids who need a bit of extra social development most.

Many school systems refuse to stream faster learners in separate classes on the pretext that streaming goes against the natural mix of adult society. We hold back students with the greatest potential for fear of offending or leaving out those with the least potential. We penalize bright kids. Unusually bright adults seldom mix socially with people of lesser intellect. Yet we force kids of vastly different intellectual abilities together during prime learning periods and expect that all will learn together without problems. It works in small doses. As a steady diet, there are unfortunate costs to the social development of the kids.

Some kids respond to this by becoming star students and learning as much as they can through alternative means that the school provides. These are a minority of children. Others who learn quickly become bored, as the school does not provide the necessary tools and encouragement for them to develop intellectually on their own. The bored kids tell their classmates that school is boring. The others will not likely tell of their good experiences because this would not stand them in good stead with their peers.

Who has the major influence here among the peers? No matter what is being learned in classes, the prevailing belief among adolescents becomes that school is boring. For some, this becomes a mantra to be repeated many times each day. This repetition is more frequent than the old school style of rote learning ever was, where the lesson to be learned was repeated over and over.

This lesson is learned well. It's burned into the brains of our young people by their peers.

Ask them why school is boring. They don't have a good answer. They just know that it is boring. They learned that lesson well. There is never an exam question asking why they think school is boring. No one asks. No one wants to know the answers.

How do students react to a situation they consider boring? They drop out or rebel. Dropping out may even be within the classroom setting. Someone who drops out of the system while remaining in the classroom either creates his own microculture opposed to the school system or he becomes more sour on his own, a loner. This is the very behavior that so many adults find bewildering and distressing about teens.

High school dropouts often have a greater than normal amount of natural ability and intellect. If they feel held back or penalized for that, they want to escape. They either escape the school or they escape within their own classes.

In the first few years of formal schooling, children come to understand that nothing much of importance is taught in school, that paying attention is not essential and that teachers have a set agenda (curriculum) that they must teach no matter what the needs of their students may be. This is sometimes reinforced or confirmed by parents who feel no twinge of conscience about taking their children out of school for a vacation of a week or two with the excuse that the kids will probably learn more while on vacation than in school anyway. Likely they will.

Then, when children are intellectually and developmentally ready to learn at a greater pace, say grade four, they aren't prepared. They've had three or four or five years of training to believe that school is not really significant for them.

We aren't preparing our young people in what to expect, both in life and in their education, in the early years of school. Why?

Because it was not needed in past centuries.

Because no one thought of it.

Because no one knows how to approach the subject.

Now that we know what's needed, it's easier for us to tell others.

A child who lacks maturity in emotional, social or physical skills and development will not likely do well in the intellectual atmosphere of a school classroom. Yet schools give short shrift to the non-intellectual elements of a child's development. There is little or no time allotted and teachers do not have a mandate to provide them. Social and emotional development are not on the curriculum.

The fourth area in the development of young people is the physical. In previous chapters we have seen how physical activity in school is offered when it's least needed. We have all heard about how physically unfit the young people of our nation are, no matter what nation we live in. Recent studies have shown that even kids believe they get more physical activity each day than they really do.

Many teachers receive very little training to prepare them to teach physical education. Now phys. ed. periods are being cut, so teacher preparation is less important. Maybe we should make each recess half an hour, so that kids can play more and get more exercise. As it is, most recesses are fifteen minutes, just long enough for the teacher to have a coffee. Is recess teacher-oriented or child-oriented?

Does physical exercise affect intellectual ability? Or does intellectual exercise affect physical ability? Yes and yes. Does it really matter which came first, the chicken or the egg? When the time comes, eat both.

If we can reasonably expect that our young people will grow and mature into good, clean, balanced adult individuals, then we must provide the opportunities for them to gain that balance. They can only do that by having good experiences from which they can learn. They're not getting those experiences in North American schools now.

We don't need to give children actual life experiences for them to learn most of these things. Stories and lessons will do. Teachers are good at that.

Many people will argue that young children are not mature enough to learn concepts, that they can only learn facts. My response would be: then how did they get where they are at that stage in life without understanding concepts? Children are hardly little walking encyclopedias. They have a clear idea of what life is about in their world. Children have the ability to assimilate facts, personal experiences and vicarious experiences told to them or shown to them by others, to absorb and understand them and create their own concepts about their world based on what they have learned.

Conceptualizing is how kids understand their world. They may not understand it fully, but they have an idea of how everything in their lives works. That's why they become so upset when their concept of their world changes, such as when their parents divorce.

Kids have the ability to learn facts and absorb concepts. The reason has to do with their need to understand their world, their drive to understand what goes on around them, to make sense of it.

It's skills that cause some difficulty if they are taught too early. Teaching skills to immature minds slows down the learning process for everyone. It's not wrong, but it makes learning slow.

Young children absorb far more than we give them credit for. They can understand concepts and they try to make sense of them. It's specific intellectual and physical skills that they may not be ready for. Yet these are the very things that we offer them in the first years of elementary school. No wonder it takes them so long to learn.

In her book *One Woman's Arctic*,[*] Sheila Burnford observes the young children of Pond Inlet, a tiny community in northern Canada, near the magnetic North Pole. She learned that the children in kindergarten had an attention span of about forty minutes, far longer than that of children in most of North America. Although she was a novice teacher at the time, this tweaked her curiosity.

We can compare Burnford's experience with our own, if we live in a more urban part of North America. Some readers of Burnford's book argue that these northern children don't have junk food to eat during a school day, thus don't become hyperactive from the chemicals in it. While that may be true to a greater extent than in the rest of North America, it doesn't explain why children who don't have junk food in southern communities have a shorter attention span.

Let's examine some possible differences. These children were taught what to expect in school. Their parents prepared them for how they should act in school and how they should approach the work they were given. They didn't have conflicting influences from television. They grew up believing that school was a place to learn and that they should get the most they can out of their time in school.

Some of these northern kids even sneaked back into their classroom after the teacher had left at the end of the school day so they could finish their projects or do some extra work. They broke school rules so they could finish their work. Feature that.

There are those who might suggest that these children have some genetic differences. That would be very hard to support. Could children of kindergarten age be genetically predisposed to pay attention in school for two to four times as long as their counterparts in the south? No. They were taught.

These children were mentally and emotionally prepared to learn and do well. They were prepared by their parents and their community and supported by their peers who also eagerly went to school to learn. They wanted to be in school.

It's part of the culture of their community that the parents teach the children to respect the school and the teacher and to learn their lessons well. The parents are also prepared to be parents. They learn how to be parents from their parents and their community. Everyone in that community is taught what family is and how to help others and to depend on others when they need them. Interdependence is considered to be a way of life. Each adult becomes a parent to any child when the situation arises.

If we want adults in our society to be different than they are now, we must teach them as children. We must prepare them for what to expect, how to manage their lives and how to cope with difficulties they will encounter in it.

If we want our children to be taught this way, we must teach their parents the importance of their responsibilities. We must not do what we do now, which is accuse the adults of being bad parents. We must actually teach young adults how to become good parents, what to do, how to act, how to be good role models, how to give their children important and effective experiences.

This will require time, at least two generations, to take full effect. There will be benefits in the shorter term, as a transition period progresses. It requires a big plan with long-term objectives. And it requires a commitment on the part of the vast majority of people in our country who want our civilization to improve.

It requires us to stop complaining about how bad things are and start doing something about it. We don't need more police, more guns, more courts and more prisons.

We need good people to exert a positive influence to make things happen the way they want things to happen.

Bad influences are still in a minority in our society. They just happen to be a very vocal and visible minority. They spread their message very effectively. Theirs is a growing minority, growing frighteningly quickly because of an increase in population and because of the success of their messages.

We need good people to speak up too. It's part of the tradition of most countries to stand up for what is right in time of war. Now it's time for good people to stand up for what is right in time of peace. If we don't, we may find a war of a different and unfamiliar sort beginning within our own borders.

The time has come. It's not yet too late.

We can build taller pyramids. We can build stronger, more substantial pyramids than we have now. We will learn how in the following chapters.

---

*Sheila Burnford, *One Woman's Arctic*

20
How to Begin

MORE than anything else in the previous chapters, we have cut through the confusion and chaos that life has thrown at us. We have tried to feel what's in our hearts, what we feel in our gut. To give more credibility to our experiences rather than to the messages the media may have sent us, each with its slant to the facts.

And to act on those feelings.

This book has already surpassed its greatest obstacle of all, getting it into existence. It happened with the encouragement and even insistence of several people in various different countries who said that these ideas should be put into a book. They said that everyone should have an opportunity to learn about them.

These people represent all continents and political preferences. They said that the problems of their countries are the same as the problems in every country. So why should the solutions not be similar? Should the problems of each country not be unique, limited within its boundaries? No. Many people in many countries suffer the same anxieties, no matter where they live. They have the same social problems.

Belief in a governing system based on the inherent goodness and beliefs of a majority of the people is a good place to start fixing things. Early supporters wanted this book to take to their own people. They wanted to address what they believed were the problems of their own countries. It turns out there are many people who will be happy to support each other to make our plan happen.

People who read this book are, for the most part, good people with honest intentions and positive wishes for our planet, our civilization, their own people. We need to see through the present mess that our world is in and try to put things right again for the future.

We can expect criticism. First, we can expect criticism from the media, as they bear the responsibility for much of the mess that our society is in. They have perpetuated the belief that our world is a disaster and there is little we can do about it. By presenting a one-sided viewpoint of life, the media have led us (and themselves in the process) to believe that life is largely negative and hopeless.

They have taught our young people that life will be hopeless for them. We all pay the price for neglecting our responsibilities to the children of our country. The media will not want to accept this responsibility, so many of their representatives may challenge the credibility of a proposal based on positive values.

Who cares about these doom-sayers? This book is about us and the future of our respective countries. It's about what we can do to make a difference in the parts of the world where we live our lives. If we believe that we can make a difference together, then we must consider that any media that criticize this book are wrong.

The media have a role in making things better. We would like them with us. But they are not essential to the program. As Milton wrote, "There are none so blind as those that will not see."* We will try to change what we can and persuade who we can, but we must bypass those obstacles that present only an emotional challenge. It's not necessary that everyone believe in this program. Good people will.

Politicians and governments can be expected to be reluctant to change until we express our collective will that they must do what we ask of them. They may be expected to delay doing the inevitable, which is to do what we want them to do. That's what governments do. We will have to insist, be firm, express our feelings and beliefs in a collective, calm but forceful way.

Politicians are not about to ignore a huge number of people who all are asking for the same thing, especially if they are asking for something that is nothing less than what democracy stands for. We are the people who are ruled by law and government. We have the right, as citizens, to participate in the governing of our country, to some extent, and of ourselves. But only if we speak up.

There will be those who insist that committees will have to be formed, studies will have to be done, time will have to be taken to consider this thoroughly and openly. This is the old way of obstruction in government. To end the life of a project, put it into the hands of a committee to study it. Death by committee is a common political and business term.

What is there about democracy that needs to be studied? Dare our politicians say that our democracy should be changed into something different? Will they say that we are not entitled to our opinions, that our wishes and wills are not important? No. They may try delaying tactics, at which they are experts. But only until they are convinced that enough people support our program.

We must tell them to avoid delay. We must remind them that a government that speaks for its people must listen to its people. It's our birthright. This is not negotiable.

There will be people who downplay our movement because they don't want anything to change. They won't know why. They are the naysayers. Naysayers may be the most dangerous because they are the ordinary people who discourage us from doing what we should do. They might be our neighbors. They never seem to have anything good to say and never have any productive suggestions. Naysayers must be ignored. They are losers. We cannot build a new world based on the destructive power of losers.

What it all comes down to is this: if we believe that life in our country is not right, then we must do what is necessary to make it right. We are part of a majority. It just seems as if we are in a minority, because we and others like us have kept quiet for so long. We have not known before that there are so many others like us around.

This book does not support any political platform. It does not support any particular party, or politician or political ideology. It asks that we find what a large majority of us have in common, then make sure that all political parties know that so many of us think alike.

We know what our differences are. They're all around us. We're reminded of them every day.

We need to discover what we have in common and focus on it. Because what we have in common is what makes us a nation. Canadians are often mocked by other Canadians because they don't know what makes them distinct from Americans, what gives them a Canadian identity. The reason is that they don't concentrate on what they have in common. When they know what Canadians and Americans have in common with each other, the differences that create identity become clearer, make more sense.

Americans are confronted with differences among themselves daily. Canadians and Americans think of the differences among the people of their respective countries as problems. That's because they don't understand how much they have in common. They have reference markers for how they're different but not for what they have in common.

This is a program to find common beliefs among people, to stress those beliefs on a regular basis and to teach them to our children.

If we concentrate on our differences, we must not be surprised if we find division and opposition all around us. If we instead concentrate on what we have in common, then we should not be surprised at how many friends we will gather.

Who would want to oppose democracy? Wars have been fought over it, to achieve it or to suppress it. Millions of people have died in wartime to preserve democracy or to gain it for their country. Now we can make it work for us.

Who would want to oppose finding what we have in common among us as a nation? Only those who have something to gain by keeping us in chaos and confusion. Who would want to oppose bringing new friends together? Only those who are incapable of making true friends.

Who would want to oppose making life better in our country? There will be some. We must ignore them and seek our goals using our collective, peaceful and productive means.

Our future and the future of our country is in our own hands. When we come together focusing on how much we have in common with each other, we can't go wrong. When we insist that these values be taught to our children, we are doing what is right. We are doing what we must.

It's time for us to come together.

---

*John Milton, "On His Blindness"

Toward a Meaningful and Lasting Future

No one knows fully what happens in schools these days. We may think we know, but we really can only know parts of the whole picture. The odd truth is that no one is fully familiar with what goes in any school now. Not even teachers or principals. A classroom is almost like a closed ecosystem. The system is so complex, the demands so high, the paperwork so intense, the curriculum so full that no one can know fully what is going on.

An administrator will tell say what he believes is happening in classrooms, but he has no way of knowing other than by the results of standardized tests that treat each student as if he or she should be part of a cloned herd. A teacher will give a positive picture that better reflects the impressions he has in his head and what he wants us to believe than reality. Some students, too many, will tell us that their teachers and they are on diverging courses, that the people who represent the school system to them, their teachers, have no idea what is going on in their heads, and don't really care.

What teachers and administrators know least is what is going on in the minds of their students. Most have been conditioned to believe that it is none of their business. They believe it should be what they are teaching and nothing else. School curriculum and experience with the judicial system (the law) work to ensure things remain this way.

If we think about what happens in a school, we will expect to find a bunch of young people of various ages learning stuff. Having experiences they won't get anywhere else. Enjoying the best years of their lives. Learning skills. Gaining knowledge. Finding out what they need to know to succeed in the world of adults. If that's true, why are there so many problems in high schools?

No matter where we may live, the problems will be similar. Ask a student what is happening in his class and we may hear a repetition of the course material being covered at the time. We will not likely hear that teachers are discussing the problems that kids have, how to act in certain situations, what feelings kids can expect to have in that time of their lives, what they should expect from their education, what is expected of them as members of their community, what they can expect in future years of school and how they should cope with problems they may have at those times.

Yet these are the very things that concern kids most, the issues that consume their time and energy, their minds, while their parents think they're at school learning the facts and skills of that grade. Their friends know too, so they cling to their friends.

Adults in the coming years will require skills that their predecessors in the past did not. Their times will demand it of them. It's not just that it would be nice. It will be necessary to give them skills and experiences that will allow them to avoid turning their lives into disasters.

People age forty or older, should think back to their years as adolescents or young adults. Life is much different now from how it was then. They survived the change from adolescence into full working adulthood. For one thing, they adapted as the times changed and their lives changed.

Our present children, the ones who are under ten years of age now, will not be able to survive the changes so easily. They won't have time to change, to grow, to develop and adapt as life around them changes in the future. They must be prepared for it before it happens. They need tools and skills to adapt, whereas we grew into change.

They must hit the ground running at full speed. Some of them will tell us that their schools are not preparing them for what they really need. As they don't know themselves what they will need, how can they know that their schools are not providing it? They know. They look around them. They are still learning about the world, so they use the bits of information and experiences they do get and expand on them. As adults, we may have stopped feeling the need to do this. They may see what we are missing. Thus they know that they require something they are not getting, even if they don't know the specifics.

It's not possible for many young people to make a spectacular change upon leaving school. They were trained for years to believe that the working world would treat them the way they were treated in school. It won't happen. Employers have different expectations of work habits than are the way of life in many in schools and in homes in North America. It's not necessary to force such shocking lifestyle and even ethical changes on these young people. They don't think that's right. The adults in the community don't realize what these young people are going through.

Consider the consequences if they aren't fully prepared for the world they'll face. What happens to the ones who are not prepared and can't make the change? Most believe, rightly so, that a radical change will not take place in them as soon as they leave school. The end of life in the protected atmosphere of school can be terrifying. Do we know that?

Childhood should be a time of innocence, a time to be carefree and enjoy everything that life has to offer, without having the burdens that adult life will impose on them later. Isn't that the way it should go?

Why? That may be the way we learned it should be. But that way does not prepare children for the many decades of adult life that will follow their leaving the classroom. Life is not easy, fun and carefree.

Where is the dividing line between the carefree ages of childhood and the more responsible age of young adulthood? In North America, each adult either does not have an answer to that question or the answers vary. In other words, we don't even agree on when a child should be treated as an adult, given adult responsibilities and expected to be accountable as an adult, except in criminal law where it is stipulated in what court a person of a particular age may be tried.

In some animal species, such as reptiles and fish, the young are left to their own devices as soon as they are born. They compete in an adult world, so to speak, shortly after birth. Mammals, in most cases, do not have more than a year or two of rearing before they must face the world of adulthood to feed and defend themselves.

That's the direction we humans are heading in. In fact, that's the way life is now for many young people. Many adolescents are leaving home before they have the skills to survive in a world of working adults. Many children live in families where the adults all work, sometimes at more than one job each. The big people come home tired and grumpy, needing rest more than to take on the responsibilities of parenthood. Kids have to look after themselves. Some leave home and live on the streets because there they have comradeship with others who have done the same.

People can't be forced to do what they don't have the strength to do. Some adults don't have the time and energy to be parents as well as income earners for the family. They are incapable of coping with both their working and their parental responsibilities. Now, parents in some jurisdictions are being forced to be legally and financially responsible for the misdeeds of their children. For example, kid breaks into a house, parent pays the bill. Many adults support that concept. Not parents with incorrigible kids, of course.

None of the supporters of this concept are parents who stand by helplessly and hopelessly as their teens run amok with addictions and afoul of the law. By the time a teen is creating havoc in some way, it's too late to change anything, impossible for the parent to do anything that will turn around both the relationship between parent and child and the attitude of the child in a reasonable period of time. The parent will be punished for something that is beyond his control because the community wants revenge, wants to punish someone. It doesn't know what to do to help the young person. It knows that imprisoning the young person won't help. So it punishes the parents who are themselves often victims of emotional abuse from their child.

Some children are treated, effectively, as miniature, incompetent adults who are given free food, clothing and shelter at home. They spend several hours each day at school learning facts and skills they are unable to make use of in their lives, either to help them to understand their lives or to cope with them.

Then they come home where it is confirmed for them that they are definitely not adults. Although they aren't adults, they have the responsibility for being their own parents, for parenting themselves as the parents are often out working to pay the bills or, if home, may not know what their children need from parents. Often there is no one else in the home to take responsibility for the child or, if there is, that person may not have the energy or the skills for good parenting.

It's no wonder that some kids have serious problems. It's no wonder that weapons appear at school, that gangs are no longer just cliques of kids who hang together at the mall and go to movies together on the weekends.

We, as a society, have forced children into this. Not only that, we have forced their parents and other adults who care about them into this. At the least they have felt forced into their uncomfortable positions out of fear and ignorance. The ignorance of what parenting is all about.

Young people can't cope. They don't know what to do. They can't learn how to manage their lives, to know what to do when they have problems and needs that are not being addressed. They have nowhere to learn such things. We don't provide such services on a broad scale.

Their parents don't have the time, energy or knowledge to be good parents. In generations past, many children learned from their parents as the parents indulged in hobbies and household chores. The kids were brought into the picture in some manner as either learners or as participants. A parent who is involved with sports might be prepared to spend time with his child doing activities related to those sports, but not so much time doing activities that don't interest him personally.

We learn most of what we know about parenting from our own parents. Unfortunately, if parents do not pass along the knowledge, skills, social training and love that kids need to be well-rounded adults and parents, they will not have access to these when they become parents themselves. Where a father fails as a parent, his children will tend to fail as parents. Where children are able to learn from their father and see what he does well, the will succeed in those areas.

Many children are not taught to respect their parents, as was the case in previous generations. On the other hand, many children do not have as much to respect in their parents as their parents or grandparents did, since parenting has become far less important in our society than it was two generations ago. They have more respect for their teachers, who can at least be seen as trying to provide for their needs.

What are children learning now from their parents? They are learning what they see. Are they learning what they should know to be good parents themselves? They're learning the inadequacies of their parents. They are internalizing the problems that their parents have, then mixing that with the problems that they face as adults, to become less adequate parents of the future. They resent the inadequacies of their parents, often rebel against them. They don't know what to expect as a child either, as no lessons about being a child were taught them, either at home or at school.

It's a pretty gloomy picture, isn't it?

Hold on! We don't have to accept this as the way things must be. We must realize that children learn from four main sources. And those sources must work together to benefit children. Together they must prepare children for the future that life has in store. We must do in the future what we are not doing now.

We must make a collective effort to have these influences work in harmony. That means we have to talk with each other. It means that one influence must provide for the needs of the child where another is unable to do so. It means that these influences must support each other, not fight each other. For example, parents, teachers, storekeepers and librarians should all know what children need and help them with it.

When parents and schools are at odds with each other, the adults fight. We know who loses, the kids. Parents must accept that schools will have to teach things that have traditionally been parental responsibilities. School systems must accept that they must teach different things than they have in the past.

School systems must give the schools the tools and resources they need to do the job.

Parents must be taught how to be good parents before they launch into the role. Children must be taught how to be good children before they get very far into childhood and form their own opinions and impressions. These must both happen early, before conditions are created that neither parents nor children can change.

At the beginning of this chapter, we learned that no one knows fully what goes on in schools. Let's take a look inside now.

Schools in North America are teaching institutions. What's wrong with that? They should be learning institutions. That is, the focus should be on the needs of the child, not on the teachers. This means what each child needs, not facts and skills that adults in some remote administrative office believe that all children need to learn.

There is a minimum core of knowledge that all children should learn and skills that they should master. There is widespread agreement with that, as it's the central function of our school systems. Children should go to school understanding that it's their responsibility to learn. If they are having trouble learning, they should make this known to the teacher.

Schools are more child-centered than ever, we may hear or read. They are. A group of learned adults sits together in a room and lists the facts and skills that children need to learn. They make these lists based on their own experiences and with input from their communities. Then they form these lists into curriculum and pass it along to teachers to teach.

What we have is schools that teach the facts and skills that the adults of our communities believe their children need to know. Why are our children doing so badly, by the standards of many adults in our communities? Why are there such problems in our senior schools? Why are so many of our high schools becoming literally like prisons, with armed guards, bells to indicate change of location and behavior, metal detectors, locker searches (some schools have eliminated lockers completely), zero tolerance for aggressive behavior and more and more rules about unacceptable behavior?

In past generations, kids used to joke about school being like a prison. Now, in some cases, it really is. The changes are bringing more rules and more fortification.

There is something wrong with this picture. Have a representative of the local police department come to a meeting of parents and talk about incidents of drugs, sex, violence and family problems in the community. Understand that the officer will not be able to give names or specific incidents, for reasons of confidentiality. Ask the officer to be honest and straightforward, but hide identities.

Or talk to a teacher, off the record. Don't ask an administrator about this subject. It's his job to prevent the public from learning the ugly side of the truth. Most teachers will try to protect their colleagues, too. Some school-related television programs show more of what the insides of schools are like today. Of course, all schools are not like this.

Is this what we have to look forward to in all schools? Is adulthood to be the reward for good behavior while in the school prison? Then what happens with those that exhibit bad behavior? Read the newspapers. Visit local schools. See how different life is now in high schools now than it was in the past.

Life in high school now is not necessarily prison-like. Prison-like *conditions* are becoming more and more common in our high schools. The more prison-like our schools become, the more students will act like prisoners.

This is not necessarily the way for the future. It's not necessarily our destiny. It's not what we want for our children and our grandchildren and great-grandchildren. However, unless we change, this is what life will be like in schools of the future.

We had better act now to change it. It won't improve on its own. Time has shown us that.

The time has come to change the earliest years of formal education to provide for the needs of children. That is, their needs of the future, not just their needs of the present.

Some major changes in focus are needed for the early years of education. This must happen at the state/provincial level, as these are the bodies of government that control education, that determine curriculum, that say what is and what will be.

Preferably, there would be initiatives over a wide area or even at a national level to determine what should be done. We should spend some money on preparing new guidelines for how our schools should be used. It would likely be a lot cheaper than how we are spending our money now.

And look at the potential benefits.

We have some serious problems in our society. It has taken us several generations to develop these problems to the extent they are now. It may take us that long to solve or overcome them. The longer we wait to begin, however, the longer it will take to fix the problems. And the worse the problems will become.

Trouble is, we may soon not be able to solve the problems at all. Study the social problems in parts of some countries of South America, Africa and parts of Europe and Asia. No one knows how to begin to solve their problems. In some places, people are in despair. Some countries, some cities, are violent. There is no jungle in nature so violent and terrifying as the human jungle, or so dangerous to life.

We may be able to help the people of other countries too by showing them the way, by example. Either we do that or risk having to defeat them by force. Or worse, risk having them defeat us by force.

We can show them that we can make major changes that really benefit our country and our society. Showing by example is good. It's role modeling, just as parenting is.

That will not be easy. We must put our own house in order first. It will require a great many people to speak up and tell our politicians that change is needed. The change should be in an orderly and organized fashion. Politicians need to be given direction.

Politicians are naturally reluctant to change. They resist change because they know it upsets their voters. Left to their own devices, politicians will remain the same, hold the fort, maintain the status quo. If they believe that the majority of their voters want change in a particular way, they will want change, too.

We have seen that the status quo cannot be held any longer. We either have to get better or allow ourselves to get worse.

We can improve.

Are we ready to make a difference? We can, but not alone. We will all have to speak up. We will have to encourage others to do this as well. Reading this book is a beginning for everyone.

We have to look for what we have in common, not at our differences. Let's accept that we have differences and concentrate on what we have in common. Focus on that and push it forward. Make our common beliefs what is most important. And we must teach them to our children.

Let's not look at what is bad and shake our heads in despair. Let's concentrate on what we want that is good and make an effort to change things in that direction. Make those good things more common among us.

The more we talk to people around the world, the more we learn that the problems they are most concerned about are exactly the same problems that we are concerned about in our own countries. The scenarios vary somewhat, but the problems and concerns are basically the same.

So are the ways to solve the problems. Mostly these ways involve people, good people with good thoughts and good ideas, talking with each other, sharing their thoughts, listening to others, speaking up for change.

There will be a new status quo for the coming century. Change will be the status quo. Change will be inevitable, unstoppable. Constant change will be a way of life.

Change can be for the better or for the worse.

Let's choose for the better. We need our voices and those of our neighbors, friends and everyone else we know.

22
They-Sayers

THEY could make life much better in our country. What should *they* do? If only they took more responsibility. There is something comfortable about asking that question. Not me. Just other people. Them, leave me out of it. To a certain extent, each of us is a they-sayer.

This kind of thinking must change. This leads to people of like minds gathering to grouse to each other. But nothing gets done.

It's easy to find fault with others. The front page of any newspaper is filled with the names and pictures of people who are faulted for something. The media are experts at placing the blame for something onto someone. Surgical targeting, the military call it. Destroy a public figure without affecting anyone else. Who wins that war? No one.

We do the same thing. No matter where we live, we find fault with the weather. We complain about our governments, our neighbors, our co-workers, others on the highway or subway, our bosses. We have no trouble finding the energy to complain.

When was the last time we said something good about another person, some praise that was not going to earn them brownie points? The last time we complimented someone on his or her work? The last time we thanked someone for helping us or told someone how much they mean to us? Most people would do it at a wake, if someone died, without hesitation or second thought. Maybe not before.

Most of us don't hear people apologize very often. Not just admitting that they were wrong, actually apologizing. "I'm sorry. I screwed up. If I hurt you, I apologize." It's one of the best ways to begin a friendship or to solidify one, but we rarely use it. We don't like to admit that we're wrong. We think it makes us weak.

We're all like this. It's a place to begin our thinking. Now let's think big again.

When was the last time a solution for a social problem was suggested in a newspaper? Oh, they're there all right. Politicians suggest a solution for something, then members of the other parties and the media take shots at it as if it were a shooting gallery. They consider it their duty to criticize. They rarely make a distinction between constructive and destructive criticism. Thus it seems as if politicians are always at war with each other.

Newspapers rarely print the full explanation of a suggested solution for a problem. Everything is slanted according to their corporate editorial policies. We don't think of our newspaper and broadcasting news as being censored. This is corporate censorship rather than government censorship. Both kinds have a clear agenda of what they hope to accomplish.

A daily newspaper should have a regular portion of one main section where it prints the details of a problem, its causes, its effects, suggestions people have about solutions, then ask for opinions. True, there are the "Letters to the Editor" pages. But these tend to cover a mish-mash of topics, are carefully edited and frequently written by people whose writing skills far exceed the reading tolerance of most readers. Many letters to the editor have a particularly strong point of view (read: extremely slanted toward one political viewpoint). They often lack balance.

Let's say there is a big feature in the Wednesday edition covering a social issue or a matter that is under consideration by the national government. Comments and reactions about the article could be submitted on paper or in digital form by email. They would be printed the following week in the Tuesday and Thursday editions, using only the space necessary to cover the input; that is, edited as letters to the editor are now to eliminate extraneous material.

In the Saturday edition following, there could be a recap of the main parts of the problem, plus solutions suggested by professionals, plus a summary of the solutions suggested in the previous week's mail. There could be a catch-up page a week later on a Monday, where late-arriving comments, observations and suggestions from readers could be included.

Governments should request a page in a newspaper where they can outline the matters under discussion in their House or legislature at the time and the various factors at play in the consideration of what to do about each. This should not be a whole section (which most people would not read anyway), just one page. Keep it brief and to the point. Federal matters could be covered on some days, provincial or state matters on other days.

Newspapers might claim that the governments should pay for this space. The government always pays for space now to make its political viewpoint, just like advertisers. That would be wrong for matters of general public interest. Newspapers search desperately for material to print each day, sometimes having to be creative with limited facts. They shouldn't charge for something that should be their civic duty.

Printing something that will enlighten and educate their readers should be considered part of their corporate civic responsibility to their readers. There shouldn't be a problem where they feel they should charge for something because they did not dig up the story themselves. They should always have the right to intercede if they believe that facts have been distorted in the government's reports.

Our media have a moral responsibility to make an honest attempt to convey the facts of matters under consideration by our governments to their readers. Of course, it would be the responsibility of these governments to put together these pieces in readable fashion, with partisan politics left out of it as much as possible.

Room would have to be left for opposition parties to insert their comments and positions. A formula would need to be worked out. Individual members and parties without sufficient representation to be an official opposition party would be given space in the "Letters to the Editor" page.

The media may claim that any material provided by a government will be edited to reflect the views of the ruling party. Newspapers and other mass media do that too. The government could have one representative of each party on a committee to review the submission for the next edition to be published.

The work of this committee would be to find as much material as possible that all parties agree is worthy of publication, then to put it into a press release or print form. By the time that the commonly agreed upon elements are aired in this committee, each party would know what else it had to put into its own section of the page allotted for its party viewpoint.

A political party could not complain that all of the facts are made available to the public. It might try to block such a program for some self-serving reason and use an emotional argument to justify their action. We must make these parties see that knowledge is good, that we have a right to it. Ignorance must be assigned to the past.

The availability of facts should not be clouded by emotional arguments. We have a right to know what our governments are doing. Our political representatives must have a commitment to make it available to us.

Radio should be another media source for our information. Virtually every car on its way to work has a radio. Those drivers who do not have a passenger talking or a cell phone plugged into their ears usually have the radio on.

A car radio should be a medium of learning, an interactive medium where the driver can choose the program he wants to listen to. A simple keypad added to the radio or on the dash could be used to connect to a distance-learning module. People could listen to course material while they are driving. They could finally make positive use of their drive time to learn what they need to better their personal lives, their work lives, their leisure time, their family time or to develop some special interest.

For service in English: press 1.

For service in French: press 2.

For service in Spanish: press 3.

To access a list of topics under discussion by the House of Representatives this week: press 1. For a list of topics under discussion by the Senate: press 2.

For a summary of the facts on the topic of water tables in the Ohio Valley: press 1. For a summary of the debate facts on the health care issue: press 2.

And so on.

Annoying? After all, we hate that on the telephone, don't we? But this is what could give us direct access to the critical information being used by our governments to make decisions about our fate on matters that directly affect us. We have never before been given such an opportunity to be plugged into a direct access to information available for decision making.

This will give us the opportunity to express our opinions to our political representatives. This also has not been practical before, as the background we required was not provided for us. It can be done easily now.

For the first time, we will have access to full information and be able to provide input to our representatives who are voting on our behalf. This is our pipeline to the center of action. Having knowledge is having power. Knowledge is something to be embraced, not to be avoided. It is a power we should have, not to be given up.

Those who take advantage of this service will be heard. Those who do not will be ignored. If we want to be heard, we must speak up.

True, this would not be possible for automobiles on the road today unless there were aftermarket modifications. But a few years of advance notice would be all that is required. Wearing of seat belts was announced ahead of time. Having headlights on at all times was announced ahead of time. Now safety and emissions testing has been announced ahead of time. It can happen easily enough with today's technology. The interested parties need to know that a program is being put together.

This would give a big advantage to small universities and colleges that have expertise but only have access to a small population base. These institutions are offering distance learning now through the Internet and some cable/satellite television channels. If they were able to pull in the interest of governments, the car makers and other private enterprise to develop the necessary hardware and software, then any institution anywhere could compete on an equal footing with the big ones, provided they could offer the courses that were needed and wanted. Even specialized courses that are not available in small cities now could be accessible in this way.

Our highways, which are now jammed with irate and impatient motorists, could be filled with mobile learners. Would they be driving too fast then? Driving fast requires concentration that would not allow the driver to pay attention to his course material. The driver would have to slow down into "follow mode" in order to not lose his place in the lesson. Driving with the flow of traffic may be boring, but not if we are learning at the same time. The keypad would also allow us to back up the lesson if we missed something, a feature that's not even possible in a classroom setting.

Someone will argue that this would distract the driver from his main job, which is to pilot his vehicle to its destination. Learning will not distract him more than his present interests with a cell phone, radio music, sightseeing or worrying about others on the road.

How would governments fit into this plan? Governments would mostly be required for coordination of these programs among the various interested parties. Some research grants may have to be provided to develop the integration of existing technology into a viable program. It's unlikely that brand new technology would need to be developed, although it may be necessary to advance existing technologies in some areas.

If education is one of the prime responsibilities of government, our senior levels of government should be expected to participate and encourage the other necessary partners in this program to come together.

There is an inherent problem with the whole idea of politicians making anything more public than it already is. Politicians are only people. We expect that somehow they should be more than people. Backbenchers are expected to know everything that goes on in their House, although they have other duties that could keep them away from the House nearly all of each working day. Leaders are expected to have impeccable morals, never make a slip of any kind, never change their minds and be completely knowledgeable about every subject about which they are questioned by the media.

That's unreasonable. It's time we stopped requiring that of our politicians. It's also time that the media stopped trying to disembowel our political representatives for the advancement of their own listenership, viewership or readership numbers. We must tell the media to stop this counter-productive behavior.

It's time that we allow our political representatives to change their minds. Facts and realities change. More information can come to light. Our representatives should be able to assess situations as they currently exist and make up their minds according to the facts of the day without having to worry that the media will skewer them for taking a different position than they did in the past. We have no trouble changing our own minds as we learn more facts. Our political representatives should have the same rights.

The best way to avoid getting into trouble is to do nothing. If we are unable to do that, then say as little as possible. Don't tell anyone what we are doing. If we make a mistake, deny and cover up as much as possible. This has been the way and the experience of politicians in the past in North America. We can see the results.

This is what we teach our children. It's what they see around them. It's no wonder that most of them lose their creative drive and entrepreneurial spirit when they are young. Our politicians have learned these lessons well. We have trained them to put up a communications wall between us and them.

We must take a different approach now. Instead of trusting that the people we elect to office will do what we want, then being disappointed when they don't, we must tell them what we want of them. We must allow that they will occasionally make honest mistakes. We must accept that they can change their minds and they should do so if they learn more about a subject and find that their stand should be changed.

We must not expect of others what we would not expect of ourselves. The Golden Rule. Only this version of it more closely resembles the words of Confucius.

We must tell our political representatives what we want and expect of them. We must tell them that we want to know about the subjects under consideration. We must be prepared to learn about those subjects. We must then be prepared to express our views about these subjects to our representatives so that our views are heard.

We must accept that politicians will make mistakes. We must allow them to give their side of an argument without holding them to it forever. If they learn more and change their minds as a result, so be it. In short, we must stop expecting them to be perfect. As long as we accept that, then we have a right to tell them what we think.

The media have taught us to think badly of any politician who changes his mind, no matter what the reason for the change. We must ask the media to change this hypocrisy, as they do the same thing themselves on a daily basis.

It's time to stop talking about our politicians behind their backs and to do something about it, about them. Understanding and agreement comes through talking, through communication among all interested parties, not through avoidance. Avoidance inevitably leads to violence or conflict.

Politicians must contribute to their local newspapers to disseminate available information more freely.

Town hall-style meetings must be held on a regular basis and knowledgeable people must be allowed to present information for the consumption of all. Four or six times a year would be a good beginning. Then we citizens must arrange to attend these meetings.

All points of view must be allowed to be presented at these meetings, within certain guidelines, such as time limits for unscheduled comments. Questions may be asked, but the questions must be information questions, not comment or opinion couched as questions. Discussion will be saved for later, when the meeting is over. At least an hour must be set aside after each meeting for those attending to share their thoughts and questions and ideas with others.

Local media must be encouraged to publicize these meetings and to cover them and report their events for those who are unable to attend. However, the media should not be held responsible for reporting fully the thoughts expressed at the meetings. The responsibility must be on each of us to attend our local Town Hall meetings. In some cases, broadcast media could record the meetings and play them on air at an hour that would not interfere with their regular programming, so that those who are housebound or who were unable to attend the meetings can catch up as best they can.

The twenty-first century will be the first in which true democracy is possible. Although we have far more people on Earth now than when democracy was first created and developed by the ancient Greeks, we have equality of all people that they did not have and we have the technology available to allow each citizen to participate in his own government.

Controversy has raged for centuries about the concept of representative government. Should the elected politician be allowed to work and vote as his conscience allows or as his party insists in the House, without consultation with his constituents, or should he be elected to portray the current views of his constituents to the House?

Today's technology and average level of education among voters should allow us to put that question to rest. We now have the ability to participate in the governing of our country. The technology exists to allow us to provide input on any topic. We don't need to depend solely on the integrity of our politicians. We need to depend more on ourselves. We need to value our own integrity and our own worth.

We need to have the will to use the technology available to us.

Governments will need to alter their voting regimen over time so that a governing party cannot be defeated and sent to an election because the people have voted differently from the ruling party, as is the case in Canada now. Each party can take a stand on issues of interest to voters and this could determine who gets elected. But each representative must be allowed to vote according to the will of his constituents if a means of polling those constituents is in place and has been used.

Party politics will have to make room for real democracy. Political parties have a valuable place in the governance of democratic countries. That place is to research facts, consider options, take positions and survey their constituents. No longer is it the place of political parties to make decisions for an ignorant constituency to follow.

Do we have the collective will to act in the best interests of our society, our community, our country, not just in our own best interests? In most cases, the will of the citizens of our community will be in our own best interests too.

If we don't, we can expect more of the same kind of government and the same kind of social ills. Only it will get worse. It's getting worse now. We know it in our heart. We know it in our gut. It worries us. It concerns us. We didn't think we could do anything about it, until now. Most of us didn't realize that the same problems worry everyone else. Just don't expect us to admit it too quickly, as everyone has been conditioned in much the same way, to deny that anything is wrong and ignore what we see.

The future is in our hands.

Don't pass the buck. It's time to invest it.

Strategies for the Long Term

WE must consider how we can prepare ourselves now for the way the world will operate in the coming years. The world will change, and quickly. Survivors will change too. Nothing dooms a country's economy faster than a government that looks backward more than it looks forward.

The present hierarchy of "developed" and "developing" countries will alter depending upon their ability to adapt the new political/economic ways of the new century. Economic and even military power in the present provides no assurance that this position will continue under new regimes. Governments that want to maintain the status quo live in the past and will inevitably be assigned to history.

Take the Internet as an example. Backward-looking political parties will want to avoid it. Static parties will want to put some information online for their many constituents to access over the Internet. Forward-looking parties, major parties of the future, will use the Internet in an interactive way to survey the thoughts and feelings of their constituents so that these may guide their legislative decisions. The "have nots" of the future will be those who do not have access to the Internet or the skills to use it.

There is no need to be frightened of the changes to come. Fear will serve no purpose but to freeze us in position, causing us to fall behind as the rest of the world advances. Change will take place regardless of whether we embrace it or reject it. Our countries will adapt to the new world regime, as the consequences of not doing so could mean economic disaster. We need only to study the rise and fall of empires throughout history to see that the warning signs for change are all in place now.

The best way to begin to prepare ourselves is to learn about what is happening now in terms of world trends. Learn about general changes in lifestyles. Accept that they are happening and join the flow. Within a generation, for example, all rich countries will be fully connected to electronic data transmission systems, such as the Internet we have now. The World Wide Web, the system of choice for commerce now, will be but one of several possible systems to select. People who live comfortably in these countries will be comfortable with the technologies of the time, despite how quickly they will change. Poor people, poor countries and countries under the control of dictatorships or other totalitarian systems will not be connected due to costs or because their leaders will fear such technologies and limit access to them.

We must understand that we will not have to become experts on any one part of technology. No one will be able to become an expert on all parts of it. There's too much to learn. The best that anyone will be able to do will be to have a reasonable idea of what is going on in the world and to try to become familiar with one or more parts of it more thoroughly. In other words, we need to be able to do what our job and our lifestyle (or the ones we would like to have) require. What we don't need, we will not be required to learn. We will need to know where we can learn more when we need it.

We must learn what we need to know now. Learn how to learn what we may need to know later. Be prepared for our own future and know what we must now. It isn't difficult. It's simply a matter of attitude. We need to accept what is happening around us and adapt to it. There is nothing to be frightened of. All we need to do is ask.

This means we must act in our own best interests. Ignorance of the law is not accepted as a defense in court if we are arrested. The judicial system expects that we will know what we must. Ignorance of what is going on in the world and failing to try to stay up with it will not be acceptable either. Failure is an option, but not a good one.

It has become a mantra to say things like, "The world is going to hell and nothing can be done about it"; "Our government doesn't care what we think"; "The world is getting too complicated"; "There's too much technology, not enough emphasis on people"; or "I'm glad I don't have to grow up in the world these days."

Notice how subjective these statements are. Each one shows a detachment from the reality around us. Each one expresses a desire to be excluded from the happenings of the day. Avoidance has become preferable to working toward solutions.

Each one is very negative, very fatalistic, very lacking in hope. Each one stresses that someone else (or some-thing outside of the control of that person) is wrong, that someone else is responsible. The speaker is not prepared to adapt. These are the words of society's losers of the future.

It's time to change that. We and the millions of others who want things to improve now have the opportunity to make a difference.

Change will be a standard, a given, for the future. We can either change to become part of the group that influences government and education or change in an atrophic sense by letting ourselves dwindle down to accepting a world that is no larger than our own living area while we wait out the rest of our lives.

There will be no standing still. Escape from change will not be an option. Change will be a way of life. A way of living. It may not be what any of us would prefer, but life doesn't come with a fixed agenda. We can optimize conditions within the situation of our lives.

Either we are working to be in or we are dropping out. But, if we choose to drop out, our excuses will no longer be valid to those who are in. No one but insiders will care about excuses. Outsiders will become sociologically extinct.

This does not mean that we will have to devote large portions of our time to preparing ourselves for life. It does mean that we will have to devote some time to knowing what is going on, to learning the facts about it, to learning the various opinions and suggestions that have been made and to putting forward our opinion in the approved manner. This will take less time daily than it takes to watch the evening news or one sitcom on television. Far less than a football game.

That's just to stay up with advances. If we want to progress through the system (climb the ladder), we will have to make further commitments.

Early in the book we established that we want our society to change, to improve, that we believe it must change and that we have a role to play in making it change in a positive way. Where can we start? The first thing to realize is that it took a very long time to get into the mess we are in now. It will take time to work our way out of it.

This is not to suggest that we are living in a terrible world. There is no need to believe that. But there are things that need to change. By coincidence, these happen to be times when people who want to participate in the formation of a new society within their country may be making changes in their own lives as well.

Let's make something clear now. It could take a generation before significant changes may begin to be felt in our society. Maybe two generations before these changes will have their full effect. Attitudes, customs and cultures require a concentrated effort to alter, and they change only over a long period of time.

Is that too long to wait? Maybe we won't be alive that long. That may well be true. But remember, we live for the future, not the past. We can't change the past. We can change the future. We can make it better for our children, our grandchildren and our great-grandchildren. That is an important function of our being a life form, of being on Earth.

To do less would be a violation of nature. A desire for continuity of our species is in common with the instincts of every living thing on this planet, plant or animal.

Most species of plants and animals cannot improve their own lives themselves. We humans can. Now we must try. Taking control of the social destiny of our society clearly distinguishes us from other animals, even while more similarities are being found between humans and other mammals.

This proposal will have two main parts to it. The first will be a long-term plan. The second will be the means to implement the various parts of the plan, for now and in the future.

We will not be proposing any prescriptive solutions for the way we would like our world to be. It's not our purpose to suggest that the same solutions apply to everyone We must decide what we want for our own home area. We and others in our respective countries must decide what we have in common and move to ensure that these values, skills and messages are taught to children as early in their lives as possible.

The role of this book will be to propose a process by which we can achieve the goals we want for our societies. Each area will have the option of accepting or rejecting or even of modifying the process with a decision. Implementing it will require a great deal of work. A few people must really care enough to devote themselves to making these changes happen. A lot of other people must lend their support, including a little effort, for it to happen.

The process is not a one-time thing, not something that can be done and over with in one shot. There will be no silver bullet, no magic pill. That is why no one is making suggestions for change immediately. Short-term solutions don't exist. Once begun, our process will be the form by which our society will update itself to reflect our wishes and those of our descendants on a regular basis, such as once each decade.

Why is it necessary to have such a long-term plan, one that will take so long to take full effect? The simple answer is that it will take a long time to both change the ways of doing things for most people and to teach our youngest generation the new ways before they grow up and experience ways we don't want them to follow.

Should we care about life fifty years into the future? Of course we should care. With recent advances in health care, all of us may well be alive in fifty years time. The changes we make in the next while could determine the future of all life on this planet. Other species are disappearing from the planet at an alarming rate. We could go too if we do not plan better than we have in the past century. We succeeded as a species through history because of our ability to adapt to current conditions.

In the previous few generations, people fought world wars because they wanted the world we live in now to be different from the way others wanted it to be. Millions of people sacrificed their lives so that we would have a decent world to live in. They cared about us, our lives, our future. We must care about generations to follow us.

The nuclear devices in silos in both known and unknown locations around the world are not just for comic book use. The good guys and the bad guys need to join forces to work things out for the best.

Where do we start? The first definitive move will have to be by each nation's government. There must be a commitment by all parties toward meeting common objectives and forming common goals. Just agreeing on that much would be a good start. The details will be worked out later. That's where we come in, remember? We are supposed to help make the final decisions. We must convince our governments to make that commitment.

It might seem unlikely that politicians and political parties could all agree on anything. That is wrong thinking. Most political parties agree on many things they don't discuss. There's no point in spending time discussing what they agree on, so they believe. So we only hear about the things they disagree about.

As individuals, as employees, as groups, as political parties, we don't discuss what we have in common. As a result, we come to believe that we have little in common. In centuries past, people discussed at length what they agreed on and the country grew from it. These beliefs made our country what it is today. Now people don't realize just how much we all agree.

Before we have some questions to decide on, we need to have the questions formulated and prepared to be put before us. This is where the commitment by the national government will be needed.

There will have to be a group assembled to formulate questions on which we will make decisions. Don't worry about those who cry, "Spare me from government by committee!" Governments do this all the time. They can make it work if they really try, and if the politicians keep their political ideologies out of it. It's up to us to tell them what we want.

Let's call this the National Formulation Commission (NFC). This august body will have to be as apolitical as possible. This is preferred to having a commission made up of representatives of all political parties, which would be a second choice. This is how the judiciary is chosen, so it is not new ground.

Selection of the NFC can be done through cooperative means, involving the various levels of government and representatives of communities making suggestions to them. In Canada, for example, a meeting of the First Ministers (premiers) of the provinces and the Prime Minister can decide how the NFC members will be selected and whether there will be provincial or regional committees under the NFC. Once these decisions are made, each participating government and party within the legislature will offer a list of candidates for the selection process. Actual selection of committee members will be made according to the process agreed upon by the First Ministers and Prime Minister.

In the United States, state governors would meet to decide how to proceed. In other countries, a similar process of meetings and decision making can take place to decide on the makeup of the committees and the NFC.

If it seems unlikely that more than one level of government could work together in this manner, remember that these people would be working toward finding common ground, things they agree about. They are used to conflict.

The existing system of government is based on confrontation, as it supposedly brings various viewpoints to the table in the consideration of controversial issues. This time they will be searching for what they agree on. Have faith that they are capable of it.

Once the decision is made by the national and state/provincial governments to follow this program and to commit to its implementation, one year will have to be set aside to select the commission members and to prepare a set of guidelines for it to follow. If the objective is made to have this commission ready for action in six months time, it should be ready within a year. They are politicians, after all, who will have to agree to this.

The decision will have to be made as to whether there will be one commission to represent the entire country or several committees, each of which would represent their particular smaller jurisdiction, such as state/province or group of states in a region.

Multiple regional committees would each make recommendations on behalf of their own region, then a representative would sit on the national commission.

Regional committees would each prepare a list of truths, virtues, ideas, feelings, thoughts and objectives that would represent their areas. The national commission would then meet to find common ground among all or almost all of the submissions by the regional committees.

Each regional/state committee would be charged with the responsibility of preparing a list of what characteristics are representative of their area and what objectives the people of that area want for themselves in the future. Think of it this way: if we had a wish list of everything we would want the people of our country to represent, what would those individual points be?

At the national level, the NFC would look for common elements within all or most of the regional submissions. After careful consideration, this commission would consult various organizations that represent communities of people for their input.

The next step would be to prepare this material for presentation to the citizens of the country or region for their consideration. Citizens would have the opportunity to vote on whether or not they want each point to be taught in schools as a characteristic or value of their part of the country.

Voting on the questions would ideally be done at the time that the census is taken. In most countries, a formal census is taken every ten years.

When a decision is reached through voting, all citizens can be made aware of the results and their implications. That decision will be final and non-negotiable until the next round ten years later. The final form of the national document will apply to every citizen in every region of the country. It would also affect how legislators prepare new laws, as these would have to reflect the will of the people.

For political bodies that make laws and bylaws, no law or regulation could be passed that would contravene one or more of the objectives, either the national ones or the ones for that region. These objectives would have the same effect as the constitution of the nation and its amendments.

The objectives would have a more pervasive impact on education systems than on political systems. One of the things that has been lacking in our education systems has been values. Values will be put back into education through this program.

For children who do receive good value training and have good role models to follow at home, a problem exists at present. These children often find themselves with conflicting feelings when they go into their own communities as they grow and find that the values taught to them by their parents were not the values they find among other people in their community.

This would be torture for these young people. Many would not be able to hold their ground against such overwhelming evidence of conflicting values. Should they follow the values of their friends and neighbors and raise the worry of their parents, thus creating the possibility of a parent/child conflict or split? Or should they hold with the values taught by their parents and subject themselves to the scorn of their peers and others in the community?

This happens, folks. It happens now among children in all kinds of families. It's no wonder we adults don't understand why our adolescent children act so strangely.

We now have the means to correct this conflict. It will take time, but we can reach our objectives. And each of us can contribute to these objectives in our own way.

These objectives will now form the basis for many of the programs of the early years of elementary school, up to grade three at least.

Remember the four bases of the pyramid of our learning system: parents, education, community and peers. If we have schools teaching the same values and objectives to all children at an early age, we have two bases of the pyramid already working together: education and the peer group. If the parents of these children voted for the values as objectives to be taught in their local schools, then we have at least support, if not actual role models for their children. The third base is covered.

This would bring us back to the fourth base of the pyramid, the community. We may recall that television and movies were included as part of the community that influences the child. Now parents will have guidelines they can use themselves when deciding which television programs and movies they should allow their young children to watch. And they'll know that they'll have the support of their neighbors.

As for older children, they should be asked to join the protest against unsuitable viewing material. When the decision is made for an adolescent and enacted on his behalf, the young person aspiring to be an adult considers that to be censorship or, more specifically, restriction of freedom which they waited so long to enjoy. But when these young people are included as part of the decision making, they feel empowered. This is what they have been waiting for. This is what they lack so much in our society, to be recognized as being able to make a positive contribution to the world they live in. They want to feel that they are responsible, connected, acknowledged.

With a significant social movement on their side, adolescent young people who are asked to join in a boycott of unsuitable viewing material will find not conflict but a spirit of mutual support. Now everyone is working together. The teens will feel part of the power group because their community has recognized that they have a right to control their own behavior. They would not do this just because their parents want them to. They would want to join a massive movement that makes them feel a part of the adult community.

Young people who have felt dissociated from their community, especially the community of adults, will now feel that they are a part of it. Indeed, they will know that they will be the leaders of it in a few years. This sort of program takes place in political parties now. There are "young" versions of many political parties that follow a similar program to the traditional versions run by the senior members.

Right now, many young people feel isolated from their communities. Estranged. Alienated. We read about them almost daily in the newspapers. Think about who is catering to these feelings of alienation. In many cases, the people who are embracing these confused and isolated young people are the very people we would not choose as role models for them. We adults have become masters at telling young people what's wrong with them and their culture. What we have not done, in many cases, is to teach them the culture, values and beliefs we believe they should adopt.

In other words, we rail against the role models we don't like but fail to act as positive role models ourselves. Young people fill the gap with whomever will accept them and teach them. But teach them what? Is it what we would want them to learn? If not, then we must make changes, to adapt to conditions that exist at present for our young people so that the environment in which they grow and learn may be better controlled or managed.

When a community of people moves together against the purveyors of viewing material that is considered to be unsuitable and anti-social in nature, those producers will take notice. If the community moves in an adversarial way, the producers will gain the support of the very young people we want to help. However, if the community moves to include the young people in the program to starve out the producers of unsuitable material, the producers will soon change their ways. They are, after all, in business to make money. And they make a huge amount of money from young people.

If those young people are demanding viewing material of a more superior nature, then producers will make it available. If a market is created, the producers will fill it. The most money is spent to fill the biggest market. So if the biggest portion of the market demands a better quality of material, the producers will comply.

Would young people demand different viewing material? They will if they have been taught what is of better quality, if they have been exposed to good examples of it when they were younger. If they have experience with better-quality viewing material and reading material when they are young children, they will expect it and seek it out when they are older. Young children must be given the opportunity to become used to good quality.

The more we deny or refuse to allow their exposure to better-quality material when children are young, intentionally or not, the more they will seek out those who will appeal to them as they get older. Media offerings almost always appeal to the lowest common denominator, the material that will attract the most people. This may not be the best that is available, but it has the biggest audience.

Young people want to learn about their culture, the culture of adults of their country. But the adults confuse them with conflicting messages, with hypocrisy. "Do what I say, not what I do." They see adults breaking laws, avoiding taxes, cheating neighbors, exhibiting behavior with no common morals or values that they can detect. So they choose a different road. They believe they are creating their own culture, one they can accept, one they feel they can control, even if it is not perfect.

They are not really creating it, as they believe. It's being created for them by those who expose their own morals and values to them, through music and visual arts and fashion. Ask an adolescent why she chooses to wear what she does and we may be given the impression that she wants to be different. But follow her to school and see how much the same all these "different" people are. Their values are being molded by commercial enterprises. Not by us. Not by the young people who buy the clothes.

The time to expose children to a unified culture of values and morals is as early as possible. If this can be done right after birth, all the better. But we should prepare a list of the morals and values that we want children to learn, so that parents will know what to stress. We had better teach parents what they need to know to be the mentors of the upcoming generation.

We had better get an organized program that includes these values and morals into our schools in the primary years of the elementary grades. At this stage, the school programs can be taught by professionals, people who are trained to teach all children to think in like ways.

We'll have to give the education systems our approval to teach values and morals, though not through religion. We'll have to give them guidance as to just what should be taught, through our voting procedure.

We'll have to support what the education systems are teaching. And we'll have to back that up with a consistent effort to portray similar values to our children at home.

In the movie *Field of Dreams* Kevin Costner's character built a baseball diamond in the middle of a corn field and coined the now famous saying, "if you build it, they will come." We can relate that to our new programs in the education systems of our country. If we teach it, they will learn. Children do learn what they are taught in school. We must see that our children are taught what we want them to learn.

The three R's are necessary, to be sure. But children need more. We need to give our educators the guidance and support they require to be able to teach what we want children to know, and insist that our curricula adopt and teach these things before the children need them, not after it is too late.

Young children can learn values and morals. They can understand concepts. They create their own concept of how their world works, based on what their senses tell them for the first few years of their lives. We need to teach them, not let them learn on their own and reach inappropriate and unacceptable conclusions because of lack of information. They understand concepts, even though they may be intellectually incapable of understanding and learning certain skills.

The brains of young children are prepared to understand concepts because their neural networks are trained from their earliest stages to comprehend these and to formulate these from what they see and hear. They can only learn certain intellectual skills later, as their brains become conditioned to that sort of learning.

Young children are ready to learn morals and values. They need and want to know what people think, how they think, what they do. They want to learn what's right and what's wrong. They should be taught what's right, not just learn it by deduction (experience). That is, if we only teach pre-school children what is wrong, by chastising them, the only "right" they know is what is "not wrong." That is, "wrong" means getting caught. Let's teach them what's right. What we believe is right. They are willing and ready learners.

Then they will have these morals and values to carry with them into their teen years. What children are not taught at home, before they go to school, must be taught in school. This must not be left to chance, as we have done for so long and to such unpleasant ends.

Even though they will not understand the subtleties and nuances of quality work in the arts, music, visual arts and so on, they will develop a concept of what's good. They will learn what's valuable. Teach them what's good and why it is. Teach them what's not good and why it fails to meet the standards of our society.

We must ensure that what we teach at home and at school is more direct and more intensive than what they will learn elsewhere. Children spend more time in school and watching television than doing anything else other than sleeping. We have the opportunity to teach them in a controlled environment just what we believe they should learn.

The culture that is dominant for them, that of their home, their school, their community and their peers, will become the culture they accept as their own. Especially if it's consistent. They won't lack for culture, such that they must seek it elsewhere. We will actually teach them what they want to know, what we believe they need to know, what we believe they should know.

Parents did for thousands of years after the beginning of our species, as part of the systems of bands and tribes of people. Somewhere the importance of a similar cultural and social training for all children got lost. Now it's time to pull ourselves together again.

There will be rough spots for the first while, as the program begins and takes effect. However, if we focus on the objectives, a new generation of young people will grow up with values that represent the large majority of citizens of the country.

Those minorities who want to make money from teaching destructive values to children will then have an uphill struggle. They will have lost their ready and willing audience.

In the past, we grew up with certain television shows that were favorites. Remember one sitcom and one drama. Now think of one recent sitcom and one drama. Set aside the technological improvements. Has the production not changed dramatically? The quality of production is far better than in the past. The writing has improved greatly because the audience has demanded it. The producers responded when the audience demanded better. When the producers failed to meet the demands of the audience, as has happened with the major television networks, substitutions came in, such as cable specialty channels, video games and the glorious world of the Internet.

Someone is always ready to satisfy the needs of an audience.

A viewer of the various Star Trek series, for example, could compare the classic series of the Sixties and the series of today. The technology improved immensely, but so did the production values. As we grew, the technology and production values of all television programs grew with us, be it drama, sitcom or sci-fi. It grew because we demanded it. We would not watch productions of lesser quality now any more than we would want to watch a television program in black and white.

If we want change, we have it within our power to make things change. We can't do it alone, and we don't need to. We can join with others who believe the same way as we do and make things happen.

We can make a difference together.

Let's do it. Let's do what no other civilization before us has even been able to contemplate, make a major change, on a national scale, in the direction of our parental and school training systems.

We have the technology to make it happen.

If we have the will, we can do it.

Preparing the Guardians of Humanity

GUARDIANS of humanity? That's us. It's a challenge to argue that the present generation of adults has done much to protect our species from itself and our home-land from degradation at our hands. We know that this is important and becoming more critical. Our only hope is to prepare our children in such a way that they will believe it their responsibility to protect and value life and our home in nature. As Major John McCrae said in his poem of the Great War, "In Flanders Fields", "To you from failing hands we throw/ The torch . . ."

During the early ages of the human species, the hunter-gatherer, pre-agricultural era, children were with their parents for almost their entire youth, twenty-four hours a day, until they reached the age of maturity. Children learned what they needed to know as they lived their lives within their tribe.

Then they took a mate, had children and stayed in almost constant contact with their family grouping within the tribe. Teaching the young what they needed to know was not just a parental role, but a tribal responsibility as well. What was good for the tribe was good for each individual member of it.

In the predominantly agricultural era, children spent time with their parents whenever they were not required to be elsewhere, such as at school or running errands or playing. They learned what life was like, what work was, how they should behave and the skills they needed to know within the family grouping. Neighbors and school helped. What was good for the family was good for each individual member of it.

In later times, children stayed at home with mother while father was out earning the daily bread at a factory. Mothers, who have always been the primary care providers for children and the parent who had the most direct influence over behavior of children in a large majority of cases, allowed their husbands to believe that the male was the head of the household.

This meant that males in the family had particular roles to fill, especially ones as income earners. This was reinforced especially when the father died as a result of disease or war injury and the oldest male child had to take a role of male responsibility in the family.

If a mother died, the father searched diligently for a replacement female figure for the family. The personal value placed on motherhood and fatherhood was so high that many women married widowed fathers and raised their children rather than go through life unmarried.

Historically, survival of the family has been a primary goal, as it is with all species. What helped the family to survive was good and was expected of and by each member of it. Family objectives were accepted.

Training of children was considered to be mostly involved with teaching males their roles as adult males (bread-winners) and females their roles as adult females (mothers and wives). Less consideration was given to their roles as parents than to their roles as adults of their particular gender. Girls would be women, boys would be men. The parenting role would be learned more than ever before by example, rather than by teaching, by the time of the industrial era.

Male children were taught to be adult males, less so male parents. What they learned about being fathers they picked up by observing their own parents. Similarly, female children were taught to be adult females, including the skills of catching the right male with whom to raise a family. There was less emphasis than before on their future roles as mothers. This was a clear change from earlier times in human history when the roles of mother and father were taught by parents and grandparents.

With this watering down of emphasis on the future roles of children as parents, the degree of parenting skills among young adults became weaker. The live-in examples that parents gave to their own children no longer had the strength of their ancient ancestors. Parents no longer knew what they should know to be parents.

In postindustrial times, particularly in the past few decades, mothers must work at jobs outside of the home to support the family financially. This means that children spend very little time with their parents. During the past half-century, working parents spent little time teaching the role of parent to their children because they believed that their parental role had been fulfilled as long as their children grew up to maturity and took their place in society.

Being a parent has come to mean ensuring that children grow to become adults. People want to be as good parents as they know how. However, many have lost the knowledge of parenting and the skill of reading the needs of children that was gained over thousands of years.

The role of parent has been diluted to the point where parent as protector and provider of food, clothing and shelter has become more important than their former role as teacher of the values and mores of the community. What is necessary to help a young person reach the age of majority without experiencing death, serious injury, self inflicted harm or prison has become the primary objective.

As parents were less available to provide these guarantees of safety and security, governments took over part of the responsibility and passed laws on an unprecedented scale to punish parents who were so careless as to raise a child who violated norms, who did not understand how to behave properly. Guilt was added to the responsibilities of parents, but not training in good parenting.

In their frustration with the rising tide of problems with young people, particularly in their teen years, governments passed laws to force everyone to be cautious about doing anything that might cause bodily injury. Seat belts, child vaccinations and workplace safety laws are examples of legislation designed to prevent physical injury and disease.

Insurance companies, at one time the providers of protection against loss as a result of natural disasters and fires, now must raise their premiums to cover the costs of liability coverage because of damages from litigation, as people consider good health their right.

Physical health is more important than social, emotional and intellectual health.

Governments, always at their best when legislating guilt and establishing punishment, continue to pass laws to fault parents who have little time to spend with their growing children due to having to earn a living to support them and not knowing what to teach the kids anyway. Politicians know it's cheaper to pass laws and punish a few parents than to teach people what they need to know to be good parents and avoid the problems in the first place. Laws cost little. Education costs more.

While we as a society have focused our attention on the physical well-being of our citizens over the past half century, we have neglected, as a society, their social, emotional and psychological well-being. The results are in the newspapers daily. We will endanger our intellectual well-being in the coming decades if we do not take corrective measures soon.

Schools are responsible for the intellectual training of our young people. But young people cannot learn properly if they are suffering from anxiety, which they get from disorientation and confusion resulting from their social alienation from the adult world around them. That anxiety can be due to social problems with peers, emotional problems originating at home, psychological problems due to long exposure to anti-social music, movies or many other possible causes.

Something was lost in the "progress" of our modern world. Responsibilities for the upbringing of our young people, the total upbringing not just physical, were not just lost, but forgotten. At this stage, many adults who are not raising youngsters themselves openly deny any responsibility for the proper, healthy growth of our younger generations. They are, however, ready and eager to acknowledge the existence of problems and to blame others. We all seem know who to blame for the problems of our society. Someone else.

If we could fault someone for everything that is wrong with our society, clear the slate completely, process it all through the courts, send hundreds or thousands to prison, nothing would have been done to correct the problem.

The solution can begin when the next child is born. That child will not wait for us until we are ready. We have to change our way of doing things.

We must face the situation as it exists today and take measures to bring our society into line with the way we want it to be, instead of the way it's drifting now. Can it be done? Not if we keep saying that it can't. We can make anything happen if enough of us want it to happen. Didn't our parents tell us when we were children that we could be anything we wanted to be? Well, we could and we can. We can be the co-architects of a new society in our country.

No one thought that a whole society could change, so our parents didn't tell us that. But this is the twenty-first century. Now it is possible. Technology has allowed us to become more connected than ever before in human history. Let us become the force for the good and the positive before someone else creates a large force for the negative. Right now, the negative forces have not united. Now is the time to bring the good guys together.

In the 1980s, the term "quality time" was invented to justify the lack of time parents spent with their children. Quality time, so the story went, was somehow better than something else, presumably non-quality time. Quality time was time a parent spent playing or doing activities specifically with his or her children. Quality time was time that parent and child enjoyed each other's company and the activity they shared.

Sad to report, quality time did not include the teaching of what kids really need to know.

Somehow it was believed that having fun together was the primary role that a parent was to play. In fact, what may be called non-quality time spent with children (presumably doing the normal chores of life) might be more important than the fun time of which there is so little.

Few parents involve their kids with those family chores because they can do them faster themselves and because the kids think they are boring and raise a fuss about doing them. Kids who were not involved with working together on family chores as young children don't want to begin when they are older. Young children think that working with mommy is fun, while older kids believe their parents are dumping new work onto them simply because they are older.

Children learn about their world by observing their parents doing everyday things, including spending time with their offspring. As the time spent with children in any form decreases, much time for learning by example (role modeling) is missed. Often children learn by example better when their parents are not at their best during the quality time. At those times kids learn what being an adult is like, not always perfect or glamorous.

Where else can young children learn about their world, the world of adults? They learn with everything they do. They learn when they spend time alone (what are they doing when they are alone?). They learn when they are with other young children (most of this time is supervised by adults who are interested in the kids being quiet and not hurting themselves). They may learn a little when they are with grandparents, family members and babysitters, but this is limited, however valuable.

This leave us with the great teacher, television. As much as we may deny that television influences children or claim that little proof has been shown of it, television is the main teacher of our children today. Ask a child who his heroes are. They will all be television characters. Ask a child who he wants to be like when he grows up. Odds are that he will answer with the name of a television character.

Ask a child to name five characters on television. Find out about those characters and see if those are people or fictional beings that we would like our children to model themselves after. Chances are good that the exercise will be frightening if we really think it through.

Some studies have suggested that a child learns half of everything he will learn in his entire lifetime by the time he reaches his fifth birthday. That comes to about twenty-five thousand waking, active hours of intensive learning during that period. Very intensive learning. What and who are the child learning from? What is the source? Is this a good source?

Television should not be abolished. It can be a very useful and helpful tool in educating children. This is about parental responsibilities. Parents need to be taught how to be parents. They need to know how to teach their children by precept and example. Education systems and governments must play a role in this before it's too late. Parents today, as hard as they may try, don't know what to do.

It has often been said that a young person of sixteen can take a course, pay a little cash and get a license to drive a car, but no training at all is required to become a parent. What happens after that statement is made? Generally a lull in the conversation, as no one knows what to do about it. The statement, however valid and sensible, is not powerful enough to prompt anyone to do anything about it. Chances are it's because they don't know what to do.

A young adult spends a small amount of time studying how a person should drive, what the rules of the road are, how to drive safely and defensively, before taking a test. But that same young person has been watching the bad habits of his parents and other supposedly responsible adults driving on the roads for many years. Which will be of greater influence?

The lessons about parenting within the family are getting fewer and shorter with passing generations, as more parents spend more time out of their homes and away from their children. Television provides children with abundant examples of dysfunctional families. Those who doubt this should imagine what life would be like if we lived in the families we see on television. We know these families are not the norm. Children do not. Television, to them, is one of their primary teachers of behavior, one of the ways that a child can see an entire family in action.

Parents can't afford to quit their jobs and stay home with their children. Yet they can't afford to be away from their children so much that they neglect their responsibilities as role models. The result is either anxiety or suppression of that concern. Many parents just pretend that everything is fine and carry on with their lives.

The only hope is for our education systems to fill a need that they have not had before, that they are not prepared for now, that they do not have the resources to provide for and for which they do not yet have the support from their communities. That support must come officially from governments. Governments will provide that support only if there is a majority of support from the people who elect them. That means us.

What do we believe that parents should be teaching their young children? We may not have all of the answers, but we likely have ideas. Other people have the same ideas. So let's get together and express these ideas to our governments and have them change our education systems to provide this guidance.

Classes in Parenting for New Parents

We can't have school classes for babies. But we can have classes for new parents and people who are about to be parents. With the popularity of pre-birth classes, there is little doubt that soon-to-be parents will attend these classes. At present, they are not offered or at least are not widely available in each community.

What specifically should be taught in those classes? Here we should be descriptive rather than prescriptive. Dr. Benjamin Spock made pronouncements about discipline of children in the 1960s and these were followed religiously by millions of parents for decades to come.* Many parents later regretted some of what they had done. Dr. Spock himself repudiated some of his statements.

The thoughts and course material suggested in Appendix A are suggestions only. What is in this book will be general content. Specific content of these courses should be decided upon in each area, in consultation among various components of the community.

What is important to realize is that the outcome of the exercise must be an attitude to be developed in a child, an approach to life and his or her place in our society. Facts, the content of school-type courses for centuries, mean little in this context. Concepts are everything. A new parent or parent-to-be must have a certain understanding about his or her role in the development of the offspring which has been created and is now in his or her charge. He must learn how to be a good parent.

A young child can learn concepts easily. That's how a child makes sense of his world. Think of it this way. A child could not devise a concept of what his world is all about by assembling facts and skills learned in school. As important as we believe the spoken word is, children learn by watching adults and their peers, by listening to what adults and other kids say among themselves, by smelling, tasting and touching.

A human cannot function properly by learning only facts taught in school or at home. A child begins to understand his world from the moment of birth, likely even before that. The child certainly begins to learn before birth, though we don't know how much at this stage.

Imagine trying to understand mathematics by learning multiplication tables and the processes of addition, subtraction, multiplication and division alone. Without putting mathematics in context of the life each of us lives, math has no significant meaning. That is certainly one reason why some children have a terrible time learning math. For them, math is a series of abstract symbols. They never learn the concepts of math, so they don't understand it as being part of their world. Two plus two equals four means little until they understand the concepts of two and four and the significance of having four of something, rather than just two.

An older child learns concepts slower, more cautiously. An adult learns them with difficulty because he has so much else in his mind cluttering the learning process, including his own experiences growing up in his own family.

The adults of today grew up in the twentieth century. That century has passed and so has that way of life. What we need is something that represents who we are, while presenting it in a manner that is fitting for life in the new century.

There will be surprisingly few similarities between the life of a child born today and the early life of the parents who conceived it. These new parents need to understand that they must conduct themselves and their lives differently from the way their parents and grandparents did. There may not have been anything wrong with the way these people were raised. But a new way of life is upon us and we must adapt to taking greater responsibility for the new lives we bring into the world. Each new child is a small step in the creation of the world of the future. We must make each step a positive one.

The course material suggested in Appendix A holds equally as well for all adults as for parents. As all adults form the part of the Pyramid of Living System side known as the community, these points are important to everyone. Only new parents and parents-to-be need to take a course. Expecting adults who are not parents to take such a course would not be practical. However, once children who are products of the new system grow to be adults, they will form an effective, positive and supportive community base for children of those years when they are adults.

This course could be prepared and conducted under the auspices of local boards of education. These people are professional teachers who have the skills to present such courses for adults in an effective manner. They know how to conduct role-playing scenes, how to present background to make their points more effective, how to repeat messages for emphasis without seeming repetitive and boring, how to explain the reasons, whys and wherefores in order that the whole program makes sense. They know how to put a professional course together.

Only teachers with experience in adult education or with a flare for it should be selected for teaching leaders for courses of this kind. No teacher should be forced to teach adults. Many would find it intimidating. They have not been trained for such a role. Some could handle it capably.

An alternative would be for a school board to engage the services of a professional human resources service organization that specializes in making inspirational presentations to adults.

The key would be effectiveness, no matter which route is chosen. The objective would be to present a course that will be remembered and implemented effectively for at least ten years, all delivered within a program that would last no more than ten evening classes. That requires some special people. A boring program will fail.

After the role of being a parent, the role of teaching new parents will be the most important one in our society.

A school board has the skills to monitor the effectiveness of the program, so may be given the resources and the responsibility to supervise this important program. Each school board would be required to have "student" parents evaluate the effectiveness of each program and instructor. Program adjustments could be made accordingly. Multiple negative comments from students should be addressed, as they signify ineffective presentation of the materials, which would mean that the course matter would not be retained by the students.

Again it should be noted that the points of the program outlined in this book should not be considered to be prescriptive or all-inclusive. They are starting points. Course content should reflect the values that the majority of the community wishes to emphasize to new parents. The list of points provided represent only values that many may believe are significant enough to be included in all courses. Majority wishes of each community (school board area, city, region, province or state) must prevail.

A program for new parents about how to be good parents should be voluntary, just as birthing classes are now. But each community should make it a social priority to encourage each set of parents to attend such classes.

There should not be a charge to attend such classes, as both provision of the classes and attendance at them should be a social responsibility for which everyone must play a role.

There should be a certificate awarded at the end of the course. Receiving this certificate should include a combination of attendance and the passing of an evaluation. This evaluation must be in a form that makes passing it accessible for everyone.

That means that students must be able to express what they have learned from the course in a way that is suitable for them. A multiple choice answer test, for example, would be a bad way of evaluating a student as it depends heavily on cultural background, intellect, memorization and test-writing skills of the student and the test-making biases of the teachers.

An oral interview is a possible way of evaluation, provided that there is not too much pressure put on the student by a panel that is socially distanced from the student during the evaluation.

Allowances must be made for people who are not literate and who have limitations in other ways on their abilities to project their knowledge in a test situation.

If possible, the test should be directed more to testing the attitude of the student parent toward the responsible position he or she will soon assume as parent of a baby. Memorization of facts for the purpose of passing a test of this sort will be a waste of time, effort and resources.

What action should be taken if a student-parent is deemed to have an attitude toward children and parenthood that would not be in the best interests of a child? This would have to be decided on an individual basis.

One thing would be clear: the soon-to-be-parent has just identified a future problem if he or she comes across as having a negative attitude during the test. Like an infection that is not cured early, this is a problem that will surely become serious in years, even decades, to come. There should be no room for passing off a guaranteed future problem on the basis that it has not yet reached full blossom. We did that in the past, in our associations with friends and acquaintances, to our peril.

Incentive can be added for each parent to attend and pass such courses by having one level of government give a significant tax reduction when both parents pass the course and something less when only one parent passes the course. Such tax reduction could be for a period of five years after the first year in which the young child appears on an income tax return.

Although attendance at this course should be considered a social obligation, we must face the reality that incentives will be needed to encourage participation by some young parents. An incentive program based on income tax reduction will increase the participation level for those who might otherwise claim that they do not have time for such a course. It also recognizes the importance that is placed on good parenting.

This course can also address a situation that is becoming more prevalent in North American countries. Most North American families where two parents work are not producing enough children to maintain the population. That is, two parents are not raising two children, in a majority of these families. Population numbers are being held closer to maintenance levels by families on long-term social assistance having more than two children. It is as important that children of these families receive the same parental advantages as those of working parents.

Population levels in North American countries are growing, rather than the reverse, because of immigration of families from other countries and other cultures. Birth rate alone is not enough to maintain the population levels. The main criterion for such immigration is often that one adult has professional skills that are urgently needed by the new country.

Culture of the country of origin of these people is not considered as a qualification criterion, and it must continue to be so. But classes of the type being discussed here would ensure than parents of immigrant families, people who have not grown up with the same cultural norms as predominates in their new country, will have the same program to prepare them for parenthood as parents who were born here.

A country can have customs and a national culture distinct from the culture that we practice at home, the one learned from parents. This is the time to ensure that there is a national culture on which everyone can agree and which immigrants and people born in the country will learn.

There is little need for the family's culture to clash with the national culture regarding parenthood and child rearing. If this national culture is taught to young children, to new parents and to new immigrants who propose to apply for citizenship, the possibilities for conflict will be minimal. The less devoted governments are to making this a part of our national culture, the greater the chance for family problems that develop into social problems in the community.

As it is in other countries where the will of the majority rules, the will of the majority of voters in our country regarding parenthood and child rearing must rule. The time for permitting emotional side issues that will put this program off the track has passed. We must look at the greater issue before us now. The future of our country is at stake. Those who endeavor to sidetrack the program will do so because they have something to lose personally from its taking full effect. Usually this will involve money.

A wise government will co-opt special interest groups by involving them in the program in some way. Movie and television producers, for example, can be helped to see how cooperating with this program is to their advantage, with a large new audience to satisfy.

Are our governments wise?

Don't answer that. It's our job to see that they become that way.

---

* Dr. Benjamin Spock, *The Common Sense Book of Baby and Child Care*

25
Preparing Citizens for the Twenty-First Century

Now it's time for our kids to hit the streets. In the previous chapter we discussed the period of a person's life that is believed to include half of all the learning that person will do in his or her lifetime. Now that the first five years of life are covered, let's look at the next few, the ones where the school system takes over the primary education of the child.

These are the years that will determine how fit a young person is to take his or her place in the world of young adults and mature adults, for education and for work, as an individual, as a family member and as a member of our society. These are the years that will prepare a young person with the attitude with which he or she will approach the rest of his or her life. The first five are years of formulation; the next few are the years that give direction to a life.

By the age of five, a child of our new generation of children has learned basic concepts about her world, at least the small part of it she has seen. She knows what is right and what is wrong, at least in how her own behavior has been treated by her parents and others who have guided her. She knows how to treat others and how not to treat them, how to make a friend (in a rudimentary sense) and what to expect when she gets to school. She also knows that she can distinguish between herself and people who do bad things, and has concluded why she should try to do good.

She understands that there are people who do wrong, but that they will not succeed if they continue to do wrong. She knows that she must be diligent about living her life the way she should if she is to become what she is capable of being. She knows it's a big world out there and there is a great deal to learn about it. She is ready to learn.

She knows it is her responsibility to learn, to take advantage of the opportunities that will be presented to her in school and elsewhere to explore and to experience, to be and to grow. She knows this and believes it because she has been taught this by her parents, the people who have loved her and guided her for the past five years, her whole lifetime to that point.

But what will she learn in the first few years of her formal education? Traditionally, the highest priorities have been the three R's: reading writing and arithmetic. We know these are the most important skills in school. How do we know this? Because it has always been taught that way. Everyone should be able to read. Everyone should be able to write clearly and in an understandable manner. Everyone should be able to do mathematics. That's how it was always done.

But this is a new age. Now each person needs much more. The three R's were first stressed in schools as education basics a century and more ago. These were incorporated into the primary school curriculum in the days when some children would not get more than five years of schooling. If a child didn't get those elementary facts and skills into him by then, he might be illiterate for the rest of his life.

Attention! Attention! Today this amount of basic education qualifies a person to be functionally illiterate. Now we know that a person's real education does not start with his formal lessons in school. It begins five years earlier, at home, before he gets to school, and it continues for the rest of his life. This is not debatable. This is not an option. This is a given. It's a starting place. It's an essential part of our existence.

A basic education of one hundred years ago could qualify a person of the today to be functionally illiterate, a person unable to function properly in today's society. That is how much the world has changed in a century. In fact, most of that change happened in the past twenty years, so even adults that grew up in the middle part of the last century may have literacy problems, may have some difficulty understanding what is needed to conduct life safely and efficiently.

Let's understand this, North American society has been stressing literacy and the three R's for everyone for the past two hundred years. Ask anyone what children should be learning in the primary years of elementary school and the answer will almost always be "the basics" or "the three R's." If this has been so important for so long, how is it that so many people are functionally illiterate now? The answer is that there are other elements of learning that are missing from our education system, key skills without which learning the basics is difficult.

In 1987, the Southam newspapers group in Canada paid for a study that showed that one in four Canadians had serious literacy problems. Statistics Canada, a federal agency, conducted further tests that showed that nearly half of all Canadians have at least some literacy or reading problems. Think about it. One of every two people we meet has problems reading, understanding, remembering and putting it to use in their lives.

That might include us and we may not know it, though it's unlikely because we have made it this far through the book. It certainly includes many people we know, even if we do not have occasion to recognize it in them. Many people who have literacy problems are not aware of it because they have made adjustments to a lower level of quality of life without even knowing it. Just because we can read does not mean that we can understand everything we need.

Some people have what we call "closed minds," people who won't change their minds for anything. Chances are they are this way because this is their way of coping with their literacy deficit.

It's even possible that a person could have a literacy problem and still read this book. This book is not hard to understand. One reading level check of the first few pages of this chapter shows that it should be able to be read by someone with a grade seven reading ability. A person with a grade seven reading level will have difficulty coping with some written material that could be important to his life. Examples might be income tax returns or written conditions on a bill of sale (small print) or even the written instructions that come with a doctor's prescription.

Is this a modern problem? No, eighty percent of Canadian seniors scored low on the literacy scale noted above. These people received their basic skills education decades ago, when the three R's were the drill in elementary school. True, many of these people have let their skills slide due to lack of use. What have they used as a substitute? Television, in many cases. These people must have someone else do their income tax returns and they do not challenge erroneous problems on invoices because they are afraid to show that they don't really understand what is on these bills. To avoid embarrassment, they pay and keep quiet. They really don't understand what is going on in the world and always have an excuse why. Usually they say it's because they are too busy or have forgotten something. Mostly they are just afraid.

More recent studies in Canada, with larger numbers of participants, show that forty percent of Canadians between the ages of sixteen and sixty-five show a low rating on literacy skills. Fifteen percent were in the lowest rating. Immigrants were not included in that rating.[*]

The same study showed that fully one in five high school graduates did not have sufficient literacy skills to get even an entry-level job. That means that twenty percent of those who graduate from high school will not likely ever be able to have a job that requires use of their brains rather than their bodies. Jobs requiring brawn rather than brain are becoming fewer in developed countries.

Are the kids at fault? Are the schools at fault? Are the parents at fault? It doesn't matter. These people cannot function properly in today's environment. We need to stop trying to point the finger of blame and start trying to correct the problem at its source. Adults who want to improve their literacy skills have programs that are available to them in most Canadian and American communities. The problem is that most of these people are either not aware of their problem, as they have been hiding it for so long and have compensated for it in some way, or they are too embarrassed to admit it and ask for help.

This book is not about to address that problem, only to make us aware of it. We can make a difference for the future by adjusting the current education programs so that similar problems are avoided as much as possible in the future. Go back to the last paragraph and read the last sentence again, the one giving reasons why people with literacy problems will not seek help. We will need to remember these later. There could be a test, the test of life as it exists in our country now.

These reasons are excellent examples of a problem that can be overcome by a new style of program, one that will be discussed later in this chapter.

What does all of this have to do with the primary grades of elementary school, grades one to three? After all, the problem is in high schools or in the upper grades of elementary school. That has been the traditional thinking. The normal way of doing things was to blame it on the child for being too lazy to learn to read properly. Maybe that's so. Maybe not. Most children are not lazy, though some cannot function well given the set of circumstances in which they live. Kids don't want to be lazy. Lazy is boring. Any young person who says that what he does is boring is sending up a red flag, shooting off flares, sounding the sirens to tell us that something is wrong in his life. He is sending us a very strong message in a very significant way.

The child may have an attitude problem that prevents him from caring about reading or anything else that takes place in school. If the child has not been taught early in his life to understand that it is his responsibility to learn as much as he can in school, that he must make an effort to learn before the teacher can have any effect with her classroom program, then he will be lost by his mid teens. He also must know that he can ask for help and receive it.

Maybe the child who is unable to learn or who is disturbing others was not ready to learn to read in the primary grades when such things were being taught intensively. It happens. Access to reading and literacy programs must be easy for people of all ages. Let's consider an example. A child may not be ready to learn to read in the primary grades. The reasons may have to do with social skills, family background or a number of other factors. Do they matter now? They didn't receive attention in the past.

With barely adequate skills, a child may be able to get through high school. But that person will not have a chance to stand as an equal with his peers until he develops the social skills of his peer group. Once past the primary grades, it is extremely difficult to improve reading skills, without help, let alone social skills.

Some children are ready to read before reaching the primary grades. They manage to read without the help of teachers in primary classrooms. Other children are not ready to read until past the primary grades. The reasons don't matter. There are programs for such young people. But not enough, apparently.

One in five Canadian young people manages to slip through to the end of high school without gaining the reading skills they need to function adequately as adults.

In the last century, these people could get along in menial jobs requiring no skills, just strong muscles. There are few jobs of that kind around now in North America, and there will be fewer still as the century wears on. These people will become those who fill the welfare rolls. Is it their own fault? It serves no purpose trying to find someone to blame. Let's just find a way to help these people to read when they need it. The faults and omissions of the past are not important to dwell on. Improvements for the future are. An adult with skills and hope can find a job.

Needed life skills are not being taught to many young people early enough to make a significant difference in their lives. Teaching of life skills in a professional way should be done in the primary grades of school. There are those who will argue that children of these ages are too young. But these people argue that no one should be taught the way life really is in the world today until they are adults. A person can't cope with life, especially its downturns, when he or she doesn't understand it before the serious problems arise.

The time to teach these skills, these lessons about life, is before the child needs them. By the time a child really needs knowledge and skills about life, it is too late to teach them. Most families that break up, for example, do so after a first child is past the primary grades of school. Since not many families have more than one child now, compared with past centuries, then the primary grades would seem to be the ideal age to teach these important lessons of life.

Understanding what happens when a family breaks up and how to cope with it is important to the functioning of anyone. Ask a divorced adult how confused and directionless she was when her marriage ended. There is confusion and groping for what to do next. Many are unprepared to cope with a devastating event that happens to about half of all marriages in western societies. For a child with no idea of why her world is collapsing, it's the end of life as she knows it.

Life skills learned young will be able to be used for the rest of a person's lifetime. Even when a person is not suffering from a downturn in the eventualities of life, there is almost always someone else he or she knows who is. These friends or acquaintances need help. We should be helping our friends when they need it, just as we would hope that they would help us in our time of need. Most people don't know how to help.

There's a greater need than ever for people to help each other so that the most personally devastating parts of these very unfortunate situations can be avoided, if possible. We can read about these tragedies in the daily newspaper or on television. By the time they hit the news, they upset everyone. We say there is too much violence in the world. Some say that people should be able to carry weapons to defend themselves. We can avoid most of these problems if we tend to what is necessary in young lives before the serious difficulties begin later. Prevention is much easier and cheaper than cure.

Many television programs or movies show a child who feels guilty because the parents broke up, feels that if he had only behaved better the family would still be together. These programs came about because the situations are around us every day. We adults know the child should not feel guilt. Parents in the process of breaking up tend to focus on their own difficulties and lose track of the lives of their most important life function, their children.

The child should have been taught that it is the parents who are responsible when a family breaks up. The child should also have been taught how to cope with the situation so that he does not become a victim of the people who have the responsibility for caring for his welfare. He needs to know how to speak up and say how he feels to his parents. He also needs to know that each of his parents loves him.

The time to learn how to cope with such a situation is before he needs it, usually in the early elementary grades. This is not to suggest that a teacher must go into gruesome details about how devastating a "messy" divorce can be to each member of a family. However, when half or more of all families are breaking up while children are still in school, we must wake up and face the reality that someone must be responsible for preparing children for this tragic event, should it happen. Parents are not doing that.

No one wishes family breakup on anyone. We can't do much about how badly the adults feel when this happens. But we can do a lot more to prevent the very bad effects that it wreaks on children who are the real victims. We may not be able to make them immune to the hurt, but we can teach them that the breakup is not their fault, that their parents still love them as much, and how to make the best of the situation so that they do not get lost in the chaos. We can teach them how to cope.

The time for this is in the elementary grades of school, grades one to three. Why not kindergarten or before? Two reasons. First, these are the years when teaching children is the primary responsibility of the parents, not of the school. Second, many social functions are already being taught in kindergarten and junior kindergarten, in some cases even in nursery schools and day-care centers. These are not necessarily authorized functions of these institutions, so they may not be covered properly or adequately.

As we saw earlier in this book, much time is wasted in the primary grades due to children not being ready to learn what they are being taught. Time can be made in the primary curriculum by changing the focus to include the teaching of life skills. The teaching time that is lost when curriculum material is pushed from the primary grades can be made up in junior and higher grades because the social problems that exist now in these higher grades will be fewer. Thus less time will be taken up with correcting behavioral problems for the rest of the years of education beyond the primary grades.

Will children be interested in learning life skills? That will depend on the way it's presented, just like anything else. If it's taught as facts to be memorized, then it will be a complete loss and will not be either absorbed or believed by the children. However, if they believe that they are learning some things that they will need to know and be able to use in the coming few years, they will play close attention. A teacher has little difficulty getting students to learn something when the kids know it's important to them. The teacher doesn't need to prove it. Children will accept the word of a trusted teacher and dig in to learn.

In general, kids love to learn about what it's like to be an adult.

Kids are asked to learn facts and skills they may not need as adults. The concepts and information they should be learning in the lower grades will help them before they even leave elementary school. They will listen and be excited about participating in discussions. Most of them will already have some information about these matters, so they will happily participate in order to learn more. After all, they will be learning about the lives they will live. The lives they live now.

The content of the primary school curriculum should be within the control of the levels of government that hold it now. These governments, usually at the state or provincial level in North America, should tell ministries and departments of education, in general terms, what they should be teaching, based on community norms surveyed at the local level. The ways of conducting these studies is covered in other chapters of this book. The ministries and departments of education will then pass directives to the local boards of education which will implement the programs.

These governments must also make available funds to cover the costs of developing and implementing curriculum changes. Citizen voters can make their wishes known on this subject at election time, if not before.

Ministries and departments of education should develop curricula to meet needs that have been identified. They must provide the tools and resources to each school board to ensure that these curricula can be implemented properly and fully. This will require a significant change from the usual form of top-down, demand-rich, resources- and tools-poor programs that school boards and senior levels of education have put forward in the past, claiming to voters that no additional tax money was required.

The fact is that school boards have put curricula into effect in the past by dictating their implementation to schools and teachers without giving them the resources and tools to do it well. It has been common for teachers to be given a new curriculum at the beginning of the school year, but nothing else to help them implement it in their classrooms. No new books, no materials, no lesson ideas, no assistance from senior educators or resource people to any extent. Just an edict, a command.

This is the government style of doing business—pass a law and expect that everyone will change their behavior. It doesn't work with the adult world and it doesn't work with schools. Teachers must be told what to teach, how to go about it, and be given the resources to do the job properly. And, importantly, they must be given instruction on how to do this new job effectively, including the reasons why it is important to their community, their children and their country.

The previous sentence should not come as a shock. Teachers need to learn too. Constantly. They need their instructors to be knowledgeable, resourceful and caring, just like all teachers are supposed to be.

The government method has not worked well in the past. If it fails, each level of the education system always had another level or two to blame. And rightly so. But this time failure cannot be an option for our future. There is too much at stake.

There is one part of the financial factor that must be considered locally in each area. Local control of the proposed program will mean that money must be raised locally, usually through taxes, in order to implement this program. If it's done on a state or provincial level, costs can be shared among all taxpayers in the jurisdiction. If it's done on a national level, sharing across many boundaries can minimize costs, but this will mean giving up local control over the curriculum. Who controls the purse controls the curriculum.

From a political standpoint, where the funds will be raised might be a sticky point. The level of government that raises the additional funds should be the level that is responsible for the outcome of the programs. This cost-benefit responsibility might make municipal governments and boards of education more inclined to want to share at least some of the responsibility with others, be they neighboring boards or across a state or province.

Just what should be taught? We should not be prescriptive about specifics of what must be taught. Citizens should have input and some level of control for their own areas. However, in order to get the process started, Appendix B offers some concepts, ideas, values and virtues that may be considered a beginning. Many more are possible and additional ones should be sought from the communities involved.

This is the time when people who are concerned about the future of education and the future of their society should have a say in the content or programs that will affect that future. This is democracy. This is government *by the people.*

New Education Program Topics for the Primary Grades

Before discussing changes to the school curricula, let's emphasize a few points. First, the list of topics suggested is in Appendix B. It's by no means exhaustive. It was not intended to be. It's meant to be a starting point for discussions of what should be taught in the new curriculum of the primary grades. Input for topics should be sought from every possible source, including parents and those who do not have children in the education systems now.

The list that is compiled for each area will have to be pared down and a method of excluding topics will have to be devised. This method should be made public, as everyone has a right to know how the decisions were made. While the decision about including or excluding each topic cannot be made by means of a plebiscite, voters have a right to know the rules for inclusion. This way they will have the tools by which they can exercise change in the rules if they feel it's necessary for their community or state.

Second, elaboration of each topic would be so long that it would require more space than this book will allow. A brief explanation will only be given if it is needed to help with understanding its intent.

Third, the list is not in any priority order of importance. Nor is it grouped in distinct sections. It was purposely left in a fairly random order so that each point can be given equal access to our attention.

Most people will think that the points listed in Appendix B will go way over the heads of children ages six to eight, in grades one to three. While it may be true that some of it will be above them, each topic that is raised at this age will be an introduction to something that adults believe children should know and understand as they get older. Much consideration will have to be given to how the material is presented. A good teacher know how to present material that her children will comprehend. They will understand if it is taught to them properly, with aids geared to their level rather than those of interest to older children or adults.

Should children be allowed to be kids, without having to learn anything about the real world ahead of them, as many people claim? Kids have lots of time to themselves for this pastime. Every young animal in nature spends its valuable and critical youth learning what it needs to know to be a successful adult. Human children must do the same. There is time for play and fun already in their lives. There must also be time set aside to teach the essentials to what they need to know for their future. The purpose of childhood is to prepare for a long and healthy adult life.

Consider this: we are prepared to teach young people the skills they need to know to function in the world of adult work. We do that in colleges, universities and special schools after high school. We try to do that in high school. But we do not teach young children what they need to know to be successful through their teen years. We don't teach them what they need to know to survive and thrive through high school, other than the academic subjects. Something is dreadfully lacking in the preparation we offer to our young people for the life ahead of them.

A guest on CBC Radio, in Canada, claimed that the top forty recordings for teenagers encourage the use of drugs.† While some lyrics were not explicit, the report said, each song had at least some words that gave the impression that drugs were good, if it did not specifically refer to some form of drug use. At what age do younger children begin to listen to this music? That is the age they are being exposed to this culture.

The report also quoted many adolescents as saying that they began their drug use because they were bored. Many television programs in both Canada and the United States have focussed on teens who have said they were bored. It's incredible that people who have a whole life ahead of them and an enormous need to learn as much as they can and experience what they are able are bored and doing nothing but wasting their time.

They have not been taught in their earlier years to believe that they must work hard to prepare themselves for life as an adult, that they have much to learn and only a limited time to learn it. They believe that they have an unlimited amount of time to waste before trying to catch up with their more aggressive peers. In fact, many do not even consider their own future. They are unable to understand that they will be required to account for their own lives within a few years. They are unwilling to accept that the responsibility for their future is their own.

The time to prepare them for what is required of them in their teen years is when they are very young. It's too late to try to repair what has been missed or improperly taught when these young people are embroiled in the anxieties of adolescence.

Each of us can do our part to help these young people learn that there is a life for them ahead, but we need help from a lot more people to help at lot more kids. There's no reason why we can't have a society of parents who know how to raise their children and young people who know what the life ahead of them is going to be like and how to manage it and cope with problems. We have to pull together to make it happen.

Young people have a different culture than the generation that employs them, either with part-time jobs during their school years or full-time later. They don't speak the same language, don't share the same values. This is an interesting point, as it tells us that we have not taught our children to join the same culture we have. Parents and the other bases of our pyramid are the teachers of culture. Children have not been taught the culture of their parents, which is one of the prime responsibilities of parents.

We assume that they will learn our culture by constant association with it. We don't actively teach our children what our culture is about in many cases.

If young people and their parents do not share the same culture, including beliefs and values, then where have the kids learned the culture they have? They learned it from the people who were more willing to teach them than their parents, the people they saw on television and in movies and heard and saw in music videos.

Think of the role models that we and our children see on television and in movies. For one thing, they rarely go to work. On the job, they are almost always playing tricks, having fun, cracking jokes. We find them cheating their employers and lying to their bosses. We laugh at these people, then expect our children will believe that they must do the opposite when they get their own jobs.

Where do kids learn what it's like to apply themselves to a work task? Where do they learn that they must be honest at work? Where do they learn that they owe their efforts and their concentration to their employers because that is why they are paid? The fact is that most kids do not have the opportunity to learn these things at home or at school. Some kids never learn. When they become like their role models on television, we wonder how they could have gone so wrong.

Though they may never have seen more than a few people in retail jobs and their own teachers actually working, we send them into the work world of adults as if they should somehow have learned a positive attitude toward work life and a beneficial set of values along the way. We expect them to be honest, upright and hard-working, though their role models on television have been anything but.

We expect our offspring to do the right things when they enter the world of work. We have no right to expect that if we have not taught our values to them. They need to know who we are, what we do, what we believe and how we act as adults. They must be taught these things or we can't expect that they should act the way we would like.

It seems simple. But we have stopped doing it.

It's time to start again.

---

*"A Nation In Denial," *Saturday Night*, September, 1999, 2-7
†*Here & Now*, CBC1, June 14, 2000

Moving to Action

WHAT can we do? Are there enough people who sincerely want to solve our worst social problems and improve the quality of life and the security of citizens to work together for change? From the point of view of an author proposing a major program such as TIA, these questions hang as critical mysteries.

The reason is that the answer depends on many people, each with the same intention to work together on beliefs and values that most of us hold in common.

Will anyone act on something that is relatively selfless, in a society amply endowed with individuals who are obsessed with their own welfare? At one time, there was doubt about whether anyone would even read a book about this topic. Many have already. They have written in with their support. Now we need at least some of the people in all communities, in all countries. We need to encourage others to read this book.

TIA is a product of the desires and wishes of people around the world, plus the author's own thoughts, plans, opinions and educated guesses. The positive thoughts and caring of one person can change an entire society, even the world, if enough people care to help. We must get other people to read this book so they will know what we know. Only when enough of us understand can we make a difference.

A few of us pushed ahead with this project, accepting that even a few people who understand and believe in the power of good people working together, with common beliefs and good intentions, can make a difference as they tell others. Within the lifetimes of most of us living now, the Berlin Wall fell, the Soviet bloc was disassembled, the United States and Russia became friends, events that few would have guessed could ever happen just five years before. They happened because enough people believed they should.

The inherent goodness of most people is real. Each of us needs hope in order to stay on the same track as everyone else. Most people do not want to destroy either themselves or other life on Earth. Many people are prepared to work together to make life on this planet livable, even better than it was when they first became aware of life around them. Buried deep within us is the same drive for survival and continuity that other plant and animal life have as their driving forces.

What we each need to do is to make a moral commitment. We must give our expression of support when it's needed. Learn about the initiatives undertaken by the groups that follow from this book and vote for the ideas we believe in. No one is asking that we blindly support something that a bunch of renegades are pushing on the government. On the contrary, renegades and extremists will only be kept at bay when there is a majority of regular folks who are stepping forward to lend their support when the time comes.

The governments of some countries have been led and influenced over the past decades by extremists, power seekers and people with their own personal agendas. That happened because the good people of those countries did not step forward to play some positive role in influencing their governments. The vocal ones win.

The wills of the majority can get lost. It's not because the politicians don't care. It's because we and our fellow citizens do not take the trouble to tell them what we want. Never underestimate how much a few committed people can accomplish in achieving change. All revolutions and other old-fashioned forms of changing social values began with a few good people who were determined to make improvements.

Good government is one where people participate in governing themselves. They agree with what their government is doing because it represents what they believe. Politicians are elected by a plurality of those who vote. Some government leaders do not have a majority of support from their citizens. So go out and vote. The renegades don't forget to vote, the special interest groups don't forget, the few people who do take the time to contact their representatives don't forget.

Good people in our community may forget to vote. They may think their vote doesn't matter. Then they blame the politicians for not representing who we really are.

Do politicians need to be defended? No, especially those who do things that they know are wrong. Nor should we fault them for situations which are not of their making. If not enough people tell their representatives what they want, then the representatives will listen to those who do the talking.

This isn't a difficult concept. It doesn't require scientific proof. Tell someone something enough times and they will believe it. It's how advertising works. It's human nature. It's also a human weakness. Look at how advertising creates empires for the industrialists. They teach us how to think, through their advertising, because it works.

A few decades of activity on the part of special interest groups have improved their skills immensely. They know how to influence politicians to follow their wishes. A few decades of apathy by good people who thought that they could not influence their politicians has made the rest of us believe that it's impossible to influence politicians positively. We deceived ourselves into believing that we were powerless.

One group knows that it can influence politicians and has the skills to lobby on their own behalf and to raise the money they need to make a success of it. Another much larger group believes that it is incapable of influencing politicians.

This is our wake-up call. It's time to get on with it. Turn it around.

At the end of this book, you will be asked to send a message of support to the author. The author may live in your country. If he is not in your country, then he will be looking for people to represent our thoughts in each country. Let us know if you know anyone who would be prepared to play any sort of role in collecting and passing along these messages of support and organizing local efforts to make TIA programs happen in their areas.

There is a common saying in the United States and Canada: everyone talks about the weather, but no one does anything about it (commonly attributed to Mark Twain). It could just as well be reworded to say that everyone talks about what bad shape our society is in, but no one is doing anything about it. Our governments haphazardly spend money and pass laws that have no effect on social problems. They build more courts and prisons, hire more judges, but problems get worse. Our education systems change curricula but still turn out a shocking percentage of adults who can't cope with their world. Violence and drugs have become a part of life for our young people.

It's time now for us to combine with others to make up a large group of people who want to make our countries better reflect our beliefs, to make our governments more responsive to the will of their citizens, to make politicians understand that people really do care about the way their country and their lives are going. Now we know the way. Let's tell others.

The first thing we will do is to collect names and contact information. This contact information will be used only for the stated purpose, to help us to contact each other so that we may act together. Security of this information will be maintained. Someone must know how to contact each of us to inform us about what is happening as a result of this book and the initiatives to follow.

(NOTE: Media reports about the Internet have made people frightened about giving their personal contact information to anyone. No one will be asked by us to provide information that is not already available on public media to anyone who is prepared to look for it. We will not share any information provided to us with anyone who is not associated with the *Turning It Around* program. We must be able to contact each when the time comes to act together. Privacy is important.)

Some people will be able to contribute their time. It will be welcome and their efforts will be used in a very positive and productive manner. Some will only be able to contribute their effort in the form of statements of support at the critical times. These people will form the vast majority and they will be welcome and critical to the project.

When the time comes to make a joint statement, every voice will be needed.

There will be expenses to contact people to bring this plan together in your country. As soon as possible, donations from each country will be kept within that country and will be used to send out information to supporters within that country. That time will come as soon as there are people within your country to play a leadership role in bringing a group together.

Similar groups in each country will have common goals and may even lend support to each other's activities when this is appropriate.

The core of each group will be volunteers, people who care. Each group will function in the best way that it can, given the resources at its disposal.

Our intention is to build a large organization of volunteers in each country. Each organization will function independently within its own national boundaries, with common goals with other similar groups elsewhere, but objectives specific to its own country. Each organization will receive skills and moral support from other similar groups in other countries. Not only will each group be beneficial and effective, it will be enjoyable. We don't have an axe to grind. We are doing this out of goodness and with good purposes and intentions. We will form ourselves into groups of good people. People who care. It will be enjoyable to be with so many people who have so much in common.

There is no intention to make this into an organized charity, with tax deductions for any and all donations. Any contributions made to each organization will be made for the benefit of the people of that country. All of the people. We will be an organization that supports a society in desperate need of help for its problems. Every person in that society will be a beneficiary.

Thank you for taking the time to read this book. You may have to re-read parts of it to get its full impact and feel the full importance of it. For most people who read this book, the majority of time they will spend on this project will have been completed already. Only a little more time will be required to lend their support when the time comes.

Please speak up when it will matter.

For others, this project will be just what they have been praying for. They will volunteer their time and effort to actually make the project happen in their country. This will be, after all, a volunteer program where you will learn a great deal as well as making a difference.

There will be some people who will complain when this organization begins to take effect. We can guess who those people will be. They will be the squeaky wheels who have been influencing their governments for years. They will be the ones who have the most to lose. They will loudly oppose our organization because they know that their views are not representative of the majority of voters in their country.

Remember, we will be trying to take away the privileged positions that these groups have paid for over the years. We will give voice to the majority.

Some minority interest groups will welcome the creation of our organization. They will support it, as we will represent with large numbers of people the views that they have been trying to express in a smaller way. Supportive groups may be less vociferous than the ones who will condemn us. That's life. We can be right without being loud. We just have to be heard and to make our views known in a meaningful way. A peaceful but effective manner. We are the majority of voters.

Anyone who is prepared to put their best foot forward runs the chance that someone will step on it. The difference this time is that we will be doing it together. We will have a massive support system. In the days of email, achieving such numbers is not difficult, if we are determined to bring them on board.

We can't start big. We can begin with the readers of this book. Each of us must play a small role in the creation of this organization.

Encourage others to buy and read this book. Give it as a gift—here's a present that really shows you care. Lend it to those who can't afford to buy it. Encourage your local library to stock copies of *Turning It Around: Causes and Cures for Today's Epidemic Social Problems*. Ask your employer to give gift copies to all employees as gifts.

Radio and television programs love to feature new ideas that will attract more viewers and listeners. Call the producers of shows in your area and have them get in touch with Bill using the contact information in this book. Magazines and newspapers you subscribe to will also be interested in the innovative strategies of the TIA plan. Ask to speak to the editor or features editor when you call.

The first important step is to encourage others to read this book. Only when they have read what we now know will they understand and want to join us. Have friends and associates ask their bookstores or libraries to order the book if they can't find it on the shelves. It will be available to everyone who wants it.

Imagine how good you will feel when someone thanks you generously for directing them to this book.

Anyone who can't find how to get the book can write directly to the author at the contact information listed later in the book. The mailing address is his real address, not a corporate headquarters. It's where he lives. The email address will reach him directly.

We will be the organization that will represent the beliefs and will of the majority of people of each country who have been without hope for so long.

What we are trying to do is to teach children how to be healthy and effective adults. We simply want to do what we should have been doing as a large civilization all along. We lost our way and now we need to get back.

We need to teach all children, not just most of them, the beliefs and values that we hold dear. We need to teach them the attitudes and approaches to their futures that will allow them to function successfully within their culture. We need to teach them coping skills so that they will be able to rebound from personal tragedies. We must do this with all children, with intent and purpose, so that the few will not fall through the cracks to become society's outcasts, its rejects and eventually its enemies, perpetrators and victims.

We need to teach parents what it means to be parents, what responsibilities they have to their children and their communities, what they need to know to raise children who will be safe, good citizens and good parents themselves. We must teach parents how extraordinarily influential they are with their young children, how they can manage that for the benefit of everyone, not the least being their own kids.

The time has come to put responsibility for setting the standards for our people into our own hands. Our politicians and education leaders must reflect our beliefs, not those of special interest groups who have different objectives from us.

The time has come to limit the influences of people who would do damage to our people, especially to our children.

The time has come for us to agree, within our respective countries, on what we believe, and to teach those beliefs to all children. It's time to make those beliefs known to everyone, before they go astray and become social problems.

The time has come for the people of each country to tell the world just who they are, what they really represent, what they stand for. First we must teach our own citizens. We can be the people we want to be. To do so, each of us must take the first step. Tell others about *Turning It Around: Causes and Cures for Today's Epidemic Social Problems*.

The world can turn at the touch of a keyboard or the stroke of a pen, if we believe that what we are doing is right and good.

The time has come to turn it around. We, the readers of this book, are part of a majority. We need to be able to contact each other to express our will, our beliefs and our needs as a majority.

Please send a message with your contact information to the addresses to follow. If you have an email address, send us that because that will allow us to contact you without incurring great expense for surface mail. Let us know we have your support. If you would like to join our team in your country, let us know that too.

Together we can do this. We invite you to join us.

Appendix A
Course Material for New Parents

WHILE it's evident that one must be cautious about stating course material of such importance, the following are matters of common interest to all communities.

1. Parents must understand that they are full-time, living, loving examples of how adults act, what adults and parents do and don't do, what their values are, what is right and wrong and what is important and unimportant for their young children. Most parents in the past have thought that their children are too young in their first five years to understand such concepts. On the contrary, young children learn by observing the people who mean most to them, their parents, during that period. Parents are live action role models for their children to follow. Parents must act as perfect examples of what they expect their children to learn during that period. That includes how to be a good parent.
2. Parents must accept that they are responsible for the learning and habits of their children, even when they are not directly supervising them every minute. This means that children's television viewing habits

and material must be monitored for every program that they watch to ensure that only material and concepts that are desirable are seen by the children. Parents must also ensure that the substitutes they choose to supervise their children (babysitters, child care facilities, etc.) exemplify and practice the ideals that the parents and the community believe are best for young children.

3. Parents must subject young children to the values and morals that represent the best of their world and their community. These may be taught directly or indirectly through reading of stories (parables and fables are good), movies, church schools, games or other events. Parents should understand and consciously be aware that every experience they have with their children is a learning experience.

4. Parents must be prepared to teach their child what he needs to know to get him safely and successfully through the coming years of his life. This must include developing a positive attitude toward learning, toward school and toward becoming the best person that the child can be. Parents should build anticipation in their child about the exciting new experiences he will have when he is in school. These attitudes should be reinforced later by each parent taking a supportive interest in what the child is learning. The child should understand that his teacher will be like a third parent, and will provide experiences for the child that his parents at home cannot.

5. Parents must teach their children that it is all right to make a mistake. There is nothing wrong with making a mistake. When we make a mistake, we learn about our mistake and we don't do it again. They don't need to feel bad if they make a mistake. They only need to feel bad if they repeat the mistake again and again. They also need to understand that doing something wrong on purpose and making an innocent mistake are very different.

6. Parents must explain to their children what is good behavior and what is bad behavior. Too often parents tell children only what they did wrong. Telling them what is wrong and what is right, then stressing that they should do the right thing next time (and repeating this message as often as necessary to make the point clear to the child) should become a natural way of dealing with bad behavior. Good behavior should be reinforced by parents.

7. Parents must help their children understand that behavior that is acceptable at home may not be the same as what is acceptable out in public. The distinction should be clear and understandable to the child and consistent over time. Examples might include differences in table manners, behavior towards siblings and acceptable standards of dress.
8. Parents should teach their children that there are limits of acceptable behavior at home, and elsewhere. These limits will include the amount of sound that the children may generate from any source, rules about hitting people, furniture, even toys, use of acceptable and unacceptable language, etc. Parents must learn what reasonable limits are for these activities and places, how to set the limits so that children will understand them and how to enforce the limits if they are broken. Threats to the children that parents do not intend to enforce must be discouraged, as they give bad impressions about the parents to their own children, specifically that their word cannot be trusted. Appropriate means of correction must be learned. Parents must be consistent with their standards and be careful to avoid breaking them themselves. A parent who screams at a child who is screaming himself is teaching a double standard. Rules and standards of the family must apply to everyone, at least the ones that are not specific for parental behavior.
9. Parents must be prepared to answer the many questions of curious children. These commonly begin at the age of three, when children gain sufficient cognitive abilities to be more aware of a larger world than they have known until then. Parents must understand that it is good for children to ask questions. It is healthy. It must be encouraged. Parents must try to answer these questions to the best of their ability, given the level of understanding of the child. Parents must learn, through this course, to anticipate the need for their child to know information about certain subjects, such as sex or violence, and to teach these to their child at the proper early age.
10. Parents should teach their children what is known in North America as The Golden Rule and in Asia as a teaching of Confucius: Do unto others as you would have them do unto you. This should be a teaching/learning process, not an opportunity for a sibling to satisfy his vengeance for having been wronged. Children should be taught to apologize for wronging another person. Parents should follow the same course themselves when

they make a mistake. There should be no opportunity for children to learn that adults have double standards, one for themselves and one for the children.

11. Parents must emphasize to their children the importance of reading, reading skills and reading as a form of self education. Adults cannot function capably in the modern world without good reading skills. They cannot even perform basic functions of civic responsibility unless they can receive and understand written communication. Parents should read not just to their children, but with their children daily or a minimum of several times each week.

12. Parents should understand and help their children understand that children are not adults and should not be judged by adult standards. However, children are adults-in-training, in the sense that children must learn the ways and responsibilities of adulthood before they reach the age where they are given the freedom of choice of adulthood.

13. Parents should expose their children to a variety of reading materials. Subject matter should always be of the type the parents approve of and want their children to understand and its values assimilated. This will include both fiction and nonfiction. Care should be taken to ensure that quality standards of reading material are maintained, so that children are not exposed to junk food for the mind.

14. Parents of school-age children should encourage them to write. This may be done using pencil and paper or a computer. Practice is critical to improving writing skills. Parents should always make time to read what their kids have written. Praise is important, much more so than even constructive criticism. However, the praise should be honest, not hollow. Good parts of the writing and good effort should be praised, but should not be overly effusive or falsified (praise for junk writing). Parental praise should be a reward for children's writing. Children will often ask how they could have written their story better. That is the time for positive and constructive suggestions. Stories, letters to loved ones and descriptions of recent events and experiences are good topics. Setting aside a time when parents and children will write their respective projects is a good family habit. If nothing else, one parent can keep a family journal.

15. Parents should teach their children how to make friends. To make a friend, you must be a friend. Children need to learn how to make friendly overtures to other children and how to accept them from other children and reply appropriately. These should be taught as soon as each child reaches the age where it is possible to have playmates.
16. Parents should expose their children to a wide variety of learning experiences. The types of experiences may be governed by limits in the family budget, but the number of experiences should not. Parents must understand that they owe these experiences to their children. Free public places are available in most communities for a wide variety of experiences.
17. Parents should teach their children, on an ongoing basis, who the children can rely on, who they can trust, and who they should not trust. Even very young children who have just learned to walk can be told again and against why it is dangerous for them to walk away out of mother's or father's sight. It is important for children to be aware of who they can trust, not just who they must not trust. Otherwise, children come to believe that they can't trust anyone.
18. Parents should teach their children at least a few times each year what they should do if they get lost. The routines should be discussed and repeated several times. One time to do this is when the child is taken to a different environment, such as a restaurant or a shopping mall where they have not been before. Parents must understand that children can get lost even in unlikely places, such as a restaurant, when they wander away in curiosity and can't find their way back. Children need to know what to do in such circumstances.
19. Parents should stress to children frequently what to do in emergencies. Anticipating emergencies will make this easier to understand. Imagine what emergencies any child could experience, then prepare the child for them. Even a very young child can be taught how to dial 9-1-1, for example, and told never to do this unless there is a big problem. If the child does not understand what an emergency might be, explain that it would be any time she is afraid. "If you are afraid, that is an emergency. Don't get upset, just do what I have taught you to do. You will have the problem over with quickly if you just do what I have told you to do." Parents should have their own plans for emergencies too. The child

should also be taught what to do if she feels uncomfortable or *funny* about a situation she is in, especially where adults or older children are involved.

20. Parents must teach their children the "rules of the road for pedestrians." Behavior on the street can mean the difference between life and death for a child. It is equally important that parents do not violate their own stated rules. Parents and children should all observe the same rules when they are walking. There should be no double standard. When someone else is seen violating these rules, this can be discussed so that the child understands that the violators are doing wrong, they are doing a dangerous thing. These family standards should be established and maintained by both children and parents from the time the children are babies.

21. Parents should show their children love and respect. Each child is a learner. Although not an adult, he is learning how to be an adult. He needs to have love and respect from those he depends on most. Parents must also teach their children that to deserve the love and respect of others, they must give it to others. Not everyone will be your friend. But even non-friends will respect you if you respect them. (This is not a perfect rule, of course, but it is a good place to start learning about how to treat people.) Teaching of what used to be called good manners, both in person and on the telephone, can be done as the opportunities present themselves.

22. Parents need to learn that bad behavior on the part of their children is often a call for attention. When bad behavior is the child's only way of getting the time and attention of his parent, then bad behavior is reinforced when attention is given only at those times. Children require a lot of attention. They deserve it. It's not just a privilege. They have a lot to learn in a short time. A child who learns that bad behavior earns adult attention will continue with such a successful method of getting attention as he gets older. The attention-getting devices get more severe over time, as the child gets older. Parents must recognize that attention is required above anything else when children act up. That attention should not be in the form of punishment, but in some constructive way of spending time together. That way the need for attention is satisfied and the fact that bad behavior brought it about becomes lost in the child's mind.

23. New parents need to understand that their children are the prime purpose for their existence and must be the focus of their attention for the next few years. Continuation and success of the human race and of their own families hang in the balance. Sacrifices may have to be made to fulfill that prime purpose. That next generation must be given everything it deserves. And it deserves a whole lot of attention and love.
24. Parents need to accept that they must give their children everything these children need and deserve, especially in love, devotion, time, attention and role models. If they are unable to provide that, for whatever reason, they should take whatever measures will ensure that the children will receive that.
25. Parents need to learn what all of the resources are at their disposal, especially in times of need. They need to know who to call, where to find resources and what sorts of matters they may want to learn about along the journey of parenthood. They need to learn to ask for help, without hesitation or reservation. They need to know that it is good to ask for help. They need to believe that they always have more to learn about being a parent.
26. Parents need to accept that their parental responsibilities supercede other responsibilities, even to their spouses and their jobs. "Quality time" can be reserved for spouses. Real time must be devoted to children.
27. Young people who will become parents need to know that the general health, nutritional intake and habits of the mother, not just during pregnancy but before the mother becomes pregnant can and will affect the health of the fetus, the newborn baby and the child. These will even affect the tendency of her child toward some diseases and other health conditions when the child reaches middle age and beyond. In terms of health, conceiving a child is a commitment of a lifetime. Parents should teach this to their children as their early commitment to their own future grandchildren.
28. The most important gift that parents can give to their children up to age 11 is their time. To a child, there is no such thing as "quality time"; it's just time together or time apart. There should be time for parent to teach child and for the child to do what they want, with the parent as a play companion. Parent-child time spent together is what the world is about to a child.

29. Love is conveyed in words, gestures and actions, but measured in touch. Each child comes into being surrounded by the comforting touch of the womb. They never outgrow their need for comforting touch by those who love them. The touch of children and parents is an unspoken line of communication of love, of security and of support.
30. Young children learn almost all of what they know about the kind of world they live in from their parents. Parents must actively teach everything they want their children to learn, then act as positive role models for their children to follow. Leave nothing to chance, as that opens the possibility for kids to learn from other, more negative influences.
31. Children need to play with other children, especially others of their own age, but also with children who are younger and older. They develop social skills and communication skills, plus they see the maturation process in play—older kids act differently, younger ones in a simpler, less mature way.
32. Young children get sick a lot. Fighting various bacteria and viruses is how their immune systems develop defenses against these same pathogens later in life. Parents should not be alarmed by this illness. Some childhood illnesses help the immune system develop protection against more dangerous diseases that adults could experience. Research suggests that making a young child's environment sterile could impair his immune system.
33. Children need to take some risks to learn the boundaries of acceptable danger. Those who have been prevented from taking risks as young children may take unreasonable risks with their lives in adolescence as they have not developed a sense of reasonable caution. When a parent stops behavior that is too risky, an explanation should be given to the child about the potential harm of doing that activity.
34. Don't worry about the behavior of your teenaged children. If you teach them well and thoroughly during the first decade of their lives and if they see you as a role model for what you teach, they will behave as you hope. Monitor what they do and discuss it with them. Worry accomplishes nothing and will often drive a teen away.
35. Trust is the most sacred bond between parent and child. If you show reasonable trust for your children when they are young and if they believe they can trust you, you will have a bond for life. If you do not

behave the way you expect them to behave, they will learn to distrust, and this will spread to everyone in their lives. Trust and love are nearly equivalent to a child.

36. Show your children who you are by showing them what you do, while they are little. The more mysterious you keep your daily life when they are little, the less they will be inclined to share with you when they are older.
37. Your young child does not care much about your bad day, your uncooperative hair, your financial woes, your nasty neighbor or your sick aunt. These are problems of your world, not hers. Your child cares about you, how you act, how you treat her, whether you are glad to see her. You are the world to your young child. You are what matters in her world.
38. Children do not always need toys to be entertained. Creativity is fostered when they don't have enough objects to do what they want to do. When they play-act other people, you can see how they think about these people. Then you can correct their misconceptions. Encourage creativity by demonstrating some of your own.
39. Some children learn best by watching, others by listening. Some can only learn by doing it themselves. If you sense a learning problem, try another learning approach. When you learn the best learning style for your child, convey this to each teacher. Teachers can adapt when they know what each child needs.
40. Your child is not better than others because he can do something they can't. By overemphasizing one skill set, you may be neglecting others. Children develop like pyramids; the best structure is one where all sides are equally strong. Aim for a balance of intellectual, social, physical and emotional development opportunities.
41. From the day your child is born, you are not just teaching and training your own child, you are the prime source of parental guidance for him, as he will be a parent himself, to your grandchildren.
42. To a child, there is no substitute for time spent with parents, for love, for loving touch (hugs) by parents or for encouragement.
43. Your child's teacher will spend more time with your child than you will. Keep the teacher informed if anything significant could affect your child's learning or his social development.

44. You have no way of knowing what words you use, what actions you make, what love you give, what time you spend with your child on any day will have a lasting impact on her life. Your child expects you to be perfect. Come as close as you can.
45. There are legal obligations associated with parenthood. There are moral obligations associated with love, particularly with those who love you and depend on you, such as children and your mate. Learn your obligations before you undertake them and strive to fulfill your obligations so you do not fail those who need you.

Parenting is the most important job you will ever have in your life. It's your key to immortality. It's the future of your community and your culture. Give it the respect, the time and the devotion it and your children deserve.

Appendix B
Program Topics for the Primary Grades

Here is a list of topics that we should consider teaching children in the primary grades of elementary school.

1. Some people are different from you. Boys are different from girls. Some people are good athletes, some are good at other things. Some people are naturally taller than others. Some people eat different foods than you eat. Some people belong to a church that you don't. Some people wear clothing that is different from yours. Some people think differently from the way you do. That's all right. Different is cool. Learn about the differences and accept them. No one is better than you. No one is less of a person than you.

2. The unknown is exciting. It is not to be feared. It is an adventure that may be explored and experienced. Sometimes you should get advice before venturing into some unknown territories and experiences. Some unknown things can be dangerous. Learn about these things before you experience them. Learn as much as you can before making a decision about anything. Only do what you believe is right for you.

3. Don't be afraid. Fear is bad for you. You can learn to overcome your fear. You can still be cautious without being afraid. Being cautious is wise. The more you learn about something, the less reason you will have to fear or dislike it.
4. Learn about what you don't understand. The world is full of mysteries. Learn as much as you can about them. You will never know everything there is to know about anything. It is important to keep learning.
5. Learn "home smarts" for the time you spend at home. Home can be a safe place or it can be a dangerous place. Learn about what is safe and what can do you harm. Understand that what you do to others can harm them.
6. Learn "street smarts" for when you are not at home. Learn what to do in as many possible situations that may arise as you can. Remember these and review them every few months.
7. Every family has its periods of crisis or disaster. Learn what to do when this happens. Learn who can help you. Learn who you should not discuss family problems with.
8. Learn how to cope with the breakup of your family, such as if your parents separate. It may not happen, but if it does, you should know what to do to help yourself. Your parents may be too upset and confused to think of what is best for you. Learn how to help them to remember what you need. Find out who you can speak with in confidence when family emergencies happen.
9. Learn how to survive and flourish in school. Understand why it is important that you succeed in school. Know that you have a long life to lead as an adult and much of it will depend on what you learned as a child. Appreciate that your future is in your own hands, to a great extent, so you have to work hard to make the best for yourself.
10. Learn what it's like to be an adult. Understand that adulthood is what is ahead of you. Appreciate that life is a lot more work than it is fun. Being happy is good, but it is not necessary to be happy at all times. Sometimes life is a lot of hard work. That includes chores you have to do at home and the work you do at school. Your life will be that way for as long as you live. Accept this and form your habits accordingly.
11. Learn what resources are available to a child. Learn how to contact those people when you need them. Understand that they will help you. Know

that it is important that you tell only the truth to these people who will help you. It is very wrong to tell a lie, as it will get you into more trouble later.

12. Learn about good habits to make you healthy and bad habits to avoid. Bad habits will shorten your life or make you sick while you are alive. They may not make you sick now, but you will be sorry later. Smoking is one example of a bad habit that will affect your health later. Non-prescription drugs and alcohol in excess can be harmful to both you and to others, such as if you have an accident or get into a fight.
13. Learn what activities are self-destructive. Some things you can do will be bad for you. Learn what they are and how they can hurt you.
14. Learn what people consider are virtues and good characteristics. Try to be that way. Understand that life is better for you and for everyone around you when you live like this. People decide who they want as friends by their virtues and positive characteristics.
15. Children should learn what a majority of citizens in their local area believe is good for their community and what the benefits are of these beliefs.
16. Children should learn what a majority of citizens believe is bad for their community and why they should believe that.
17. Children should be taught, with examples, how advertisers and even adults and other children can influence them by playing on their minds. They can learn how to recognize that others are trying to influence them wrongly and how to get themselves out of the situation. If they have a "funny feeling" about something, chances are good that it is the wrong thing to participate in.
18. Children should learn what we believe constitutes the civic responsibility of each citizen. They learn what their society owes them. They should be taught what they should be giving back to their society as their contribution to its welfare. To do otherwise is to, by omission, teach greed as an accepted value, as they can see on television. We have seen how effective this has been in the past few decades in our country, beginning with the "Me" generation of the 1970s, followed by the "Gimme" generation of the 1980s and the "Gimme-or-else" generation of the 1990s.

19. A child should learn what his responsibility is to himself, especially as it relates to his physical health, his mental health and his future as a member of his society. Learning this automatically gives the child a feeling of self-worth, of importance, of meaning. Since he has no way of knowing what he will be in his future, he will better prepare himself to be the best he can be, since he owes that to himself.
20. A child should learn to build, not to blame. This means focusing on improving the conditions in which we and others live, not to dwell on past problems. The past cannot be changed. Mistakes, errors and faults are in the past. They should be kept there.
21. A child should learn that only the future can be changed, not the past. We can plan for the future and work to make it better than the present. We can avoid the mistakes of the past by knowing our own history. We use our knowledge of the past to build a better future, not to suffer anxiety over times that were different from our own.
22. Children should be taught to take pride in their neighborhood, their city, their state/province and their country. Children who take pride in something other than themselves respect others. They know enough to direct their attention away from themselves at times. They should learn that the world does not center around *me*.
23. Children should be taught why it is necessary for us to stand up for what we believe is right. The old saying is: those who don't stand for something will fall for anything. This country was built by those who believed in justice and doing the right thing. It is time to return to those values. People gave their lives to make our country what it is today. We owe it to our country to stand up for what we believe is good and right now.
24. Children should learn who their neighbors are and why they should care about them. Even if their neighbors don't care about themselves or anyone else, the children should learn to care about others. Every successful relationship begins with one party making a positive move first. You have to reach out to make a friend.
25. Children should learn what it means to be successful as a person. That must be determined by a majority of citizens. Now we teach that success is equated to money. This has produced a greedy society that does not want to help anyone else. Success as a person really means more than

the value of one's financial net worth. It means how good you feel about yourself inside.

26. Children must learn that voting in elections is a moral responsibility for citizens of a democratic country. By not enough good people voting, we have turned the running of our country over to minority interest groups. Even our entertainment is dominated by people of values different from those of the majority of the population. We have lost control by losing interest. The minority interests know enough to speak up and to make their wishes known. That is why they are listened to by politicians. Good people should always be prepared to speak up.

27. Children should learn that mistakes are learning situations. No child should be punished for an honest mistake. Repeating the same mistake is negligence, which is another matter. A child should learn something from each mistake she makes. If possible, a child should learn from the mistakes of others too, be they mistakes of brothers and sisters or even of her parents. If we are honest about admitting our mistakes as adults, children will learn not to be hypocritical about hiding their mistakes. No one should feel guilty about having made an honest mistake.

28. Children should learn what the people of their community and their country care about as being important. Most children learn this as they grow, but some miss out because they are not exposed to such matters. Each child should be taught and have these points stressed through all the years of formal education.

29. Children should learn how other people can help them when they need help. This is different from knowing who can help. Knowing what to expect or ask for from others is equally important. Most children now do not understand that they can ask for help and that people will help them if they ask.

30. A child should learn how she can recognize that she has a problem in her life. Children have little experience with problems, so they often do not realize that they have them. They can be taught to recognize clues, such as fear or apprehension.

31. A child should be given reasons why he should help another person who needs his help, why he should care about others. So many adults do not understand this now that they would be unable to teach their children. Children should grow up with these values.

32. A child should learn that he will never know everything about any subject, but he should learn something. At least a little knowledge of many subjects is useful in understanding how the world works. It is a hedge against ignorance. It also provides a launching place when a person wants to learn more. People tend to believe that anything they don't know is either too hard to learn or is not important. Both beliefs are wrong. The time to learn a positive attitude toward learning is when a person is very young.
33. Each child should learn how to work with others in a group situation. This can be either as a group participant or as a team member. We tend now to overstress individual achievement and downplay group participation. This is why many meetings fail, as the participants do not feel compelled to be a part of the group action. Interdependence, each group member depending on each other member, is a skill that must be learned. It also builds trust and bonds among people.
34. Each child should have some experience with presenting her viewpoint to a group. This is very frightening to many children. Most adults have bad memories of presenting a speech to their childhood school classes. Being prepared to present one's point of view in a discussion is something that should be developed through all the years of school, at least to the end of high school. This requires practice, which comes almost exclusively in school.
35. Each child should be taught that learning is a lifetime project. They should be taught why it is important, even essential, that each person continues to learn throughout his lifetime. The world is changing, medicine and science are changing, social relationships are changing, politics is changing, jobs are changing so fast that only a person who continually prepares by learning steadily can be ready to cope with constant change. Learning to cope with constant change is essential to self-confidence and to many other parts of our lives.
36. Children should be taught, with repeated emphasis, why reading, writing and speaking clearly and effectively are important skills to develop. Many people have difficulties with these skills, but they can become good with hard work and practice.
37. Children should be taught what it means for someone to become an expert in a particular subject or field. That could be athletics or medicine

or research, but the important thing is for them to understand what kinds of skills and devotion are necessary to achieve such a goal. Other school programs should aim to develop such skills and attitude. Anyone can become an expert on a subject if they are prepared to work hard to reach that level of knowledge and skills.

38. Children should be taught that childhood is the beginning of a person's life, not the end of it. Each person lives for several decades after childhood is over. Childhood is the training ground to prepare each person for the kind of person he will be for the rest of his life. Some things about childhood should be taken seriously.

39. Children should be taught survival skills in their own environment and in other situations in which they might find themselves. This should include any situation where they are not in familiar territory, including such things as school and family trips.

40. Children should be taught the differences between cultures and the fact that each culture has its own value. These differences are to be appreciated for what they add to the richness of the country, not to be feared or hated. Learning about these cultures will help with understanding and accepting them.

41. Children should be taught about differences in religions among people in their own class and elsewhere in their community. While there should not be an emphasis on one religion over any others, teaching about the different religions aids in understanding and acceptance of others who practice these religions. They should be taught that most religions have many characteristics and beliefs in common with each other. Often it is just the way these are practiced that makes them different.

42. Children should be taught what it means to have a true friend. A life without friends is a life with problems. Having at least one good friend is valued highly in our culture.

43. Children should be taught what it means to be a true friend and how to act toward another person who is their friend. Friendship, as with any relationship, often has each party feeling as if they contribute 85 percent to the other's 15 percent. This perception is as close to a balance as most relationships require in order to sustain themselves. We don't always appreciate what our friends contribute to our friendships, but we always understand what we contribute to them.

44. Children should be taught what they must do to make and keep a friend. In order to improve their chances of success at making a friend, they must be given the tools to decide what sort of person they would like as a friend.
45. Children should be taught what their expectations of life should be. And they should also be taught, by extension, what they should not realistically expect of others in their lives and of society itself.
46. Children should be taught what the world owes them and what it does not. There is a perception that, as a member of the human race, certain benefits should be accorded to each person. Kids should be taught the reality of this perception and how it affects them.
47. Children should be taught what they owe to the world, their country, their home community, their neighbors, their friends and their families. These values will vary from one place to another and must be selected within each area, such as a state or province.
48. Children should learn what is required to make the world safe for the future. As these values will vary over time and from one area to another, they will have to be selected to represent local values of the time. As this is when many values about ecology will be taught, this must be an important part of the program.
49. Children must learn what is required to make our planet last in such a way that it is habitable for all existing animal and plant life. This will include lessons in sustainable industrial and personal activity. While this cannot be taught in depth for primary grade children, this is the time to introduce the concepts they will learn more about as their school life continues and they mature.
50. Children need to understand the privileges of wealth. Some of these privileges are real, such as the power to buy things that others cannot, while some of them are false, such as some people with lots of money to spend believing that they are better than others or that they deserve more recognition or better service than others. As wealth is one source of what may be called class discrimination, this is a good time to teach that wealth does not grant personal privileges over other people.
51. Children need to learn what discrimination is, how it demonstrates itself and why it is wrong. This is the time to squash ideas of discrimination that may be developing in kids. People may be different from each other, they may dress differently, act differently, eat different foods, practise

different religions, but they are all to be understood and not to be classified as being better or worse than each other.

52. What is courage? What is the difference between courage and foolishness? This will reflect local values and perhaps national values.
53. How do we recognize a bully? How should we act if someone is bullying us or a friend? What should we do if we know someone is bullying?
54. What does it mean to cheat? How do we recognize a cheater? What should we do about it if we know someone has cheated? What problems will result have if we cheat?
55. What are the social values of my community and my country regarding use of alcohol, drugs, gambling and other addictions? How can these harmful habits affect my body and my life?
56. Children should learn the value of nature to our planet and the role we should play in preserving nature. They should learn the results of our abuse of nature in the past.
57. Children should learn the complexity of natural life and where we humans fit into this matrix of nature.
58. Children should be taught how complex our lives can be and some general ideas about how to cope with the good and bad things that happen in our lives.
59. Children should be given the opportunity to learn about the range of human emotions and the complexity of them. Some people experience and show emotions in stronger ways than others. Children need to be able to understand that shows of emotion are natural. They need to learn how to cope with the show of negative emotions by others.
60. Children need to understand and appreciate that being different (if they feel that way) is not bad. It is necessary to find others who share some things in common with them, so that they can feel less alone than they may otherwise. No two people like all the same things and no two people are entirely alike.
61. Children should learn the need for kindness, both their own and their ability to accept kindness from others.
62. Children should learn the need for devotion, dedication and perseverance in whatever they do so that they may do as well as possible at it.
63. Children should learn to appreciate their own need for understanding from others and the need of others to be understood. Often differences are misunderstandings of similar ideas expressed in different ways.

64. Children should learn what it means to be an employer, an employee and an entrepreneur. If they learn the characteristics of each, they will be better able to recognize these in others, especially adults, and may be able to see into which of these roles they seem to fit best. They can be given opportunities to experience each situation by working with others in small groups and even by role playing exercises. Having visitors who represent each of these categories might help.
65. Children can be helped to understand how there will be downturns in their lives, such as having problems with their friends or at school, and how to cope with these problems. They need to be taught to understand that these problems happen to everyone from time to time and what steps to take to get past them. They need to know that downturns in their lives always come to an end. At its worst, life always gets better.
66. Children need to understand that they are not personally responsible for problems their parents may be having.
67. What should we do if we have been abused or if we learn that someone else has been abused?
68. Children should learn that death is a part of life. They need to understand how they can help themselves through a period of their lives when someone close to them has died. They need to know how to be understanding and helpful with others who have experienced this.
69. Children need to learn how to recognize and to cope with their own fears.
70. Children need to understand what worry is, how to recognize it in themselves and others and how to overcome this destructive activity. Being sensitive and caring does not mean having to worry.
71. Self-esteem comes from knowing who we are, what we do well, what possibilities we have ahead of us, not from what we own or what we can make others do for us, or from thinking that we are better than others.
72. Children need to be taught the rules and realities of the road for vehicles, for pedestrians and for those on bicycles. That is, a pedestrian may have the right of way over a vehicle, but a vehicle can kill the pedestrian if the driver makes a mistake.
73. Children need to understand the need for safety in their lives, that they can be injured or killed if they are not careful and what effect that would have on others that love them. They need to know the difference between adventure and dumb or risky behavior.

74. How can children learn about themselves? How can they get to know themselves, what they do well and what things they need to improve about themselves? This is important, as most schools do not teach this. Many schools evaluate children for the teachers' and parents' purposes. They do not think that children want to know about themselves. They do not understand that a child that understands himself has a better chance of improving than one that is told he needs to work harder.
75. How can a child overcome shyness, stuttering, reading difficulties, uncertain feelings about the need to wear glasses or a wardrobe that is not as nice as that of others in their class?
76. How can a child learn to be proud of herself?
77. What are the important lessons that each child should know about life?
78. Why should a child be good, if being bad is more fun? What are the risks of being bad?
79. Children need to understand that it's all right if someone dislikes them. Not everyone has to be liked by everyone else. This is normal. It's acceptable. It is not something to worry about. Worrying about someone who dislikes them is one of the most destructive activities that children and adults can do.
80. What should a child do if they have a big problem and their parents or teacher can't help them or if they don't want to tell those people about it? Is there anything that child can do, anyone else who could help them? Who can they turn to who is not threatening and could be depended upon to help them?
81. Children must be given the opportunity to learn the laws of the country and state/province in which they live and the bylaws of their municipality. This is not just fair, but essential in a country where ignorance of the law is not accepted as an excuse for breaking it, but no provision is made for the learning of laws on an organized basis. We live under three sets of laws. We have a right to know what they are.
82. Children should be taught how to recognize a person with a problem and what to do about it. This could include someone who could be dangerous in school, someone with a physical difficulty, someone who seems to be not as smart as they are (but may or may not be in reality), and so on. They need to know how they should act around such a person and whether they should tell someone else about this person.

Resources

Learn more about the beliefs and values that humans hold in common and one possible future for humankind in:

The Celestine Prophecy, James Redfield, Warner Books, 1993

See how much human organizations have in common by studying the basic principles (not rituals, but the principles that guide them) of all of the major religions and philosophies of life. They teach the same basic concepts about how to live our lives.

To join others who want to begin TIA programs in their home communities or to contact the author (including for personal appearances) and the *Turning It Around* team of volunteers please use the following information:

turningitaround@sympatico.ca
Turning It Around
c/o Bill Allin
R. R. # 1
Buckhorn, Ontario, K0L 1J0 CANADA

Find out what's happening in the TIA world by joining our Internet community of TIA supporters at: http://groups.yahoo.com/group/turningitaround

The *Turning It Around* web site will be a continual work-in-progress as we make changes and additions to keep you informed about the worldwide progress of the TIA program. Find us at: www.billallin.com

Commentaries there will be changed regularly and news posted about what's happening with TIA organizations as they build and grow around the world. There will be listed links to sites that promote TIA materials and thoughts and useful stuff our various groups will be giving away free.

You can also sign up to receive the TIA newsletter. The online (email) version will be free. Make sure you send us your email address so you can see how the organization grows. Your address and other personal information will be safe with us. The newsletter will be a real-time history of one of the greatest movements for change in the past two thousand years.

Bookmark our site on your computer and visit regularly. We promise to make it a valuable investment of your time.

For the first time in history you will be able to meet people who have regained their hope for a better world and will have a plan in hand for accomplishing that change. You'll make some new and interesting friends, too. You'll be surprised at how many people hold the same values as you.

We'll also have dates for online chats with Bill and other TIA representatives, plus locations for upcoming personal visits and presentations.

Please remember, we can't do this without you. Don't leave it to someone else. Ask libraries and bookstores to stock this book. Speak to group leaders about having a TIA representative as a guest speaker. Ask that TIA information be added to your newsletters. We will write articles tailored to your group, if you ask. Encourage your local media to write or broadcast information about *Turning It Around: Causes and Cures for Today's Epidemic Social Problems*.

The future of your community is in your hands. We'll help you if you'll help us spread the word.

Bibliography

Saturday Night, "A Nation In Denial," St. Joseph Media, Toronto, September, 1999

Macleans, *The Quest for Literacy*, MACLEANSBEHINDTHESCENES, Rogers Media, October, 2002

Stern, Christopher, *FTC concludes entertainment industry ignores own warnings*, The Washington Post, Washington, August 27, 2000, and Archives of Pediatrics and Adolescent Medicine 2000;154:366-369

Glausiusz, Josie, *Brain, Heal Thyself*, Discover, Buena Vista Magazines, New York, August 1996

Harris, William Torrey (1889), Quoted John Gatto (1992) *The Tyranny of Government Schooling (audiocassette)*

Burnford, Sheila, *One Woman's Arctic*, Little, Brown; [1st American ed.] edition (1973)

Milton, John, *On His Blindness*

Spock, Dr. Benjamin, *The Common Sense Book of Baby and Child Care*, Duell, Sloan and Pearce (USA), 1946

CBC1, *Here & Now, June 14, 2000*

About the Author

BILL ALLIN has lived toward the creation and development of the TIA concept his whole life. A near-feral child until the age of five, he was a social outsider during his elementary and high school years as his social immaturity and hidden disabilities went undiagnosed by his teachers.

During three years at what is now Ryerson University, he caught up to his peers socially while studying Radio and Television Arts. After a few years working in print and broadcast media, he became an elementary school classroom teacher.

Sixteen years later, after teaching children from a variety of socioeconomic backgrounds and achieving his Masters of Education in sociology, he began his own business, where he spent much of his time teaching adults. When chronic fatigue syndrome ended his traditional working career, he studied business and cultures around the world. He returned to writing when he discovered not just that people around the world suffer from the same social problems, but that they all responded positively to his unique ideas about how to solve them.

Turning It Around: Causes and Cures for Today's Epidemic Social Problems is his first book for general distribution. Bill and his wife live in a wilderness area of Ontario, Canada, where he is working on his next book of discussion topics of common interest to parents and their teenaged children and a followup book about what new parents need to know about young children and how they learn.

Index

A
abstinence, 19
accidents, 7, 13, 109–11
addictions, 24
adolescence. *see* teens/teen subcultures
adult education, 227
adults
  coping skills for, 186
  expressing emotions as, 169
  interdependence role of, 178–79
  parental responsibility of, 222
  parenting skills for, 133, 135–36, 153–54, 160, 224–30
  as role models, 61, 220–21
  see also parents
advertising
  manipulating group behavior by, 71–72
  media fear mongering and, 55
  psychological violence and, 56
  selling of love through, 172
  socialization through, 172
  see also propaganda
Africa, 25, 48, 57, 63, 192
African-Americans, 84
aggressiveness
  desensitization to violence and, 59–61
  establishing hierarchy by, 67
  outlets for non-athletic, 58–59
  in sports, 58
  zero tolerance for, 122, 191
alcohol
  aggression threshold and, 80–81
  as extreme behavior, 24
  fight reflex and, 78
  motor vehicle accidents and, 7
  societal attitude toward, 2
  teens and, 62, 120, 148
alliances, economic vs. military, 31–32
American Academy of Child and Adolescent Psychiatry, 59
American Academy of Pediatrics (AAP), 59
American Medical Association (AMA), 59
American Psychological Association (APA), 59
anarchy
  anti-social behavior and, 2
  politics to avoid, 93
  in schools, 127
  social problems leading to, 153
  tabloid media and, 9
anger, 33–35, 81
anti-social behavior
  desensitization to violence and, 59–61
  as social problem, 11–13, 124
  societal systems for dealing with, 2

anxiety
  adolescent, 242
  causes of, 222
  educational success and, 81
  group behavior and, 152
  helplessness and dealing with, 5–7
  parental, 225
  toward social problems, 181
  understanding fear and, 122
apathy, 15–16, 89, 97
Asia, 28, 63, 145, 192, 255
athletic competition, 58–59, 80–81
  see also sports
attention span, 178
attitudes, 2, 208–10, 235
authority, 69, 72, 121
automobiles
  accident liability and, 109–10
  alcohol and, 7
  potential for teaching behavior, 199
  road rage and, 33–35, 81
  speeding as social norm and, 13
avoidance, 23, 49, 207

B
behavior
  ancient moralities and societal, 14
  crisis and unpredictability of, 82
  dealing with anti-social, 2
  group, 40–41
  laws to control, 172–73
  parental influence on children, 160, 219–20
  parental skills for teaching, 253–62
  phobias and individual, 68
  role of government in, 92–93
  self-destructive, 35
  socially unacceptable, 23–24
  taking responsibility for personal, 17–18
  zero tolerance, 122, 191
  see also anti-social behavior
beliefs and values
  building, 10, 62
  creating system based on, 182–84
  failure to teach, 213–18
  in forming a new society, 208–10
  freedom and equality, 116–17
  goals for teaching, 125–26, 132–34, 152–53
  learning, 44–45, 136–37, 164, 216–18
  loss of parenting skills in, 220–21, 224–30
  role of government in, 101
  society, 3–4
  work ethic and, 64
  see also common beliefs; moral codes/morality

Berlin Wall, 246
bigotry. see discrimination; prejudice
birth rate, 229–30
blame
  education, 154, 222, 234–39
  the government, 92
  group behavior, 70
  learning not to, 207, 266
  of others, 47, 195
  parents, 120
  politicians, 247
boundaries of acceptable behavior, 170, 260
Britain. see Great Britian
British North America Act, 105
bullying
  aggressiveness and pecking order in, 67
  vs. defensive fighting, 77
  disguising fear by, 122
  human nature and, 53
  victimization by, 33–35
Burnford, Sheila, 178
business
  globalization and, 103
  Internet role in, 206
  as warfare, 80
  women in, 66–67
  see also corporations; employment

C
Cambodia, 57
Campbell, Kim, 3
Canada
  changing society in, 248–52
  crime in, 19
  entertainment media, 241
  ethnic diversity in, 84–85
  independence and establishing, 25, 105–06
  literacy skills in, 233–34
  NFC proposal for, 210
  politics in, 92, 99, 202
  "politics of inclusion", 3
  Pond Inlet school, 178–79
  Quebec separatism and, 30–31
  as role model, 6
  social problems in, xiii
  world perceptions of, 41–42
Celestine Prophecy, The, 275
censorship, 196
change
  bad influences in society, 179
  education role in behavior, 92–93
  educational system, 119–22, 190–93
  fear of progress and, 73–74
  and future expectations, 85–87
  improving society by, 36–38, 206, 218

individual participation in
  government, 98–99
from past expectations, 84–85
in politics and future world
  leadership, 87–89
Pyramid of Living System and,
  164–65
socialization of children and, 64
toward national education program,
  218
Town Hall meetings and, 201–02
understanding the need for, 45–46
as a way of life, 193, 207–08
Charter of Rights and Freedom,
  Canada, 105
children
  attention span, 178
  coping skills for, 2
  educational goals for, 132–34
  educational objectives for, 142–57,
    240–43
  educational process for, 134–42, 159
  importance of love to, 137–40
  learning about the natural
    environment, 44
  learning as a responsibility of,
    125–26, 190–91, 231–32, 235
  learning from entertainment media,
    44–45
  learning morals and values, 216–18
  learning parenting skills, 186–90,
    224–30
  long-term planning for, 104
  parental influence on behavior in, 160
  past expectations of, 84–85
  Pyramid of Living System and,
    161–63, 167–68
  school failure and, 121–22
  socialization and violence, 64
  societal change through, 37–38
  survival instinct and, 78–79
  teaching inhibitions to, 35
  teaching survival skills to, 186–89
  television violence and, 60–61
China, 106
church. *see* religion
citizenship
  democracy and participative, 98–99
  goals for teaching, 132–34, 155–57
  "politics of inclusion" and, 3–4
  representative government and,
    96–97
  role in long-term planning and
    change, 9–10, 208–10
civilization
  and future of society, 128, 182, 218,
    251

long-term plans for, 208–10
morality and, 14
and the natural world, 39
power to change, 218
responsibilities of, ix, xiii
society as a form of, 15, 25, 46, 88,
  153
violence and, 26, 64
as a way of life, 2–3, 35
see also society
civilized behavior
  self-destructive actions and, 35
  societal change and, 36–38
  teaching, 25–27
clothing
  dress code, 70, 122
  group conformity and, 69
  as measure of success, 68
  morals and values from, 215
code of ethics, 69–70
collective will
  political power and, 72, 117, 131,
    182–84
  problem solving and, 14–15
  of society, 10, 128, 203
  special interest groups and, 98
  for teaching behavior, 189–90
  violence and the, 35
  worldwide, 32, 181–84
Columbine, 55, 61, 82, 148
commitments
  to educational goals and change,
    132–34
  in forming a new society, 209–10,
    245–52
  maintaining, 18–19
  recognizing, 259
  teaching children about, 125–26
common beliefs
  agreement on, 210
  preserving, 3, 10
  recognizing, 184, 193
  working toward goal of, 245–52
  see also beliefs and values
communications
  Internet and worldwide, 106
  mass media and government, 197–98
  social interaction through, 173–74
  with the unborn and newborn child,
    134
communities
  anti-social behavior in, 1–2
  commitment to changing, 8–10
  concepts of, 84–85, 115–16
  educational goals of, 144–45
  future economic order and, 87
  NFC objectives and, 212–14

punishment of parents, 188
Pyramid of Living System and, 161–63, 213–15, 227
reshaping society into, 5–6
responsibility toward children, 219–20
responsibility toward parents, 253–62
role in education, 130–32, 172, 178–79
teen alienation from, 213–18
see also society
computers
as abstraction or for learning, 44–45
role in education, 129–30
vulnerability of, 51–52
see also Internet (Information Highway); technology
concepts/conceptualizing
for changing government, 247–52
formation of, 45
learning, 130, 150, 177, 231–32, 255
need to understand, xi, 215–17
for a new way of life, 275
parents role in, 226, 253–54
teaching, 138, 238, 270
conflict
defensive fighting and, 77
desensitization to violence in, 59–61
establishing hierarchy by, 67
in group behavior, 70
humanity vs. nature, 39–40
NFC objectives and, 212–14
conformity, 68–70, 173, 215
Confucius, teaching of, 201, 255
conservation, natural resources, 43
consistency, 160, 173, 215–18, 255
consumer society, 67–68
coping skills
anti-social behavior and, x
children and, xi, 2, 150–51, 179, 188–89
for dealing with anger, 82
divorce, 237
education and, 93, 133, 139, 147–49, 248
fear and, 65, 74–75
ignorance and, 48–49
illiteracy and, 13, 233–34
learning, 141–42, 186, 236–37
school system, 124–26
society and, 242
teaching, 263–72
violence and, 54, 78
workplace, 34, 131
corporations, 86–87, 103
see also business; employment; technology

corruption, 24, 92
Costa Rica, 57
court system, 2
crime/criminal organizations, 18–19
see also organized crime
culture
failure to teach, 213–18, 242–43
learning foreign, 146, 230
planning to alter, 208–10
curriculum development
change needed in, 141, 148, 192
educational system and, 135–38, 191
government involvement in, 238–40
growth and overload, 119–20, 126, 185–86
history of, 124–25
illiteracy and, 232
Internet and, 51, 130
life skills and, 236–37
for a new education program, 240–43
politics and, 93
pyramid of living and, 162, 167
student motivation and, 176
see also education system

D

date rape, 24
death
alcohol-related, 7
by committee, 183
conflict and politics of, 29
coping skills, 133, 147–48, 221
fear of, 33, 66
PTSD and, 56
survival instinct and, 79
teaching children about, 272
television and depiction of, 61–62
war and the risk of, 57–58
decision making
access to information and, 198–99
by committee, 183, 210
ignorance and, 48–49
NFC and, 210–13
Declaration of Independence, U.S., 98, 105
defensive fighting, survival instinct and, 77–78
defiance of authority, 69
see also authority
democracy
behavioral change in a new, 32
defined, 96, 131
future of education in, 240
future of true, 202–03
rights of citizens in, 181–84
understanding the forms of, 98–99

deoxyribonucleic acid (DNA). *see* genetics
developmental disabilities, 64
deviance from acceptable behavior, 170
dialogue as alternative to war, 30
disasters, natural, 54–56, 182
discipline
   childhood learning of, 137–38
   for deviance, 170
   failure to learn, 119–21, 140
   parenting skills and, 225
   Spock, Benjamin on, 225
   teaching conformity and, 173
   see also curriculum development
discrimination, 84–85, 270
   see also prejudice
disease, 54, 86
   see also health care
dishonesty, 1
divorce
   children and, xi, 177
   coping skills for, 147, 236–37
   as a social problem, 12–13
   women in the workplace and, 66–67
DNA. *see* genetics
domestic conflict, 7, 24
dominance, social, 53
double standards, 112, 256, 258
   see also behavior; standards of behavior
drive-by shootings, 33
drug use
   community awareness of, 191, 271
   as community characteristic, 1, 7
   entertainment media and, 44, 241
   as extreme behavior, 24, 40
   fight reflex and, 78
   media fear mongering and, 55
   organized crime and, 14
   schools and, 62, 147
   teens and, 6, 120–21, 248
   television and, 172

E

economic development, 106–07
economic power, 27–32
education
   adult, 227
   children and expectations of, 176
   children and goals of, 129–34
   children and objectives for, 142–57
   children and process of, 134–42
   connection between humans and nature in, 44–45
   functional illiteracy and, 231–34
   historical development of system of, 123–24
   improving the state of, 122–23
   influence on extreme behavior, 29
   long-term planning in, 9–10, 208–10
   past expectations of women, 85
   "politics of inclusion" and, 3–4, 99
   Pyramid of Living System and, 161–63
   role of government in, 92–94, 96
   school failure in, 119–21
   success and importance of, 62–64, 81, 125–27
   taxation and social problem, 14
   see also learning; schools; teaching
education system
   behavioral change and the, 19
   changing the, 9, 93, 131–32, 154–57
   curriculum and the, 148–49, 263–73
   dealing with anti-social behavior in, 2–6
   failure of the, 120, 126–27
   job training and the, 144–45
   NFC objectives and the, 212–13
   parental responsibilities of the, 190, 222
   proposal for a national, 210–15
   reordering priorities of, 135–41
   teacher support in, 155–56
   teaching morals and values in the, 215–18
   teaching parental skills in the, 225–30
   technology and the, 130
   zero tolerance, 122, 191
   see also curriculum development; national program in education
emergencies, anticipating, 257–58, 264
emotional skills
   childhood learning of, 140
   human nature and, 40
   Pyramid of Living System and, 168–71
   unacceptable behavior and, 34–35
employment
   education and, 126–27
   generational gap in, 242
   impact of technology on, 142–43
   international, 144–46
   literacy skills and, 6, 13, 234–36
   school failure and, 187
   see also business; corporations; workplace
England. *see* Great Britian
entertainment media
   celebrity publicity in the, 112
   drug use and the, 44, 241
   learning beliefs and values from, 44–45
   Pyramid of Living System and, 213

socially unacceptable behavior and, 214–18
violence and the, 59–61
see also mass media
environment, natural, 44–45, 54
see also natural world
equality
  beliefs and values in, 116–17
  democracy and individual, 202
  educational, 144–46
  racial, 116
  sexual, 60, 79
ethnic minorities, 84–85, 116–17
Europe, 30, 74
European Union (EU), 31, 106
experience
  assimilating and understanding, 177
  child development and, 160, 216–18, 257
  emotional health and, 168
  importance of school, 174
  learning and, 162
extreme behavior, 23–24, 31–32

F

family
  divorce and the, 237
  future economic order and, 87
  interdependence role of, 178–79
  past concept of, 84
  Pyramid of Living System and, 163
  "quality time" in the, 223
  role in developing social skills, 172, 219–20
  teaching children about, 125–26
  violence in the, 24
  see also domestic conflict
fathers
  concept of family and, 84, 143, 220
  newborn babies and, 134
  as role models, 60, 160, 189
  survival instinct and, 78–79
  teaching behaviors, 171, 257
  see also parents
fear
  of change, 205–06
  as community characteristic, 1, 7
  dealing with, 5–6, 14, 151–52
  in group behavior, 68–75
  ignorance and, 49
  irrational, 67–68
  school failure from, 121
  understanding, 65–67, 122
female roles, understanding, 220
  see also adults; mothers
"fight or flight". *see* defensive fighting

friendship
  building, 196, 257
  childhood social problems and, 162
  common interests and, 115
  emotional extremes and, 168–69
  social interactions in, 173–74
functional illiteracy
  education and, 232–33
  employment and, 6
  social immaturity and, 140–41
  as a social problem, 13
future
  education and the, 62–64, 121–22, 190–93
  expectations of the, 85–87
  long-term planning for the, 101–02, 208–10
  predicting the, 83–84

G

gambling, 24
gangs
  anti-social behavior and, 13
  as community characteristic, 1, 63, 188–89
  extreme behavior in, 24
  group behavior in, 68–70
genetics
  DNA and, 78
  and future expectations, 86
  learning differences and, 178
  modified foods and, 54
  survival instinct and, 78–79
genocide, 57–58
globalization, 103
Goebbels, Joseph, 57
Golden Rule, 142, 201, 255
goodness
  in beliefs and values, 182
  of common goals, 249
  in others, 113, 246
  recognizing, 195–96
government
  commitment to behavior change by, 18–19
  commitment to changing, 246–52
  by committee, 183, 210
  dealing with citizens as voters, 71–72, 91–92, 95–96
  democracy in, 31–32
  educational involvement of, 238–40
  individual participation in, 15–16, 98–99, 202–03
  long-term planning and changes in, 9–10, 101–02, 107
  manipulating group behavior by, 50–51

mass media and the, 197–201
NFC objectives and, 210–12
parental responsibilities of the, 221–22
political parties and the mechanism of, 93–94
"politics of inclusion", 3–4
rights of citizens in, 181–84
role in forming a new society, 209–10
role in the future, 86–87
system of beliefs and values, 182–84
taxes and income from social problems, 14
see also politics; representative government
gratuitous sex, 24
Great Britain, 42, 98
Greece, 96
group behavior
   emotional inhibitions in, 34–35
   fear and, 68–73
   rules for, 70–71
group fears, 73–75
group therapy, 151–52
groups
   counseling programs for, 151–52
   learned behaviors, 161
   patterns and values of, 68
   recognizing sub-groups within, 69–71
   social behavior in, 40–41
   taxpayers as, 71–72
guilt, xi, 109–14, 221–22, 227, 237, 267

H

habits, 2, 17–18
Hague, The, Netherlands, 18
happiness, 115, 168–70
hate, 23–24, 50, 115
health care
   dealing with social problems and, 14
   functional illiteracy and, 13
   future genetics and, 86
   media fear mongering and, 55–56
   stress and fear in, 34
   teaching children about, 259
   see also disease
hearing loss in teens, 6
helplessness, 5–6, 67
hierarchy
   children in the education, 156
   of countries, 205–06
   establishing pecking order in, 67
   group rules and formation of, 70–71
   species survival, 78–79
history, learning from, 51, 116–17
Hitler, Adolf, 24, 61, 107

holidays, 12
Holocaust, 57
home invasion, 1, 7
   see also privacy
homelessness, 13, 66, 120
hopelessness
   about the future, 63–64
   apathy and, 16
   media fear mongering and, 182
   quality of life and, 2
   toward changing the future, 89
human life, value of, 62
human nature
   in conflict with the natural world, 39–41
   fairness in life in, 114
   "fight or flight" and, 77–78
   objectives for the future and, 45–46
hypocrisy, 112–13, 201, 215

I

ignorance
   of laws to control behavior, 172–73
   of parenting skills, 186–90, 224–30
   of responsibilities toward children, 164
   role in education, 51–52
   role in government, 93–97, 198
   school failure from, 121
   toward change, 206–07
   Town Hall meetings as solution to, 201–02
   victimization through, 47–49
illiteracy as a social problem, 13
   see also functional illiteracy
immaturity. *see* maturity; intellectual skills
immigration, 229–30
immune system, 34, 260
India, 27–28, 48, 96, 106
individual nature, group behavior vs., 40–41
individuality, group behavior and, 69
Industrial Revolution, x, 123
inhibitions, emotional, 34–35
instincts, basic, 66, 134, 208
   see also survival instinct
instinctual behavior, 42
intellectual skills
   learning, 216
   Pyramid of Living System and, 168, 174–76
   societal role in creating, 222–25
interest groups, 20
   see also special interest groups
International Adult Literacy Survey, 6

International Criminal Court, 18, 57–58
International Monetary Fund, 28
Internet (Information Highway)
    dealing with ignorance with the, 49–50
    distance learning, 199
    future trends and the, 205–06
    individual privacy and the, 248
    as learning medium, 20
    resources for the TIA program, 275–76
    role in education, 130
    worldwide communications and the, 106
    see also computers; technology
intolerance, ignorance and, 49
invasion of privacy. *see* home invasion; privacy
Ireland, 51

J
Japan, 27–29
jobs. *see* employment; workplace

K
Kashmir, 27
Kennedy, John F., 55
knowledge
    expansion of human, 49–50, 126, 141–43
    as a function of schools, 190–91
    government and the electorate, 93–99
    Internet as reservoir for, 49
    Middle Ages and the loss of, 50–51
    parental influence on children, 160
    as power, 199
    role of computers in, 51–52
    school failure in teaching, 185–86
Korea, 28, 57
Kosovo, 29, 63

L
language
    obscene, 24
    Quebec separatism and, 30–31
    usage patterns, 19–20
lawlessness, 1
leadership
    for dealing with social problems, 50–51
    power of government, 91–93
    right to privacy in, 112–13
    role in education, 131–32
    Town Hall meetings for identifying, 201–02

voting for good, 247
women and future world, 87–88
learned behaviors
    acceptable vs. unacceptable, 23–25
    attention span as, 178
    group fears and, 73–75
    men asking for directions, 142
    newborn babies and, 161
    violence as, 53–54
learning
    beliefs and values, 216–18
    early childhood, 135–36, 159–60, 219–20
    education and, 31
    emotional skills, 168–71
    experience and adaptation for, 146–47
    Internet potential for, 199
    from the life force of plants, 86
    as a lifetime activity, 132, 142–44
    motivation for, 174–76, 178–79
    physical exercise and, 176
    by social interactions, 173–74
    social skills, 171–74
    standardized tests and rote, 51–52, 120, 185
    from television, 60–61, 172, 178, 199, 224–25
    topics for a new system of, 263–73
    trends for future, 206–07
    by the unborn and newborn child, 134
    see also education; schools
learning disabilities, 64, 279
legislation, behavioral change by, 19
    see also government
life
change as a way of, 193
    change for a better way of, 2–6, 36–38, 227
    fairness in, 114
    fear as part of, 73–75
    finding happiness in, 115
    genetics and a future way of, 86
    human-nature connection in, 44–45
    media depiction of way of, 62
    past concepts of way of, 83–85
    preparing adults for, 186–87, 221
    preparing children for, 219–20, 240–43
    Pyramid of Living System and, 163
    in schools of the future, 190–93
    teaching children about, 125–26, 176
    see also quality of life
life skills, x, 120, 138, 236–38
lifestyles
    dealing with changing, x, 66, 187

education and choices in, 133–35, 152–53
learning about new, 206–07
predicting the future of, 20–21
Lincoln, Abraham, 116–17
literacy skills
in Canada, 233–34
combating ignorance by, 52
importance of, 256
reading ability and, 6–7
see also functional illiteracy
litigation
government regulation and, 221–22
greed and hypocrisy of, 113
school failure and, 122
lobbying. *see* special interest groups
long-term planning
business, 103
in forming a new society, 208–10
in government, 101, 103–07
individual, 102
love
advertising and the selling of, 172
family relationships and, 125
importance to children, 137–40
parents teaching how to, 189, 232, 237–38, 258–62
peer acceptance as, 69–70
survival instinct and, 79

M
Magna Carta, 98
male roles, understanding, 220
see also adults; fathers
marriage, xii, 79, 84, 173
see also divorce
mass media
attitudes as influenced by, 2
dealing with social problems in, 196–97
fear mongering and the, 54–57, 182
gratuitous sex in, 24
individual privacy and the, 248
language changes in, 19–20
political perceptions and, 94–95
politics and the, 3, 200–203
in positive role for change, 8–9
for promoting TIA program, 250
right to privacy in, 112–13
role in government, 95–96, 197–98
special interest groups and, 130
violence as a way of life in, 62
see also entertainment media
maturity
intellectual, 130, 174–76
restricting emotional growth and, 171
social skills and, 140–41, 219–21

McLuhan, Marshall, 59
mental illness, 7
Middle Ages, 51
Middle East, 57, 63
military power, 27–30, 106–07
see also warfare
moral codes/morality
building common beliefs and, 10
commitment to supporting, 246
loss of parenting skills in, 220–21, 224–30
and mass media responsibility, 197–98, 215–18
organized crime and, 14
tabloid media and, 9
see also beliefs and values
mothers
concept of family and, 84, 143, 220
pre-natal concerns and, 133–34, 259
survival instinct and, 78–79
teaching behaviors, 68, 123, 139, 160, 171, 257
working, 60, 66, 121
see also parents
motivation
of fight reflex, 78–80
for learning, 174–76
toward behavior patterns, 59–60
murder, 7, 23

N
National Formulation Commission (NFC), 210–13
national program in education
changes to create a, 190–93
course materials for a, 253–63
curricula for primary grades, 240–43
curriculum development, 121–22
government involvement in, 238–40
objectives for a, 152–53, 192
policies for a, 144–46
resources for a, 275–76
topics for a, 263–73
Town Hall meetings and, 201–02
Town Hall meetings for input on, 201–02
see also education system
natural resources, 43
natural world
disasters as violence in the, 54
establishing hierarchy in the, 67
life force of plants in the, 86
survival instinct in the, 78–79
see also environment, natural
needs, personal, 39–40
negligence, accidents and, 109–11
negotiation as alternative to war, 30

neighbors. *see* communities
networking. *see* special interest groups
neuroses, 13
newspapers. *see* mass media
NFC. *see* National Formulation Commission (NFC)
North American Free Trade Agreement (NAFTA), 31
North Atlantic Treaty Organization (NATO), 57–58
North Korea, 28
Northern Ireland, 29, 63
nuclear weapons, 106
nurture vs. nature, 39–41

O

obscene language, 24
oppression, 49
organized crime, 7, 13
   see also crime/criminal organiza-tions
ostracism, 23
ownership, 43, 116–17

P

Pacific islands, 63
Pakistan, 27–28, 106
paranoia, ignorance and, 50
parenting skills, 133, 190, 224–30
parents
   as behavioral influence, 160, 186–89
   education for, 153–54
   parenting skills for, 220–21, 224–30, 253–62
   Pyramid of Living System and, 161–63
   responsibility for teaching, 45–46, 122–26, 135–36, 242–43
   role in education, 178–79
   role in guiding children, 2, 12, 37–38, 126, 219–20
   suppressing emotions in children, 171
   teaching how to love, 189–90, 232, 237–38, 258–62
   see also adults; fathers; mothers
peace, 18–19, 30–31
peer groups
   children and, 164, 172, 212
   group behavior and, 68–70
   help from, 152
   love and acceptance from, 69–70
   motivation for learning and, 175, 178–79, 235, 242
   Pyramid of Living System and, 161–63
personal habits, anti-social behavior and, 2

personal interests, problem solving and, 14–15
personal problems, 11–13
personal violence, 60
phobias, 68
   see also fear
physical maturity, 168, 176–79
physical violence
   disguising fear by, 122
   fear of, 33–35, 56
   in our personal lives, 54
   sports and, 58–59
   warfare and, 57–58
police, 2
political correctness, 12
politicians
   anti-social behavior, dealing with, 2
   apathetic citizenship and, 15–16
   citizens vs. special interests and, 91–93
   democratic government and, 32
   educational system and, 120–21, 130–32
   long-term government planning and, 107
   manipulating group behavior by, 50–51, 71–72
   mass media representation of, 94–95
   media scrutiny of, 3
   needs of society and, 46, 181–84, 193
   Pyramid of Living System and, 164–65
   right to privacy by, 112–13
   social illness solutions and, 7–8
   unrealistic expectations of, 200–203
   women as future, 88–89
politics
   economic and military power in, 26–32
   extreme behavior in, 24
   mass media and government, 197–98
   NFC objectives and, 212
   role of women in future, 88–89
   of societal change, 37
   societal change and, 181–84
   Town Hall meetings and, 201–02
   victimization of ignorance in, 48–49
   see also government
"politics of inclusion", 3–4
pollution, 39–40
Pond Inlet school, 178–79
population growth, x, 179, 229–30
pornography, 24
postindustrial era, 103, 221
post-traumatic stress disorder (PTSD), 56
poverty, 66–67

power
    of anti-social behavior, 61
    to change civilization, 218
    economic and military, 27–32, 205
    education as, 99
    government, 91–94, 98–99, 103–07, 129–31, 154
    knowledge as, 183, 199
    media and political, 71–72
    of social problems, 6–8
    special interest groups, 247
    of survival instinct, 78
prejudice, 23, 25, 49, 73, 85
priorities
    of behavioral change, 19, 139–41, 228
    educational, 155, 232
    human needs as, 39
    for a new education program, 240–41
prisons
    in Canada, 19
    for dealing with social problems, 82
    schools viewed as, 154, 191
    in United States, 19
    violence and increase in, 59
privacy
    individual right to, 112–13
    invasion of, 7
    maintaining individual, x, 248
problems. see personal problems; social problems
professional sports, 58–59
propaganda
    mass media and, 79
    violence and hatred in, 57–58
    voting for government and, 97
    see also advertising
prostitution, 14
psychological development, 44–45
psychological disorder, 169
psychological violence
    invasion of privacy as, 7
    media fear mongering as, 55–56
    in our personal lives, 54
    see also violence
psychoses, 7
public policy, apathy and, 15–16
punishment
    as deterrent, 18–19, 155
    in group conflict, 70
    of parents for their children, 188, 221–22
Pyramid of Living System
    community and the, 227
    defined, 167
    identifying the sides of the, 161–63
    infrastructure, 168
    NFC and the, 213

Q
quality of life
    education and, 129
    hopelessness and, 2
    long-term planning for, 104, 208–10, 245–52
    and social illness, 7–8
    see also life
"quality time", 223, 259
Quebec separatism, 30–31

R
racial equality, 116–17
radio as medium for learning, 198
    see also mass media
rage, victimization by, 33
    see also anger
rape, 24
reading ability. see functional illiteracy; literacy skills
Redfield, James, 275
religion
    basic principles of, 275
    discrimination and, 270
    ignorance and, 49
    morality and, 14
    parents role in, 123
    schools role in, 125–26, 215
    teaching children about, 269
    violence and hatred in, 29
representative government, 96–97, 201–02
    see also government
resources for a new system of education, 275–76
respect
    for life, 62
    for others, 125, 266
    for parents, 189
    in politics and the media, 95
    for school, 178, 189
    for self, 102, 115
    teaching, 12, 258
    for wealth, 27
    for work, 64
responsibility
    accident liability and, 109–11
    of adults toward children, 164
    for changing behaviors, 17–18, 38
    educational system, 121–26
    government legislating, 221–22
    for maintaining knowledge, 52
    and the mass media, 182
    and role of citizens, 3–4, 155–57
    to teach parents, 178–79, 253–62
    of wealth and ownership in society, 43

risk
  anxiety and, 65
  heroism and, 62
  learning to take, 260, 272
  life skills to avoid, 142, 273
  relationships and, 35
  in schools, 82
  stress and, 13
  of war and death, 58, 79, 153, 192
ritualistic behavior, 41
road rage, 33–35, 81
role model
  adults as, 61, 139, 172
  Canada as, 6–10
  entertainment media as, 243
  fathers as, 160
  gender, 12
  parents as, 136–37, 179, 212, 223–25, 253–60
  pyramid of living and, 213–14
  society as, 192–93
  television as, 164, 172, 242–43
Russia, 30, 57, 106

S

sadness, dealing with, 168–70
schools
  anti-social behavior in, 2
  childhood adjustment to, 135
  drug use in, 6
  failure of, 119–20
  increasing anger in, 81–82
  learning vs. teaching in, 190–91
  NFC objectives and, 212–14
  political correctness in, 12
  restricting emotional growth in, 171
  student drop outs, 175–76
  violence as a way of life in, 62
  weapons in, 121, 152, 189
  see also education; education system; learning; teaching
self-esteem
  children and, 62
  fear and the loss of, 67
  through war and violence, 63–64
self-interest, 4, 144, 245
sexual behavior, 24
sexual equality, 60, 79
silent majority, 16
slavery
  as extreme behavior, 23
  Lincoln and, 116–17
  ownership attitudes and, 43
social agencies, 14
social behavior, 40–41
  see also behavior

social interaction, 173–74
social policy, 15–16
social pressure, 34–35
  see also peer groups
social problems
  defined, 14–15
  education for coping with, 147–48
  homelessness as, 13
  ignorance and growth of, 50–51
  impact on schools, 119–21
  mass media and, 196–97
  recognizing, 11–12
  role of government, 101
  solving, a plan for, 245–52
  taxes and income from, 14
  worldwide anxiety toward, 181, 192–93
social skills
  childhood learning of, 140–41, 235
  Pyramid of Living System and, 168, 171–74
socialization
  advertising and, 172
  human nature and, 39–42
  propaganda as, 57
socially unacceptable behavior. see extreme behavior
society
  aggression as a danger to, 82
  agricultural vs. industrial, 42–43
  behavioral inhibitions in, 34–35
  commitment to changing, 8–10, 18–19, 208–10, 245–52
  dealing with social problems in, 12–15
  dealing with violence in, 54
  educational system history in, 122–26
  effecting change in, 36–38
  future of education in, 240
  group fears in, 73–75
  knowledge in a functioning, 50
  measuring success in, 67–68, 81
  objectives for the future of, 45–46
  parental responsibilities of, 222–25
  system of beliefs and values, 182–84
  teach worthlessness in, 62–64
  see also civilization; communities
South America, 57, 63, 192
Soviet Union. see Russia
Spain, 57
special interest groups
  politicians and, 92
  role in education, 130–31
  role in government, 98–99, 101, 247
Spock, Benjamin, 225
sports
  community identification with, 115–16

violent behavior in, 58–59
warfare in, 80
see also athletic competition
Stalin, Joseph, 24, 57
standards of behavior, 19
see also behavior; double standards
starvation, fear of, 66
status quo, 193, 205
street gangs. *see* gangs
stress, 34, 56
suicide, 1, 62
support groups, 12–13, 152, 174
survival instinct
fear and the, 65–66
"fight or flight" and the, 77–78
love and, 79

T

tabloid media, role of, 9
see also mass media
taboos, 84
taxation
for education, 121
group behavior and, 71
impact of crime on, 13–14
for a new education program, 239–40
social illness solutions and, 8
teaching
attention span and, 178
beliefs and values, 42, 214–18
increased demands placed on, 126–27
parenting skills to parents, 225–30, 253–63
propaganda as, 57
relationship with nature, 43–44
rote learning and effectiveness of, 51–52
school failure in, 185–87
worthlessness in society, 62–64
see also education; learning; schools
technology
impact on jobs and employment, 142–43
participation in government by, 98–99, 202–03
"politics of inclusion" and, 3–4
potential for teaching behavior, 200
role in education, 129–30
role in societal change, 206
teens/teen subcultures
alienation from community, 1, 213–18
education and coping skills for, 151–52
educational goals for, 132–34
increasing anger in, 81–82
learning parenting skills, 137, 186–90, 224–30

past expectations of, 84–85
preparing for adult life, 241–43
as school drop outs, 175–76
telephone as medium for information, 198–99
see also mass media
television
advertising and violence, 56
aggressiveness in sports on, 80
childhood learning from, 137, 237
desensitization to violence and, 59–61
literacy skills and, 234
Pyramid of Living System and, 163–64, 213
as teacher and babysitter, 60–61, 178, 224–25
for teaching behavior, 172, 199, 242–43
see also entertainment media; mass media
terrorism
economic world order and, 86–87
as extreme behavior, 23
fear of unknown, 65
media fear mongering and, 55–56
military power and, 106–07
violence and, 26–27
tobacco, 2, 14
tolerance, ignorance and, 49
torture, 23
Town Hall meetings, 201–02
tribe. *see* communities
Trudeau, Pierre Elliott, 3
trust
building, 150, 255, 257, 268
loss of, 2, 88
in politics, 201
as sacred bond, 260–61
as victimization of ignorance, 47–48

U

United Nations, 19, 30, 41–42, 57–58
United States
Civil War, 30
economic and military power in, 28, 106
independence and democracy in, 98, 105
NFC proposal for, 211–13
politics of, 93
prisons in, 19
racial equality in, 84, 116
schools, 148, 156–57, 242
TIA implementation in, 245–52
world perceptions of, 41–42, 106
U.S. Supreme Court, 125

V

value systems, 10, 41–42
vandalism, 23
victimization
  by accidents, 109–11
  by desensitization to violence, 59–61
  by fear, 33
  fear of strangers and, 13
  by ignorance, 47–49
  of parents, 188
video games
  intellectual maturity and, 81, 130
  learning and, 44–45
  negative effect of, 61
  technology and, 217
Vietnam, 28, 57
violence
  as community characteristic, 1
  defensive fighting and, 77–78
  desensitization to, 59–61
  as extreme behavior, 24, 26–27
  group behavior and fear of, 72–73
  human nature and, 53–54
  impact on quality of life, 7
  media fear mongering and, 55–57
  punishment as deterrent to, 18–19
  thresholds for, 56–57
  worldwide social problems and, 192–93
  see also psychological violence
volunteers for the TIA program, 245–52, 275–76
vote, right to, 98

W

war games, 81
"war on terrorism", 65
  see also terrorism
warfare
  as aberration to civilized behavior, 25–30
  beliefs and values in, 42, 209
  commitment to behavior change and, 18–19
  human nature as, 54
  Lincoln and Civil War, 116–17
  mass media and, 79
  physical violence and, 57–58
  women and, 79
  see also military power
wealth
  knowledge as, 143–44
  litigation and, 113
  society and creation of, 42–43

weapons in schools, 121, 152, 189
women
  as future world leaders, 87–88
  past expectations of, 85
  sexual equality and, 60
  sports and, 80–81
  survival instinct and, 78–79
  in the workplace, 66–67
workplace
  anger and bullying, 34
  future economic order and the, 87
  importance of education in the, 126–27
  increasing anger in the, 81
  Industrial Revolution impact on the, 123
  role in education, 133
  warfare in the, 80
  women in the, 66–67
  see also employment
World Bank, 28
World Trade Center, 55
World War I, 26
World War II, 25–27, 58, 79
World Wide Web. *see* Internet (Information Highway)
worry, dealing with, 5–6, 14, 151–52, 260
writing skills, 196, 228, 256
  see also literacy skills

Y

young people. *see* teens/teen subcultures
Yugoslavia, 29, 57

Z

zero tolerance, 122, 191